ENGLISH in Common

6

with ActiveBook

JJ Wilson with Antonia Clare

Series Consultants
Sarah Louisa Birchley and María Victoria Saumell

ALWAYS LEARNING

PEARSON

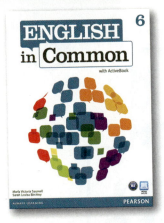

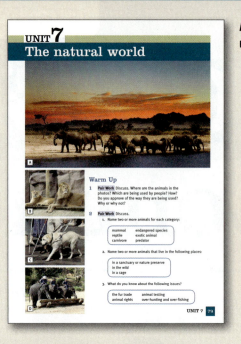

English in Common 6 has ten units. Each unit has twelve pages.

English in Common is a six-level course that helps adult and young-adult English learners develop effective communication skills that correspond to the Common European Framework of Reference for Languages (CEFR). Every level of *English in Common* is correlated to a level of the CEFR, and each lesson is formulated around a specific CAN DO objective.

There are three three-page lessons in each unit.

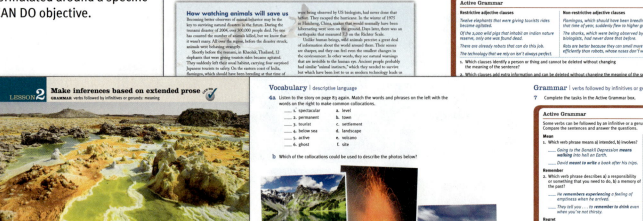

A Unit Wrap Up ends each unit.

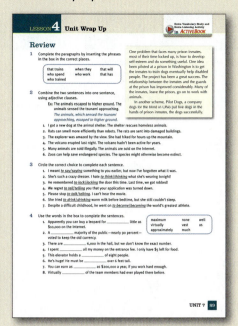

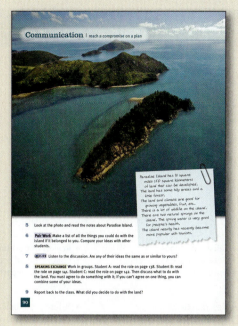

Back of Student Book

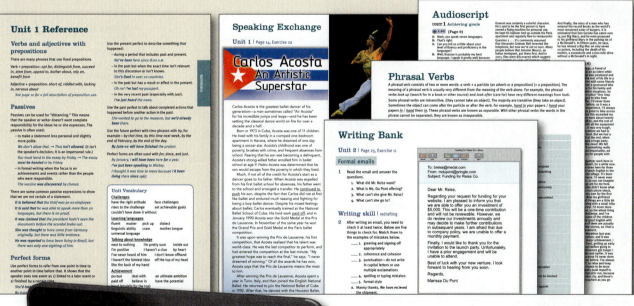

- Each Student Book contains an **ActiveBook**, which provides the Student Book in digital format. *ActiveBook* also includes the complete Audio Program and Extra Listening activities.

- An optional online **MyEnglishLab** provides the opportunity for extra practice anytime, anywhere.

- The Teacher's Resource Book contains teaching notes, photocopiable extension activities, and an **ActiveTeach**, which provides a digital Student Book enhanced by interactive whiteboard software. *ActiveTeach* also includes the videos and video activities, as well as the complete Test Bank.

Contents

UNIT	CAN DO OBJECTIVES	GRAMMAR	VOCABULARY/ EXPRESSIONS
1 Achieving goals page 7	• Discuss your language learning experiences • Say how much you know or don't know • Talk about your achievements	• Verbs and adjectives with prepositions • Passives • Perfect forms	• Challenges • Learning languages • Talking about knowledge • Achievement
2 Places and communities page 19	• Give advice and make recommendations about places • Use features of formal and informal language • Describe a place	• Gerund and infinitive review • Comparisons • Adjectives	• Qualities of communities • Recommending places • Adjectives to describe places
3 Stories page 31	• Tell an anecdote • Describe a person in detail • Tell a joke	• Review of past forms • Compound adjectives • Phrases with participles and gerunds	• Stories • Synonyms • Books • Humor
4 Moving forward page 43	• Describe the chances of something happening • Talk about plans and arrangements • Follow an extended piece of discourse	• Future probability • Future forms: review • Subject / verb inversion	• Progress • Arrangements • Special abilities
5 Making money page 55	• Talk about professional relationships • Discuss financial decisions and regrets • Express priorities	• Emphasis • Conditionals: review • Sentence adverbials	• Money, achievement, and charity • Expressing priorities • Expressing quantity • Describing a job
6 Understanding power page 67	• Describe an important building or structure • Take notes from fluent connected speech • Write an autobiographical statement	• Articles • Clauses with *whatever, whoever, whenever* • Logical connectors of time and contrast	• Power • Fashions and fads • Personal characteristics
7 The natural world page 79	• Explain procedures • Make inferences based on extended prose • Write an ad for an object	• Relative clauses • Verbs followed by infinitives or gerunds: meaning • *as . . . as*; describing quantity	• Animals and their environment • Descriptive language • Buying and selling
8 Problems and issues page 91	• Stall for time when asked a difficult question • Discuss lifestyle • Explain everyday problems	• Reporting verbs • Continuous forms • Fronting	• Global issues • Positive and negative opinions • Lifestyles • Cause and effect
9 People with vision page 103	• Express a degree of certainty • Use colloquial expressions to explain your tastes • Respond to hypothetical questions	• Collocations with prepositions • Discourse markers • Unreal past	• Describing art • Expressing certainty or uncertainty
10 Expressing feelings page 115	• Discuss how feelings affect you • Make guesses about imaginary situations • Describe a childhood memory	• Modals (and verbs with similar meanings) • Modals of deduction (past and present) • Uses of *would*	• Idioms and phrases for feelings • Outlook and attitude • Strong feelings

READING/WRITING	LISTENING	COMMUNICATION/EXTRA VOCABULARY STUDY
Reading texts: • an article about polyglots • articles about two incredible athletes • a personality quiz **Writing task:** write a news report based on a picture	**Listening texts:** • an interview with a polyglot • a radio show about "famous firsts" • news stories • descriptions of personal achievements • analysis of answers to a personality quiz	**Communication:** take a personality quiz **Extra Vocabulary Study in *ActiveBook*:** prefixes
Reading texts: • an article about Wikipedia • formal emails • descriptions of travel destinations **Writing tasks:** • write recommendations for travelers to your country • write a formal email • write a description of a favorite place	**Listening texts:** • descriptions of life abroad • a debate over the value of the Internet • descriptions of two clubs to which people belong	**Communication:** collaborate on a plan **Extra Vocabulary Study in *ActiveBook*:** phrasal verbs
Reading texts: • an article about famous hoaxes • a biography of Groucho Marx **Writing task:** write a description of someone	**Listening texts:** • descriptions of favorite fictional characters • an abridged biography of Groucho Marx • a joke	**Communication:** tell a story **Extra Vocabulary Study in *ActiveBook*:** metaphors
Reading texts: • an article on scientifically generated "superpowers" • an article on child geniuses • descriptions of new technology **Writing task:** summarize a story from a listening	**Listening texts:** • news stories • a conversation about superheroes • an interview with the creator of Spider Man • telephone conversations about future plans • an interview about child geniuses • discussions about discoveries and inventions	**Communication:** make an argument for research funding **Extra Vocabulary Study in *ActiveBook*:** two-part expressions
Reading texts: • an article about a unique business model • true "riches to rags" stories • an article about famous philanthropists • an article about *Fortune* Magazine's 100 Best Companies to Work For **Writing task:** write a paragraph supporting an opinion	**Listening texts:** • advice on choosing a business partner • an interview with the CEO of a successful company • a discussion about a hypothetical business situation	**Communication:** negotiate **Extra Vocabulary Study in *ActiveBook*:** idioms 1
Reading texts: • an article on architecture as a symbol of power • an article about the power of charisma **Writing tasks:** • write about two important pieces of architecture • write an autobiographical statement	**Listening texts:** • descriptions of important architectural structures • an interview about the influence of teens on technology • conversations about limits on teenagers	**Communication:** evaluate personal characteristics **Extra Vocabulary Study in *ActiveBook*:** idioms 2
Reading texts: • an article on using animals to save human lives • an article about illegal online animal sales **Writing tasks:** • explain procedures in your home • write an ad for an object	**Listening texts:** • advice on choosing and caring for pets • a description of a travel adventure • a description of an unusual job • a discussion about how to develop a piece of land	**Communication:** reach a compromise on a plan **Extra Vocabulary Study in *ActiveBook*:** suffixes
Reading texts: • opinions on necessary future inventions • an "online" advice column **Writing tasks:** • write an essay on a problem or issue	**Listening texts:** • descriptions of imaginary inventions • explanations of career choices • conversations about problems with machines	**Communication:** summarize opinions on issues **Extra Vocabulary Study in *ActiveBook*:** academic English
Reading texts: • an article about famous visionaries • an article about fine art theft • advice for aspiring travel writers and photographers **Writing tasks:** • write about thoughts and actions inspired by a photo • write a story based on a hypothetical situation	**Listening texts:** • an interview about geniuses' "aha" moments • conversations about works of art • histories of two important inventors	**Communication:** collaborate on a proposal **Extra Vocabulary Study in *ActiveBook*:** confusing words
Reading texts: • an article about a blind photographer • a book review • an excerpt from a novel **Writing task:** write about a childhood memory	**Listening texts:** • an interview about optimism and pessimism • deductions about feelings in the past • recollections of childhood • explanations of strong opinions	**Communication:** express strong feelings about an issue **Extra Vocabulary Study in *ActiveBook*:** phrasal verbs and particles

1 Read the paragraph and match each underlined word or phrase to a part of speech below.

In 1967 Allen and Beatrice Gardner embarked on an experiment (**1.**) to train a chimpanzee to talk. Realizing that chimpanzees don't have the vocal apparatus to be able to speak like humans, but that they (**2.**) can use gestures easily (**3.**), the Gardners decided to train the (**4.**) animal in ASL, American Sign Language. Their subject was a chimpanzee called Washoe. The Gardners brought up (**5.**) Washoe like a child, giving her regular meals and getting her to brush her teeth before sleep. At first, Washoe made meaningless hand gestures, similar to the meaningless babbling of baby humans learning a language. But after four years, Washoe had learned over 150 signs. She could (**6.**) also combine the signs on some occasions, such as when she made the signs for "water" and "bird" on seeing (**7.**) a swan on a lake. Linguists and scientists, however (**8.**), are skeptical (**9.**) about the Gardners' research (**10.**), and question whether Washoe can really "speak." They say that her "language use" is simply imitation.

_____ **a.** present participle		_____ **f.** phrasal verb
_____ **b.** linking word (contrast)		_____ **g.** adjective
_____ **c.** non-count noun		_____ **h.** adverb
_____ **d.** count noun		_____ **i.** pronoun
_____ **e.** article		_____ **j.** modal verb

2 Find and correct the grammar mistake in each sentence.

1. By this time tomorrow, we will have arrive in Peru.
2. We were hot because we'd run.
3. If I would have seen you, I would have stopped.
4. It mustn't have been John; John's tall and that man was short.
5. We haven't been knowing her long.
6. The conference will held in the theater tomorrow.
7. I had my purse stole yesterday.
8. She persuaded me buying the car.
9. He climbed up the Mount Everest.

3a Complete the word maps with words and phrases from the box.

step-sister	culture shock	uncharted territory	soulmate
career path	spending spree	be laid off	gamble

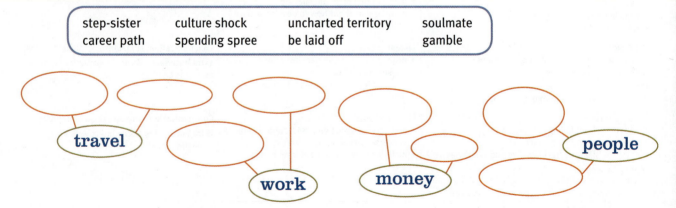

b Underline the main stress in each word or phrase.

c Add three more words to each word map.

UNIT 1
Achieving goals

A

B

C

D

Warm Up

1 **Group Work** What type of challenges are shown in the photos? Have you ever faced any challenges similar to these? What happened? How did you feel?

2 Complete the sentences. Write the letter on the line.

1. I like to **set achievable goals,** ____
2. It's important to **face challenges,** but ____
3. She usually **rises to the challenge,** even if ____
4. I **couldn't have done it without** help, so ____
5. It's important to **have the right attitude,** because ____

a. I'd like to thank my family and my sponsors.
b. so before starting, I always think about my objectives.
c. if you are a positive person, it will be easier.
d. you mustn't be afraid of them.
e. it's something very difficult.

3 **Pair Work** Discuss. What are your goals for your career or your personal life? What challenges do you think you will face in achieving these goals?

Reading

1 **Pair Work** How many languages do you speak? When did you learn them?

2a Read about some amazing language learners.

Great Language Learners

1 Cardinal Giuseppe Mezzofanti (1774–1849), who spoke 72 languages, is said to have once learned a language overnight in order to hear the confession of two condemned prisoners the following morning. Modern linguists laugh at this story, but they admit that there are some phenomenal polyglots out there.

2 The greatest is probably Francis Sommer. Sommer, who grew up in Germany and died in 1978, was fluent in 94 languages. He began learning languages as a young boy, starting with Swedish, Sanskrit, and Persian. He went on to master all of the major European languages as well as languages from other parts of the world. David Perlmutter, Professor of Linguistics at the University of California, says, "People like Sommer are amazing examples of human achievement."

3 Another great polyglot is Kenneth Hale, a linguistics professor who speaks roughly 50 languages. "I didn't do very well as a student," he says. "I wanted to learn languages, and I let everything else slide." Hale says that he and other master linguists learn languages not for money or recognition but for the pleasure that comes with mastering each new language. "When I found I could speak Navajo at the age of 12," says Hale, "I used to go out every day and sit on a rock and talk Navajo to myself."

4 Some studies suggest that people with a talent for languages may actually have a slightly different brain structure than the rest of us. Polyglots may have more white brain matter, which is involved in connecting different parts of the brain together. Faster language learners have more white brain matter in the area of the brain where sound is processed, which could result in an increased ability to process sound.

5 Stephen Wurm, linguistics professor at the Australian National University at Canberra, speaks 48 languages. He believes the best way to learn a language is to hear it spoken regularly from a very early age. Wurm's parents and grandparents, each of whom came from a different part of the world, spoke different languages with him when he was a child. His father spoke to him only in English, his mother in Hungarian, and his grandparents in Norwegian, Finnish, and Mongolian. Wurm also traveled with his father, who worked in Germany, Russia, China, Argentina, and Turkey, so he picked up those languages as well. He recalls, "By the age of six, I spoke ten different languages."

6 The greatest of today's polyglots is Ziad Fazah. Fazah, a Lebanese in his 50s who has been living in Brazil for over 20 years, is fluent in 56 languages. In addition to Arabic, his mother tongue, he learned French and English as a child. After that, Fazah taught himself German, then Mandarin Chinese, Cantonese, and Japanese, and on and on. He says that Mandarin was the most difficult language to learn.

7 Fazah teaches several languages, including English, Arabic, Farsi, French, and German. In addition, Fazah's abilities have had some unexpected uses. Several years ago, police in Rio called him to help with an illegal immigrant who spoke a language that they could not recognize. "I soon realized he was from Afghanistan and spoke a dialect called Hazaras," Fazah said.

8 TV fame also arrived unexpectedly. He appeared on TV shows in Spain and Greece, where his linguistic abilities were tested by people from Thailand, Hungary, Korea, Japan, China, and other countries. The US consulate in Brazil was less impressed, however. Because of his ability to speak Chinese and Russian, they feared he was a spy and asked the Brazilian police to bring him in for questioning. "After two hours I was let go," he says.

9 So do polyglots ever get their languages mixed up? Yes, says Kenneth Hale. He says that sometimes he starts speaking in one language but ends up speaking in a different one. He points out that if he's not paying attention, it's easy to mix up similar languages. Likewise, Francis Sommer stopped learning new languages in his old age, saying, "I am afraid to cram any more words into my head." Fazah, however, has room for at least one more language. He would like one day to create a new universal language that would be written as it is spoken.

b Now answer the questions.

1. Why do polyglots keep learning languages?

2. How might polyglots' brains be different from most people's brains?

3. What do polyglots sometimes worry about?

4. What positives and negatives has Ziad Fazah experienced because of his linguistic abilities?

3 **Pair Work** Discuss.

1. What are the benefits of being a polyglot? Are there any drawbacks?

2. In your opinion, what personal qualities are necessary to become a polyglot?

> *I think it would be amazing to be able to speak many languages. On the other hand . . .*

Vocabulary | learning languages

4 Match the words and expressions from the Reading with the correct definitions.

____ 1. fluent (adj.)
____ 2. master [something] (v.)
____ 3. pick up [a language] (v.)
____ 4. mother tongue (n.)
____ 5. dialect (n.)
____ 6. linguistic ability (n.)
____ 7. cram (v.)
____ 8. universal language (n.)

a. put too much into a small space
b. level of skill in learning languages
c. to learn something so well that you understand it completely
d. able to speak a language very well
e. the first language you learn
f. a form of a language that is spoken in one area
g. a language spoken by everyone
h. to learn something without much effort

Listening

5a ▶1.02 Listen to Mark Sorok talk about his experiences as a language learner. Make notes about the following:

1. The number of languages he speaks

2. Special techniques he uses

3. How he feels about language

b Compare your notes with a partner. Listen again to check your answers.

6 **Pair Work** Discuss your own language learning experiences. What problems have you had? What do you like best about learning languages?

> *I learned to speak Portuguese when I was a child . . .*

Grammar | verbs and adjectives with prepositions

7 Match the pictures with the sentences below.

_____ 1. Marco found he was very short on opportunities to use his English.

_____ 2. Tanya tended to rely on translation when she learned new words.

A

B

8 Read the rules and answer the questions in the Active Grammar box.

> ### Active Grammar
>
> 1. There are many expressions that use a fixed preposition. Which sentence in Exercise 7 contains *verb + preposition*? _____ Which contains *adjective + preposition*? _____
>
> 2. Prepositions after verbs, nouns and adjectives always have an object. What is the object in each of the sentences in Exercise 7?
>
>   1. _____   2. _____
>
> 3. When the preposition is followed by a verb, the verb is usually a gerund.
>
>   *I look forward to **meeting** you.   She apologized for **taking** the camera.*

See Reference page 127

9 Add the correct prepositions from the box to each sentence. Check any new expressions in your dictionary.

from (x3)	to	in (x2)
about	for	with (x2)

1. Do you think you'll succeed _____ passing your next test?
2. If you could improve your English by watching DVDs, living in an English-speaking country, or studying from books, which would you opt _____?
3. Do your problems in English stem _____ poor grammar, or are there other problems?
4. Do you feel you are lacking _____ opportunities to practice speaking?
5. Some students' spoken English is riddled _____ errors. Do you think this matters, or is fluency more important?
6. What distinguishes your first language _____ English?
7. What types of classroom exercises appeal _____ you?
8. Do you think pronunciation is worth bothering _____?
9. Are you nervous _____ giving presentations in English?
10. How can your fluency benefit _____ watching TV?

Speaking

10a **Pair Work** Ask and answer the questions in Exercise 9. Explain your answers.

b Tell the class what you learned about your partner.

> *Yes, I'm sure I'll pass my next test. I've studied a lot.*

Say how much you know or don't know

GRAMMAR passives

Vocabulary | talking about knowledge

1a Complete the sentences with words from the box.

> | | | |
> |---|---|---|
> | nothing | sure | head |
> | positive | hand | know |
> | heart | clue | out |
> | certain | idea | of |

1. A: Who won the match last night?
   ___ B: **I haven't a** _____ .

2. A: Who wrote *Silas Marner*?
   ___ B: **I don't know off the top of my** _____ .

3. A: Which nation has the smallest population?
   ___ B: **I'm pretty** _____ it's the Vatican.

4. A: Where did Elisha Gray come from?
   ___ B: Who? **I've never heard** _____ **him**.

5. A: Do you know Paris?
   ___ B: Yes. I lived there for years, so **I know it like the back of my** _____ .

6. A: When did a man first go to the Moon?
   ___ B: **I don't** _____ **offhand,** but I can look it up.

7. A: Do you know Eliot's poem about cats?
   ___ B: **I know it by** _____ . I learned it at school.

8. A: What do you know about corporate law?
   ___ B: **I know it inside** _____ . I have a Ph.D. in it.

9. A: What do you know about Belgian politics?
   ___ B: **I know next to** _____ about it.

10. A: Which country has the biggest population?
    ___ B: **I haven't the faintest** _____ .

11. A: Are you sure Russia is the biggest country in the world?
    ___ B: **I'm fairly** _____ it is, but it might be China.

12. A: Are you sure Mt. Everest is the highest mountain in the world ?
    ___ B: Yes. **I'm** _____ it is.

b Think about the meaning of the expressions **in bold**.
Write ✓ next to the expressions that mean *I know*.
Write ✗ next to the expressions that mean *I don't know*.

Speaking

2 **Pair Work** Ask a partner how much they know or don't know about the topics in the box.
Try to use the expressions from Exercise 1a.

> | | |
> |---|---|
> | Antonio Meucci | classical music |
> | the World Cup | the North Pole |
> | Alexander Graham Bell | computers |
> | the history of flight | the Tango |
> | Leonardo da Vinci | jazz |
> | Isabel Allende | sports |
> | global warming | sailing |

Listening

3 **Pair Work** Take the quiz. If you disagree, discuss your answers. Use the vocabulary from page 11.

WHO DID IT FIRST?

1. Who was the first to fly a plane?
   a. Alberto Santos Dumont
   b. the Wright brothers
   c. Von Zeppelin

2. Who invented the telephone?
   a. Thomas Edison
   b. Alexander Graham Bell
   c. Antonio Meucci

3. Who first reached the North Pole?
   a. Peary
   b. Cook
   c. Amundsen

4. Who invented the light bulb?
   a. Edison
   b. Bell
   c. Leonardo da Vinci

5. Which country won the first World Cup (and hosted it)?
   a. Brazil
   b. Uruguay
   c. Germany

6. Which was the first country to allow women to vote?
   a. Switzerland
   b. New Zealand
   c. the United States

7. Who was the first woman to sail solo around the world?
   a. Ellen MacArthur
   b. Amelia Earhart
   c. Naomi James

8. Which country held the first Olympic Games?
   a. Italy
   b. France
   c. Greece

4 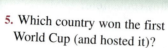 ▶1.03 Listen to the radio show to find answers to the quiz. Does anything surprise you?

Grammar | passives

5 Read the Active Grammar box and circle the correct answer to item 1.

Active Grammar

1. The passive is often used to show that a statement is ____.
   a. not our own opinion
   b. a personal opinion

   It is said that . . .

   It is believed that . . .

   It is claimed that . . .

2. If we aren't sure that the information is 100 percent true, we can use the passive to put "distance" between ourselves and the statement.

   He is said to be the richest man in England (but I don't know if this is accurate).

   He was thought to have left the country (but I'm not sure if this is true).

   Other verbs for "distancing":

   It appears/seems that . . .   *It seems as if/though . . .*

See Reference page 127

6 Complete the sentences using passives and the verbs in bold.

> Ex: People say that Edison invented more machines than anyone else in history.
>
> **say** Edison ___is said to have___ invented more machines than anyone else in history.

1. The evidence suggests that Edison didn't invent as much as we thought.

   seems It _____ though Edison invented fewer things than we thought.

2. People believe that da Vinci invented the helicopter.

   think Da Vinci _____ invented the helicopter.

3. Some historians assert that the Wright brothers flew first.

   assert It _____ by some historians that the Wright brothers flew first.

4. Many journalists in the late 19th century said that William Dickson had "invented" the motion picture in 1891.

   claim It _____ that William Dickson had "invented" the motion picture.

5. We think Joop Sinjou and Toshi Tada Doi invented the CD player at the same time.

   believe Sinjou and Tada Doi _____ invented the CD player simultaneously.

6. Newspapers of the time reported that Felix Hoffman had invented aspirin.

   report It _____ that Felix Hoffman had invented aspirin.

7. We now think that aspirin was first used by ancient Egyptians.

   believe It _____ that aspirin was first used by ancient Egyptians.

Listening

7a ▶1·04 Listen to the radio news headlines. Take notes on the stories you hear.

b **Pair Work** Retell the stories in your own words. Do you think these are important achievements? Discuss why or why not.

Speaking

8 **Pair Work** Look at the pictures and answer the questions.

1. Which story do you think is the most interesting? Why?
2. Which is the most likely or unlikely? Why?

> I think the man who lived with lions is the most interesting because it seems impossible . . .

FIRST WOMAN TO SKATEBOARD AROUND THE WORLD

FIRST MAN TO LIVE WITH LIONS

FIRST TWINS TO REACH 125 YEARS OLD

Writing

9a Write a news report based on one of the pictures in Exercise 8 (about 100–150 words). Use at least two passive constructions.

b **Group Work** Read your news reports to your classmates.

Reading

1 **Pair Work** Discuss. Which sports are typically dominated by men? Which by women? Why do you think this is?

2a **Pair Work** Student A: read the article on page 15. Student B: read the article on page 137 in the Speaking Exchange. Make notes in the chart.

Name		
What is/was their ambition?		
To what extent have they achieved it?		
What challenges have they faced?		
Who has helped them achieve their ambitions? How?		

b Tell your partner about your article. What similarities are there between the two stories?

3 **Group Work** Discuss.

1. Carlos Acosta got teased for being a boy ballet dancer. Do you think that there is a prejudice that ballet is not for boys? Do you think it is the same in all countries?

2. What do you think of the fathers' behaviors in these two cases? Would you have reacted similarly? Do you believe that parents should influence the ambitions of their children?

Vocabulary | achievement

4a What do the following words and expressions from the articles mean? Use the context to help you establish the meaning.

1. head (straight for the top)
2. pursue (a dream)
3. deal with (chauvinism)
4. believe in (what you can achieve)
5. have the potential (to do something)
6. continue to push someone (to do something)
7. (something) paid off
8. an ultimate ambition

b Complete the sentences using the Vocabulary.

1. It was obvious that Venus Williams _____ to become a tennis champion when she was very young.
2. Ralf Schumacher had to _____ criticism from his colleagues.
3. Ellen MacArthur _____ her dream of sailing solo around the world.
4. If you _____ yourself, you can achieve almost anything.
5. Her _____ is to be the best tennis player in the world.
6. Encourage your kids to try new things, but don't _____ them too hard.
7. All of his hard work _____ when he won the race.
8. That young singer is _____ for the top.

Brazilian Racing Star

Meet Bia Figueiredo, who is set to join the ranks of her country's great racing drivers—Senna, Piquet, Barrichello. She has already beaten the boys from Brazil at their own game. Now she competes in the US, in the IZOD IndyCar series.

As the swarm of race cars completes its final warm-up lap and hurtles across the starting line, the race is on. Thirty minutes later, when the winner's helmet is removed, a wave of dense dark hair flows freely. For the champion is a girl, Ana Beatriz Figueiredo—Bia, for short—and she is <u>heading straight for the top</u>.

I first met Bia Figueiredo in May 2001. She was 16, and her rivals in São Paulo's kart scene—all male—had been suffering the obvious taunt for eight years: "Beaten by a girl . . . again?"

She is still winning. One day soon, the image of her long hair spilling out of her helmet could open motor sports to new audiences, sponsors, and perhaps a whole new lease of life. For as Bia <u>pursues her dream</u>, she is being spoken of as the possible future of racing, the woman to transform an increasingly predictable sport.

"The first time I went to the kartodrome," she tells me, "I was five or six. I begged my father to take me and fell in love with the noise and the crashes. He told me I had to be seven before I could learn to drive. Somehow I managed to wait."

Money pressures are inherent in motor racing, even for a family that is well-off by most standards. Compared with other drivers at this level, Bia is disadvantaged. Bia's father, Jorge, says that Bia was already dreaming of Formula 1 at the age of six. And having encouraged his daughter's passion, he has accepted the financial burden with good humor. "I once heard a Formula 1 team boss say it costs $10 million to become a Formula 1 driver. I said to myself, 'OK. I'm only $9,990,000 short!'"

Because of the expense, Bia could only do two 50-minute tests before each race, when other drivers did four. She went to one of the best schools in São Paulo, which meant she was doing school work when other drivers were on the track. "Given these constraints, she has done very well," her father says. "She was born with a forceful personality, and today she's still forceful and has a caustic sense of humor. I feel a little sorry for anyone in her way!"

Motor racing would not be every father's chosen career for his daughter. "Yes, it can be dangerous," Jorge concedes. "But the element of risk can be controlled. I'm much more afraid of Bia not doing what she loves. By pursuing what they enjoy, I think people have more chance of being happy."

Yet Bia will have to <u>deal with</u> chauvinism. Not the least of the barriers facing her is whether motor sports are prepared to accept a genuine female contender. "A beautiful woman is always welcome," Alex Dias Ribeiro says, smiling and then adds: "But she will have to be quick and mentally tough, because Formula 1 is a pressure cooker."

One man who believes in Bia's potential is her mechanic and mentor, Naylor Borigis de Campos, who is better known simply as Nô. Nô has worked closely with most of Brazil's best drivers. He compares Bia favorably with the best of his protégés. "She's as cool, aware, and determined as Rubens Barrichello and as any other driver I've ever worked with."

As for Bia herself, she <u>believes in</u> the future and in <u>what she can achieve</u>: "I have a lot to learn, but my temperament is right: I've got plenty of animal instinct. I believe I <u>have the potential</u> to reach Formula 1 and perhaps one day be a great driver."

Listening

5 **Pair Work** Talk about something you have done that was difficult. How did you prepare for it?

6 ▶ **1.05** Listen and answer the questions.
1. What has each person achieved?
2. What challenges did they face?

Grammar | perfect forms

7 Read the Active Grammar box. Match sentences a–c to the timelines on the right.

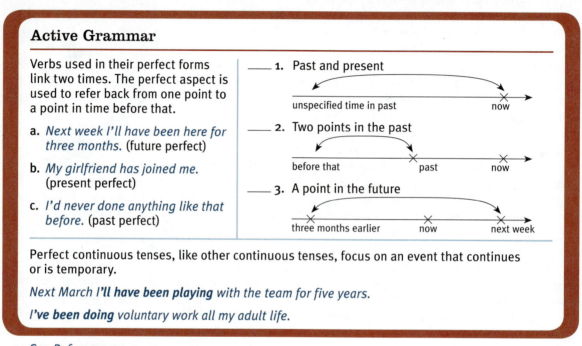

Active Grammar

Verbs used in their perfect forms link two times. The perfect aspect is used to refer back from one point to a point in time before that.

a. *Next week I'll have been here for three months.* (future perfect)

b. *My girlfriend has joined me.* (present perfect)

c. *I'd never done anything like that before.* (past perfect)

_____ 1. Past and present

unspecified time in past   now

_____ 2. Two points in the past

before that   past   now

_____ 3. A point in the future

three months earlier   now   next week

Perfect continuous tenses, like other continuous tenses, focus on an event that continues or is temporary.

*Next March I'**ll have been playing** with the team for five years.*

*I'**ve been doing** voluntary work all my adult life.*

See Reference page 127

8a Circle the correct choice.
1. Jake, this is my friend Amy, whom I've *been knowing/known* forever.
2. I asked what had *happened/been happened*, but nobody could tell me.
3. I chose this school because *I've heard/I'd heard* it was the best.
4. Before I came to the US, *I've/I'd* never been abroad.
5. I'm so exhausted. *I've/I'd* been working really hard.
6. By the time she retires, she'll *have been working/had been working* there for more than 50 years.

b ▶ **1.06** Listen and check your answers.

Speaking

9 **Pair Work** Think about your greatest achievement. Make notes using the language in the How To box. Then tell your partner. Try to use perfect verb forms in your story.

How To:

Talk about an achievement

Problems	• *I didn't know what to expect.* • *It was tough/a challenge.*
How it felt	• *It exceeded my expectations.* • *I felt like I'd accomplished something.* • *It was a great experience.*
Results/ follow up	• *I've learned a lot.* • *I'm looking forward to . . .*

Extra Vocabulary Study and
Extra Listening Activity
▶ in *ACTIVEBOOK*

Review

1   Complete the article with words from the box.

> distinguished from   challenging   relied on   faced
> benefited from   succeeded in   intelligible   pick up

The Hawaiian Creole language was invented through necessity. In 1880, thousands of immigrants from Europe and Asia went to work for the English-speaking owners of sugar plantations in Hawaii. Among all the other challenges these immigrants _____ (**1.**), the most _____ (**2.**) was to understand each other, to understand their bosses, and to understand the Hawaiian people. After a short time, they were able to _____ (**3.**) some English, but barely enough to communicate. Instead, they _____ (**4.**) body language and a simple code of sounds.

However, things changed fast, and by 1910 a new language had emerged: Hawaiian Creole.

This included words and sounds from other languages, but it could be _____ (**5.**) all of them by its different grammar. With this new easily understood language, everybody _____ (**6.**) increased communication.

Many years later, Derek Bickerton studied the origins of Hawaiian Creole. He was amazed that within one generation, the immigrants had _____ (**7.**) creating a language that was _____ (**8.**) to all. In fact, in his book *Roots of Language*, he says that the children invented the language while playing together.

2   Add one word to each news headline to make it correct.
1.   Sci-Corps Company seems to abandoned its research into cloning.
2.   Former president Michael Nkrumah is said be recovering well from the stroke he suffered last Thursday.
3.   The explorer Michaela Barker has been found in Brazil. It believed that she had drowned during a storm.
4.   Baseball star Alex Hanai appears to finally retired at the age of 40.

3   Complete the sentences using a perfect form of the verb in parentheses.
1.   By the time she finishes her degree, she _____ (be) in school for ten years.
2.   I feel healthier now that I _____ (take up) kickboxing.
3.   Where were you? I _____ (wait) here for at least an hour!
4.   I _____ (run) for years before I entered my first marathon.
5.   We _____ (use up) all the world's oil long before 2100.

4   Put B's words in order to complete the conversations.
>   **Ex: A:** What is Pelé's real first name?
>   **B:** pretty I'm Edson it's sure. *I'm pretty sure it's Edson.*
1.   **A:** Have you ever been to Prague?
     B: yes, I of the hand like my back it know _____
2.   **A:** How many women have succeeded in Formula 1 racing?
     B: I many know not but offhand, don't _____
3.   **A:** Can you help me with my homework? I need some information about space travel.
     B: know nothing it to next about I _____
4.   **A:** Who's Michael Vaughan?
     B: never him heard I've of _____

Communication | take a personality quiz

5 **Pair Work** Complete the questionnaire. When you have finished, compare answers and think of another question to add.

DO YOU LIKE A CHALLENGE?

1. You are climbing a mountain with some friends. It is cold and wet, and you are halfway up. You ____ .
   a. turn around and go home to a hot bath.
   b. keep going. Nothing will stop you once you've started.
   c. see what your friends want to do. It doesn't really matter if you reach the top.

2. You get an offer to work abroad for a year. It means you have to learn a diffcult new language and live in an isolated place with no nightlife. You ____ .
   a. refuse politely. You'd have to be crazy to live in the middle of nowhere.
   b. accept. Who needs nightclubs? And you may love it.
   c. ask your colleagues, friends, and family what they think.

3. You are asked to perform in a local play. You will have to learn some lines and act in front of a large audience. You ____ .
   a. say no. You aren't going to make a fool of yourself in public.
   b. jump up on stage and start singing. This is your chance at fame and fortune.
   c. ask exactly what you'll have to do, then think about it.

4. Your friends decide to learn to skydive. They want you to join them. You ____ .
   a. refuse, saying you're too young to die.
   b. immediately book lessons. It'll be fun.
   c. find some statistics on the mortality rate of skydivers before committing yourself.

5. You are asked to cook for 15 people. You ____ .
   a. immediately find out the name of a good caterer.
   b. start dreaming of the delicious feast you will prepare. It could be a great night.
   c. consult some cookbooks and figure out how much it will cost.

6. You are offered the chance to sail around the world. You ____ .
   a. say no. You can't take the time off work.
   b. get ready to go immediately.
   c. ask for additional information before you commit.

6 ▶1.07 Listen to what your answers say about your personality.

7 **Pair Work** Discuss.

1. Which would be the most difficult challenge for you? Which would be the easiest? Why?

2. How would you prepare for each challenge?

3. Which do you think are harder—mental or physical challenges? Give examples.

> *Performing in a play would be the most difficult for me. I get really nervous speaking in front of large groups of people.*

Places and communities

A

B

C

D

Warm Up

1 **Pair Work** Discuss. What types of communities do the people in the photos belong to? What are the positive and negative aspects of each community?

2a Unscramble the underlined words and expressions and read the definitions. Then mark each item positive (+) or negative (–).

_____ 1. reasonable octs of glinvi—not too expensive

_____ 2. ldim climate—not extreme weather; not too hot or too cold

_____ 3. personal ermefod—you are allowed to do what you want

_____ 4. efficient ecraehalht system—plenty of good hospitals

_____ 5. good addsarnt of ilgniv—you can have a good lifestyle

_____ 6. high emcir reta—many crimes per year

_____ 7. high level of pnmletouneym—many people don't have jobs

_____ 8. ria ooitpulln—dirty air

_____ 9. no utllruac life—lack of theaters, concert halls, art galleries, etc.

_____ 10. vibrant ihilgfetn—many good nightclubs, restaurants, movie theaters

b **Pair Work** Discuss. Which four qualities from the list are the most important to you in a community? Why?

Personal freedom is really important to me. Also . . .

Give advice and make recommendations about places

GRAMMAR gerund and infinitive review

Listening

1 **Pair Work** Discuss.

   1. Have you ever lived abroad? Where? Describe your experience.

   2. What problems might people living in a foreign country have?

2a ▶1.08 Listen to the descriptions of living abroad. Complete the chart.

	Speaker 1	Speaker 2	Speaker 3
1. Where did he or she live?			
2. What was he or she doing there?			
3. What did he or she like about the host country?			
4. Was there anything he or she didn't like or that was difficult?			
5. What are his or her favorite memories of the country?			

b Which of the speakers (1, 2, or 3):

   ____ 1. got a few surprises?

   ____ 2. was there at the wrong time?

   ____ 3. is from a small town?

   ____ 4. would like to return?

   ____ 5. learned about the culture by talking to the local people?

   ____ 6. says the place was multicultural?

   ____ 7. has lived in many countries?

   ____ 8. doesn't mention the scenery?

c Listen again to check your answers.

3 **Group Work** Discuss.

   1. Which of the places in Exercise 2 would you most like to live in? Why?

   2. Would you like to live abroad for a while? Why or why not?

   3. Why do you think the speakers talk mainly about food, scenery, and people? Which of these do you think is the most important in a place?

Grammar | gerund and infinitive review

4 Complete the sentences. Use an infinitive or gerund and a preposition if necessary.

1. I'm **thinking** _of taking_ (take) a break.
2. If you can't **afford** _____ (eat) in expensive restaurants, Vancouver has many cheaper ones.
3. I can't **imagine** _____ (live) there.
4. You can **avoid** _____ (offend) people by learning the host country's customs.
5. I don't **mind** _____ (stand) in line.
6. She doesn't **want** _____ (miss out) on "fusion cuisine."
7. I can't **stand** _____ (travel).
8. If you **object** _____ (pay) lots of money, don't shop there.
9. I **encourage** all foreigners _____ (try) some real sushi.
10. I **urge** you _____ (see) Stanley Park in Vancouver.
11. I'd **recommend** _____ (go) to Tokyo Art Gallery.
12. She **persuaded** us _____ (visit) Austria in the spring.

5 Complete the Active Grammar box, using the verbs in bold in Exercise 4.

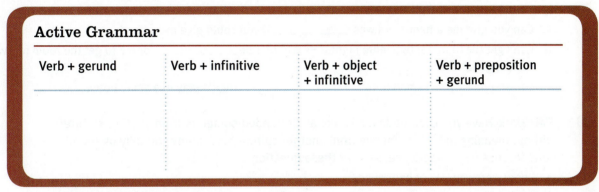

Active Grammar

Verb + gerund	Verb + infinitive	Verb + object + infinitive	Verb + preposition + gerund

See Reference page 128

6 Rewrite the sentences below, using a gerund or infinitive with the verb in bold. Begin each sentence with *I* or *I'm*.

Ex: You must go to the National Gallery. **urge** *I urge you to go to the National Gallery.*

1. I don't have the money to go to the theater. **afford**
2. You should go to the museum on Sunday. **advise**
3. I think people ought to use the parks more. **encourage**
4. You should buy tickets early. **recommend**
5. I never take the train. **avoid**
6. I may go to Thailand in February. **think**

7 **Pair Work** Think of a place you have visited. Make recommendations to your partner. Use some of the language in the How To box.

> *Toledo, Spain is a must-see. My favorite part is . . .*

How To:

Give advice/make recommendations about places	
Saying it's good	• *It's a must* or *a must-see.* • *It's a good value for the money.*
Saying it's not so good	• *It's a little bit overrated* or *overpriced.* • *It's not all it's cracked up to be.*
Recommending	• *If I were you, I'd go to . . .* • *Don't miss . . .* or *Make sure you go to . . .* • *You should try . . .*
Warning	• *Watch out for . . .*

Speaking

8 **Pair Work** Discuss.

    1. What do you think "cultural awareness" means? Can you give any examples?

    2. Do you think cultural awareness is important? Why or why not?

    3. What cultural mistakes do foreigners sometimes make in your country?

    4. Do you know of any customs or habits that are acceptable in your country but impolite in other countries?

9 Make the sentences more polite, using the words in the box.

> please   mind   were   was   wondering   think   possible

    1. Move your bag. → Would you _____ moving your bag?

    2. Be quiet. → Could you _____ be a little bit quieter?

    3. Slow down. → Do you _____ you could slow down a little?

    4. I thought you could give us a ride. → I _____ hoping you could give us a ride.

    5. Can you give me a hand? → I was _____ if you could give me a hand.

    6. Can I get the room for two more nights? → Would it be _____ for me to get the room for two more nights?

    7. You should stay in a small hotel. → If I _____ you, I'd stay in a small hotel.

10a **Pair Work** Have you ever made a mistake and offended someone from another culture without meaning to? Has someone from another culture ever unintentionally offended you? Discuss your experience. Answer these questions:

- Where were you? What happened?
- Did you (or the other person) realize at the time that a mistake had been made?
- What did you do to resolve the issue?

> *I was traveling in Indonesia for business last year. A colleague there asked me how much money I make. I was startled and said that that was private. I think I offended him—I didn't realize that it's common for people there to ask each other about their salaries. I later went back and apologized . . .*

b Would you have made the same mistake as your partner? Why or why not?

11 **Group Work** Use your experiences from Exercise 10a to compile a "cultural awareness guide." Include advice on what people from your country should expect and how they should behave in other countries.

Writing

12 Write a "web page" with advice for visitors to your country. Include information on food, places to go, the best methods of transportation, holidays and festivals, and cultural advice. Use language from the How To box on page 21 and some of the verbs from the Active Grammar.

Use features of formal and informal language

GRAMMAR comparisons

CAN DO ✓

Listening

1 **Pair Work** Discuss.
1. How often do you use the Internet? What do you use it for?
2. Do you trust what you read on the Internet? Why or why not?

2 ▶1.09 Listen to the conversation. What issues do they discuss?

3 Listen again and check (✓) the phrases you hear.

_____ 1. (It's) so much . . . (than)
_____ 2. (It's) far . . . (than)
_____ 3. (It's) not nearly as . . . as
_____ 4. the less we . . . , the less we . . .
_____ 5. the more we . . . , the more we . . .
_____ 6. It's not quite as . . . as . . .
_____ 7. It's considerably . . .
_____ 8. It's slightly . . .
_____ 9. (It's) almost the same as
_____ 10. It's the same as
_____ 11. It's a little bit . . . (than)

American English	British English
not nearly as . . .	*nowhere near as . . .*
so much (easier)	*miles (easier)*

Grammar | comparisons

4 Complete the chart in the Active Grammar box, using the phrases from Exercise 3.

Active Grammar

1. A big difference	
2. A little difference	
3. No difference	
4. *The* + comparative + *the* + comparative	

See Reference page 128

5 Complete the sentences with words or phrases from the Active Grammar box. Some items have more than one possible answer.
1. It's _____ (easy) to communicate by email than by telephone.
2. Buying things in stores is _____ as cheap as shopping online.
3. Writing on a computer is _____ (fast) than writing by hand.
4. The more you use your smartphone, _____ you will rely on it.
5. Buying things online is _____ (risky) than face-to-face transactions.
6. Information on the Internet is not _____ (reliable) as information in books.

Speaking

6 **Pair Work** Do you agree or disagree with the statements in Exercise 5? Discuss.

Reading

7 **Pair Work** Have you ever heard of or used Wikipedia? What is special about it?

8 Read the article. Then answer the questions below.

The Internet's largest encyclopedia

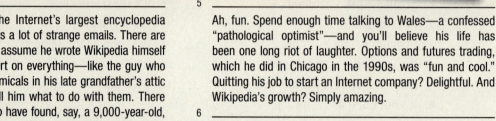

1 Being the founder of the Internet's largest encyclopedia means Jimmy Wales gets a lot of strange emails. There are the correspondents who assume he wrote Wikipedia himself and is therefore an expert on everything—like the guy who found some strange chemicals in his late grandfather's attic and wanted Wales to tell him what to do with them. There are wackos who claim to have found, say, a 9,000-year-old, 15-foot human skeleton and wonder if Wales would be interested. But the emails that make him laugh out loud come from concerned newcomers who've just discovered they have total freedom to edit a Wikipedia entry at the click of a button. "Oh my gosh," they write, "you've got a major security flaw."

2 Wikipedia is a free open-source encyclopedia, which means that anyone can log on and add to it or edit it. And they do. It has millions of entries in 281 languages—and counting. Academics are upset by what they see as info anarchy. A print encyclopedia editor once likened Wikipedia to a doorknob because you don't know who touched it last. But loyal users claim that collaboration improves articles over time.

3 But what exactly is a wiki and how does it work? Wikis are deceptively simple pieces of software that you can download for free. You then use them to set up a website that can be edited by anyone you like. Need to solve a thorny business problem overnight and all the members of your team are in different time zones? Start a wiki. And the name? Believe it or not, the name came about because the inventor of the wiki had his honeymoon in Hawaii, where you catch the "wiki wiki" (quick) bus from the airport.

4 Anyway, in 2001, Jimmy Wales was looking for a way to combine his two major hobbies: perusing the Encyclopedia Britannica and surfing the Internet. "I met all these great people online," he says, "and we were all discussing things on mailing lists no one ever looks at. I thought, why not build something more long-lasting, more fun and entertaining?"

5 Ah, fun. Spend enough time talking to Wales—a confessed "pathological optimist"—and you'll believe his life has been one long riot of laughter. Options and futures trading, which he did in Chicago in the 1990s, was "fun and cool." Quitting his job to start an Internet company? Delightful. And Wikipedia's growth? Simply amazing.

6 Wikipedia is the cumulative work of 16,000 people, the bulk of it done by a hard-core group of around 1,000 volunteers. Its over 3 million entries in English alone make it far larger than the Encyclopedia Britannica. And Wales pays just one employee, who keeps the servers ticking.

7 Naturally there are many who take advantage of Wikipedia's open system to deface, delete, or push one-sided views. Sometimes extreme action has to be taken. For example, Wales locked the entries on John Kerry and George W. Bush for most of the 2004 presidential election campaign. But for the most part, such action is not necessary. According to an MIT study, obscene comments randomly inserted on Wikipedia are removed within 100 seconds, on average. Vandals might as well be spray-painting walls with disappearing ink.

8 As for edit wars, in which two users with opposing views delete each other's assertions over and over, well, they're not much of a problem these days. All kinds of viewpoints co-exist in the same article. Take the entry on Wikipedia: "Wikipedia has been criticized for a perceived lack of reliability, comprehensiveness, and authority." Indeed, Larry Sanger, Wikipedia's former editor-in-chief (now a university professor), still loves the site but thinks his fellow professionals have a point. "The wide-open nature of the Internet encourages people to disregard the importance of expertise," he says. Sanger doesn't let his students use Wikipedia for their papers, partly because he knows they could confirm anything they like by adding it themselves.

1. What is Wikipedia?
2. What is a wiki?
3. Who is Jimmy Wales?
4. What problems has Wikipedia had?
5. What criticisms has it faced?
6. What do people like about it?

9 **Pair Work** Look at the How To box. Then discuss items 1–2.

1. Find other examples in the article of a) informal vocabulary, b) spoken English, and c) humor.

2. Are the following generally used in formal or informal texts: full verb forms, lots of phrasal verbs, sentences beginning with *and* or *but*, repeated use of the passive?

10 Read the two formal emails below. Some of the words and phrases used are too informal. Replace them with a more appropriate word or phrase from the box below.

How To:

Recognize features of a colloquial writing style

Informal vocabulary	• *guy* (paragraph 1) • *wackos* (paragraph 1)
Spoken English style	• *say* (paragraph 1) • *Oh my gosh* (paragraph 1) • Short forms: *who've* (paragraph 1)
Omitted words	• *Need to solve a thorny business problem . . .* (paragraph 3). The full question = *Do you need to solve . . .* • *And the name?* (paragraph 3)
Humor	• *A print encyclopedia editor once likened Wikipedia to a doorknob because you don't know who touched it last.* (paragraph 2)

will be very happy to attend	will be unable to attend	requested
we would be grateful if you could	a previous arrangement	concerning
could you please confirm your attendance	don't hesitate to	follow

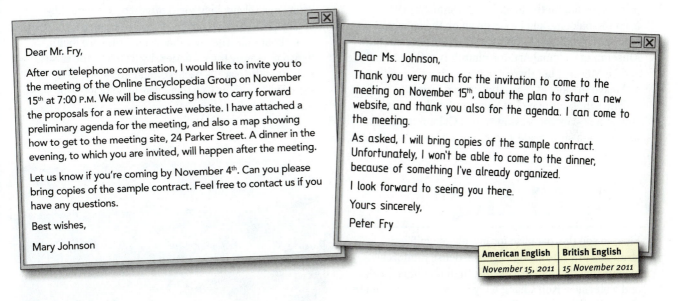

Dear Mr. Fry,

After our telephone conversation, I would like to invite you to the meeting of the Online Encyclopedia Group on November 15th at 7:00 P.M. We will be discussing how to carry forward the proposals for a new interactive website. I have attached a preliminary agenda for the meeting, and also a map showing how to get to the meeting site, 24 Parker Street. A dinner in the evening, to which you are invited, will happen after the meeting.

Let us know if you're coming by November 4th. Can you please bring copies of the sample contract. Feel free to contact us if you have any questions.

Best wishes,

Mary Johnson

Dear Ms. Johnson,

Thank you very much for the invitation to come to the meeting on November 15th, about the plan to start a new website, and thank you also for the agenda. I can come to the meeting.

As asked, I will bring copies of the sample contract. Unfortunately, I won't be able to come to the dinner, because of something I've already organized.

I look forward to seeing you there.

Yours sincerely,

Peter Fry

American English	British English
November 15, 2011	15 November 2011

Writing

11a Read the formal email in the Writing Bank on page 144 and do the exercises.

b Read the information in the box and write a formal email. Pay particular attention to greeting and signing off, coherence and cohesion, punctuation, spelling, and style.

You are a celebrity. A Wikipedia entry about you contains some extremely negative comments and a number of factual errors. You tried to edit the Wikipedia entry, but it was "locked," so you were unable to change it. Write a letter of complaint to Wikipedia. Make sure you include corrections of the facts and explain why you think the comments about you are unfair. Ask for the changes to be made as soon as possible.

Cali, Colombia

Reading

1   **Pair Work** Discuss. What do you know about the places in the photos? What do you think they are like? Would you like to visit them? Why or why not?

2   Read the descriptions.

Cali

1   In Cali, they say, even the ghosts dance salsa. Its rhythms, born in Cuba, nurtured in New York, and carried on the winds all the way to hot Cali, can be heard in bars, on buses, along the avenues of Juanchito and Plaza Caicedo, and here, too, in a taxi moving at the speed of light, taking me to the heart of the bustling city. The driver slows down at a traffic light, turns to me and says, "*Las calenas* (the women from Cali) are the most beautiful women in the world!" And we're off again, driving past groups of *mulatto* men laughing in the street.

2   My hotel is a run-down old building whose blue paint is peeling in the heat. It has a stunning view from the balcony, and I gaze down on the square. The guidebooks tell you to visit the Gold Museum and the Museum of Colonial Art, the churches of San Antonio and La Merced, but there's only one thing on my mind as I leave the key at reception: salsa dancing.

3   The *salsotecas* don't get busy until midnight, so I stop at a restaurant serving typical Colombian food: *sancocho*—a stew made with chunks of beef, vegetables,

cassava (a tropical plant with edible roots), and plantain (a type of banana but not as sweet) served with rice. Then I must choose from the amazingly diverse selection of Colombian fruit. I settle for guanabana and maracuya, and I'm not disappointed. I stroll for a while, tempted by dark smoky cafés, the fans spinning weakly on the ceilings. This is the old, unspoiled Cali, which lives side by side with a newer version, the Cali of junk food, Internet cafés, and vast touristy nightclubs. I walk past the trees and sculptures that line the river and into San Antonio park, a tranquil spot off the beaten track.

4   Later, on Avenida Sexta—Sixth Avenue—I find what I'm really looking for: a *salsoteca*. Some friendly young Colombians teach me a few dance steps, and we chat about Cali. They say that when times are tough, they dance away their worries. By 2:00 A.M. the salsa is swinging, the place is packed, and I know one thing for sure: I've found the Cali that I was looking for—the salsa dancer's paradise.

Koh Chang

5   I had to see this paradise for myself: magnificent stretches of white sandy beaches, dense rainforests, exciting wildlife and marine life, high mountain peaks, and waterfalls. Koh Chang truly is heavenly—a remote, charming, island unspoiled (as yet!) by the modern world.

6   It wasn't easy getting to Koh Chang. My wife and I boarded a rickety overnight bus in Bangkok. We rode for five uncomfortable, sleepless hours to the town of Trat, where we caught an early morning ferry to Center Point Pier in Koh Chang. There we squeezed in the back of a pick-up truck with seven other people and experienced a wild, bumpy ride over the steep winding peaks of the island to our destination: White Sand Beach.

Koh Chang, Thailand

7   And it was truly that—a pure white sand beach. We were engulfed by the tranquility, and our bare feet didn't part with the white sand for three full days. We roasted under the hot sun, gazed at the blue ocean, strolled along the endless beaches, paddled in

canoes along the coastlines, and at night retired to our humble beach hut. We had opted for the simplest of accommodations over the more luxurious villas and resorts that the island also offers.

8   Day four, however, the jungle called, and we ventured away from sun, sand, and sea. A guide walked us through the vast rain forests. We met face-to-face with a tarantula, studied a venomous snake from a distance, and admired a barking deer and a wild pig. I performed a daring high jump into a waterfall that was so clean and refreshing that I then drank from it. My wife was not so brave as to jump, but she did swing on a vine Tarzan-style, waving to the wild monkeys and the exotic birds around us. The guide also showed us a tree used to extract rubber—one of the livelihoods of the inhabitants of Koh Chang. I had no idea rubber comes from trees!

9   The biggest treat was an evening boat tour on our last night. We were met with magical blinking lights on the vast ocean horizon. Our guide informed us these were the boats of local fishermen catching squid. The inhabitants of Koh Chang come from generations of fishermen who still live traditionally, surviving on fishing (as well as growing fruit and rubber). Their ideal balance: go fishing at night and hike or kayak during the day. Sounds like the perfect life to me!

Cape Town

10 The first thing I can tell you about Thabo, my South African guide, is that he is the world's worst driver. From the airport to the heart of the city, he averages 60 miles per hour, swerving around trucks, motorcycles, and taxis crammed with people. The second thing is that he knows everybody and everything about Cape Town. This is good, because I am trying to complete Mission Impossible: see Cape Town in just three days.

11 On the first day, Thabo takes me to the wealthy suburbs with unpronounceable names—Tamboerskloof and Oranjezicht—where you can watch the sun go down on Africa. The views are stunning.

12 The next day we go off the beaten track to Cape Flats, the run-down township where the buildings are made of cardboard and corrugated iron. It is the poorest part of the city and it is vast—nearly a million people live here, side by side. Skinny dogs slide out of the way as Thabo zooms along mud roads lined with trash. Some people wave, others stare. Children run barefoot by the car.

13 Later that night we walk around the bustling Victoria and Alfred Waterfront, Cape Town's most fashionable area. The contrast from the township could not be more stark. As we stroll, the smells of cooking drift up from the kitchens—Asian, French, Italian, and of course

Cape Town, South Africa

South African. The restaurants are packed, and I soon find out why. Cape Town is a paradise for gourmets, seafood-lovers, and people like me, who just like eating. Thabo tells me I can't leave Cape Town without trying some Cape seafood, so I do. It's delicious.

14 On my final morning, we spend a tranquil hour sitting outside a café. I gaze at Table Mountain, which forms the backdrop to the city, while Thabo shouts greetings to everyone who passes by. Then we are driving again, experiencing the diverse landscape—sandy beaches, mountain slopes, and green valleys unspoiled by tourism. It's a great way to say goodbye to a place I've known only too briefly. I promise myself, and Thabo, that I'll be back.

3   **Group Work** Discuss.

1. Each place is described as a type of "paradise." Which aspects of these places sound perfect to you? What makes them unique?

2. Which place would you prefer to go to for a vacation? Why?

3. Do you think tourism is good for these three places? What problems might it bring them?

Vocabulary | adjectives to describe places

4 Work in groups. Find words in the article on pages 26–27 that mean:

1. not damaged in character or atmosphere _____ (paragraphs 3, 5, 14)
2. having variety _____ (paragraphs 3, 14)
3. extremely large _____ (paragraphs 3, 8, 9, 12)
4. in poor condition, uncared for _____ (paragraphs 2, 12)
5. amazingly beautiful _____ (paragraphs 2, 11)
6. very busy, crowded _____ (paragraphs 4, 13)
7. peaceful (n. peace) _____ , _____ (paragraphs 3, 7, 14)
8. in areas people don't normally go to (usually outside the city) _____ (paragraphs 3, 12)
9. energetic and noisy, full of life _____ (paragraphs 1, 13)
10. extremely impressive and beautiful _____ (paragraph 5)

5 Use the vocabulary in Exercise 4 to complete the sentences.

1. The roof is falling off, and the windows are broken; the old house looks very _____.
2. It's hard to find the little cabin in the countryside because it's _____.
3. You can hardly move during carnival time because the streets are _____.
4. There are many different nationalities living there, so the culture is very _____.
5. The Sahara Desert is 3,630,000 square miles. It's _____.
6. We're going to spend a few _____ days camping, far from the noisy city.
7. The town remains _____, despite the tourists. It hasn't changed at all.
8. The lake is simply _____—it's one of the most beautiful things I've ever seen.

6 **Pair Work** Talk about a place you have been to that a) has stunning views, b) is off the beaten track, c) is tranquil, d) is bustling on the weekends, or e) is unspoiled.

Writing

7a Write a paragraph or two about a favorite place. Think about atmosphere, landscape, things to see and do, and food.

b **Group Work** Exchange paragraphs. Ask questions to learn more about your classmates' favorite places.

> *How do you get to Silver Beach? What's the best time to go?*

LESSON 4 Unit Wrap Up

Extra Vocabulary Study and
Extra Listening Activity
in **ACTIVEBOOK**

Review

1 Complete the sentences, using the gerund or infinitive form of words from the box. You may need to add a preposition.

> take   pay   spend   hear   apply   consult   go   buy   live   wear

1. I encouraged the architects _____ the community about their new project.
2. We didn't mind _____ a few days in the town, but we didn't want to live there.
3. We urged them not _____ a house in that area.
4. She's thinking of _____ for a job as a tour guide.
5. I object _____ such high rent.
6. They persuaded us _____ to Koh Chang on our next vacation.
7. I can imagine _____ here for the rest of my life. I love it.
8. To relieve stress, I recommend _____ a long vacation once a year.
9. I look forward _____ from you soon.
10. Members of the ski club are advised _____ helmets while skiing, for safety.

2 Add one word to complete each sentence.

> **Ex:** Prague is pretty as Vienna.
>
> *Prague is <u>as</u> pretty as Vienna.*

1. Paraguay is as large as Brazil—Brazil is much larger.
2. Switzerland is the as it always has been: safe, clean and expensive.
3. The more cars we use, the polluted our environment becomes.
4. Poland quite as cold as Norway, but its climate is similar in the northeast.
5. France is a little bit larger Spain.
6. China is far populated than Greenland.
7. Traveling by train is considerably comfortable than traveling by bus.

3 Put the sentences in the correct order. The first two have been done for you.

<u>_1_</u> Paris is one of the great tourist destinations. Its mild

____ pollution, with a hot air balloon that serves two purposes: it monitors air quality and provides people with stunning

____ of living and have an efficient

____ nightlife, though the crime

____ living is not too high, compared to most of Western Europe. Paris is famous for its cultural

____ healthcare system. Paris has a vibrant

<u>_2_</u> climate is perfect for relaxing and strolling along the wide streets. Parisians enjoy a good standard

____ life. There are so many wonderful things to do and see. Paris is working to control air

____ views of the city.

____ rate has risen in the last few years. The general cost of

Communication | collaborate on a plan

4a Read the article. Do you think the club is silly, funny, or a good idea?

THE NOT TERRIBLY GOOD CLUB

IN 1976, STEPHEN PILE formed The Not Terribly Good Club. To qualify for membership, you had to do something badly and attend meetings. During these meetings, people gave public demonstrations of things they couldn't do, such as painting or singing, and gave presentations on things they knew nothing about. Stephen Pile kept a record of these unsuccessful events, and then published them as *The Book of Heroic Failures* in 1979. The stories included examples of incompetence, such as "the world's worst tourist," who spent two days in New York, believing he was in Rome; "the slowest completion of a crossword" (34 years); and the burglar who wore metal armor to protect himself from dogs. The armor made so much noise that he got caught, and it was too heavy for him to run away. Included in *The Book of Heroic Failures* was an application form for membership to The Not Terribly Good Club. Amazingly, within two months of the book's publication, the group had received 20,000 applications to join, and the book appeared on various bestseller lists. As a result of his sudden fame, Pile was kicked out of his own club, and the club itself soon disbanded: it had become too successful.

b **Pair Work** If you were joining The Not Terribly Good Club, what would your presentation be about?

5 ▶1.10 Listen to two people describe clubs they belong to. Take notes as you listen. Then compare your notes with a partner.

Alumni club
1. The main purpose of the club
2. Other things that members do
3. Type of meeting
4. Who can be a member

Ballroom dancing club
1. Number of people in the club
2. When and where it meets
3. Things members have learned

6a **Group Work** Imagine that you are going to form a club. Think about the following questions.
1. What type of club is it?
2. What events will you organize?
3. What are the goals of the club?
4. What is the name of the club?
5. Where will you meet?
6. How often?
7. What rules will the club have?

b Present your ideas to the rest of the class. Which clubs would you like to join?

Stories

A

B

C

D

Warm Up

1 **Pair Work** Discuss. Can you identify any of the stories illustrated by the pictures? What types of stories do they illustrate?

2 Think of an example for each of the story types listed below. Use your dictionary if necessary.
   1. a fake   2. a myth   3. a tall tale   4. a fairy tale   5. a legend   6. a joke

3 **Pair Work** Discuss the meanings of the phrases in bold. Then answer the questions.
   1. Do you think it's OK to **tell a white lie** if it makes life easier?
   2. Have you ever taken part in (or heard about) **a hoax**?
   3. When you describe things, do you sometimes **exaggerate**?
   4. Do you know any **good storytellers**?
   5. Were you told **bedtime stories** when you were a child? Which were your favorites?

Reading

1 **Pair Work** Look at the photos and discuss the questions.

1. What can you tell about Manuel Elizalde from the photo?
2. Who do you think Sidd Finch was?

2 Read the article. Then answer the questions that follow.

Manuel Elizalde and the Tasaday people

HOAXES THAT FOOLED THE WORLD

In 1971, while he was working as a government minister in the Philippines, Manuel Elizalde announced a great discovery. He had found a Stone Age tribe, the Tasaday, living in a remote part of the country. They lived in caves, used stone tools, and ate any food they could find. This isolated tribe, just 27 people, had been living this way for many generations. Journalists arrived from all over the world, a documentary about the tribe was filmed for TV, and thousands of dollars were spent on research trips. The Philippine government, however, not wanting to destroy a way of life that had existed for thousands of years, allowed only a few people to visit them.

It was only years later that the truth came out. Researchers found the tribe living in villages, wearing Levi's jeans and communicating happily with other people. They explained that they had been pretending all along; Elizalde had paid them to act like a Stone Age tribe.

Elizalde's hoax was just one in a long line. Anthropology has been a particularly rich field for hoaxers, including Fujimura Shinichi, the Japanese archaeologist who faked vital discoveries for years before being found out in 2000.

But perhaps the most interesting hoaxes are those that involve fictitious people. Piotr Zak was, as reported by the BBC, a Polish composer. An avant-garde modernist, he was not well-known among the public. At least not until 1961, when the BBC broadcast his piece *Mobile for Tape and Percussion*. Some music critics hailed it as a great work. Unfortunately for them, the piece had consisted of BBC staff making strange noises, edited by BBC technicians. It was a classic hoax.

Nearly a quarter of a century later, on April 1, 1985, another great hoax was to shake the world of American sports. In the United States, April 1 is April Fools' Day, a day for playing practical jokes. *Sports Illustrated*

ran an article about Sidd Finch, a truly extraordinary baseball player. The subheading of the article read: "He's a pitcher, part yogi and part recluse. Impressively liberated from our opulent lifestyle, Sidd's deciding about yoga—and his future in baseball." Read the first letters of these words again, carefully. They spell out "Happy April Fools' Day." On April 15, the magazine came clean: They had fooled their readers. Finch was an invention. The writer of the article, George Plimpton, then extended his article into a novel, published in 1987.

Just a year later, British writer William Boyd published *Nat Tate*: *American Artist, 1928–1960*, the tragic biography of a New York painter. A number of prominent critics claimed to remember Tate's work, claiming that he had been one of the greatest artists of the century. He'd never existed. The name Nat Tate is derived from two of Britain's most famous art galleries: The National Gallery (Nat) and the Tate Gallery.

Sidd Finch

1. Why do you think people were so excited about the discovery of the Tasaday tribe?
2. Why do you think the people in the reading created these hoaxes?
3. Why do you think that intelligent people such as journalists and academics fall for hoaxes?

Grammar | review of past forms

3a Read the first paragraph of the article in Exercise 2 again. Find examples of the simple past, past continuous, past perfect, and past perfect continuous.

b Look at the pairs of sentences below. What are the differences in meaning (if any)?

1. a. When the truth came out, Elizalde had already left the country.
   b. When the truth came out, Elizalde left the country.
2. a. People believed the tribe had been living the same way for centuries.
   b. People believed the tribe had lived the same way for centuries.
3. a. When researchers arrived, the people from the tribe weren't living in caves any more.
   b. When researchers arrived, the people from the tribe didn't live in caves any more.

4 Complete the rules in the Active Grammar box with words from the box.

progress	length
chronological	before

Active Grammar

1. Use the simple past for past finished actions. Use it to describe a sequence of events in _____ order.
2. Use the past continuous for actions in _____ when something else happened.
3. Use the past perfect for actions completed _____ other events in the past. Use it when you are already talking about the past.
4. Use the past perfect continuous for actions already in progress before the main events happened. Use it to emphasize the _____ of the action.

See Reference page 129

5a Complete the descriptions of some famous hoaxes with the correct form of the verbs in parentheses.

¹ In 1957 a news program called *Panorama* broadcast a story about spaghetti trees in Switzerland. While the reporter told the story, Swiss farmers in the background _____ (1. pick) spaghetti from trees. Following this, thousands of people _____ (2. call) the show, asking how to grow spaghetti trees.

² In 1998 large numbers of Americans went to Burger King asking for a new type of burger. The food company _____ (3. publish) an ad in *USA Today* announcing the new "left-handed Whopper," a burger designed for left-handed people. The following day, Burger King _____ (4. admit) that they _____ (5. joke) all along.

b ▶ 1.11 Listen and check your answers.

Speaking

6a Prepare to tell a story about something that has happened in your life. Include in your story two or three details that are *not* true. Think about the following:

1. What were you doing when it happened?
2. Where were you? Who were you with?
3. What had happened before this?
4. What happened next?

b **Pair Work** Tell your story. Try to guess which details in your partner's story are invented.

> *It was the summer of 2009. I had been hanging out at the pool with my friends all morning, when suddenly . . .*

Vocabulary | synonyms

7a Read the newspaper excerpts. Think of synonyms for the underlined words and phrases.

1 The president is under pressure to <u>combat</u> illegal immigration after another state took <u>drastic measures</u> to <u>deal with</u> the problem yesterday.

2 Two men have been <u>detained</u> by police in connection with a bank robbery. The police stopped a truck <u>loaded</u> with cars that may have been <u>purchased</u> by the thieves.

3 In order to <u>keep track</u> of cows, which are <u>considered</u> sacred in India, authorities in Delhi are <u>placing</u> microchips in the animals.

4 The government has <u>initiated</u> a series of <u>talks</u> to <u>settle</u> the dispute that <u>led to</u> chaos on the trains.

5 A PROMINENT doctor <u>claims</u> that the country's failure to <u>prevent</u> the yearly outbreak of flu <u>arises</u> from a lack of hygiene in schools.

b Match the words to the underlined words and phrases with similar meanings in Exercise 7a.

1. stop _____
2. fight _____
3. resolve _____
4. follow the movements _____
5. extreme actions _____
6. asserts _____
7. arrested _____
8. stems _____
9. packed _____
10. putting _____
11. thought to be _____
12. formal discussions _____
13. cope with _____
14. caused _____
15. bought _____
16. started _____

8 **Pair Work** Complete the crossword puzzle. All of the words are from the article on page 32.

Across
1. faking (v)
2. alone (adj)
4. extremely important (adj)
5. freed (adj)
7. ruin (v)
10. tricked (v)

Down
1. well-known and usually well-respected (adj)
3. imagined/invented (adj)
6. expanded (v)
8. extremely sad (adj)
9. a big, elaborate trick (n)

LESSON 2 Describe a person in detail CAN DO ✓
GRAMMAR compound adjectives

Vocabulary | books

1 **Pair Work** Discuss.

1. What kind of books do you like reading?

2. What are your three favorite books?

2 Match the sentences with similar meanings.

_____ 1. I couldn't put it down.

_____ 2. It's very readable.

_____ 3. It's a page-turner.

_____ 4. I found the story very moving.

_____ 5. The characters are one-dimensional.

_____ 6. It's based on a true story.

_____ 7. I'm a real bookworm.

_____ 8. It's a best-seller.

a. I'm an avid reader.

b. I was hooked.

c. It was gripping.

d. It depicts real events.

e. It has a nice, easy style.

f. It has sold many copies.

g. I was emotionally involved in it.

h. They didn't really come alive for me.

3 **Group Work** Think of different books that could be described by the words in Exercise 2. Tell other students about them.

> The Road Home *isn't a best-seller, but I thought it was a wonderful story. I couldn't put it down.*

Listening

4a ▶1.12 Listen to three people answering some of the questions below. Complete the chart.

	Speaker 1	Speaker 2	Speaker 3
1. Who is your favorite fictional character?			
2. Why do you like or admire this character?			
3. What do you think the character looks like?			
4. What personal traits does he or she possess (type of character)?			
5. What problems does he or she overcome?			

b Listen again to check your answers.

5 **Pair Work** Who is your favorite fictional character? Spend a few minutes thinking about your own answers to the questions in Exercise 4a. Then discuss.

Reading

6 Read the book excerpts and answer the questions. There may be more than one possible answer.

1. Which excerpt describes a dangerous character?
2. Which excerpt describes a middle-aged and not very handsome character?
3. Which excerpt describes a character who is probably bossy?
4. Which excerpt describes a character who probably spends a lot of time outdoors?
5. Which excerpt describes a character who is old but has a young mind?

1 For one thing, he was unlike any other man we'd ever seen—or heard of, if it came to that. With his **weather-beaten** face, wide teeth-crammed mouth, and **far-seeing** blue eyes, he looked like some wigwam warrior stained with suns and heroic slaughter.

(*The Edge of Day*—Laurie Lee)

2 My father is still living, but less and less. Judge James Charles Endicott Jackson . . . that tall, lean, **hollow-cheeked** man who had made such a religion of the law, preached from the head of our dining-room table each evening of my young life.

(*The Best Revenge*—Sol Stein)

3 He was fifty-five, but he could have been ten years either side of that. Thin sandy hair, a big awkward mouth. Bad teeth, crooked and dark when he smiled, jug-handle ears. As a **self-conscious** boy he'd tried different things with those ears. He'd made an elasticized band with elaborate leather flaps to flatten his ears while he slept. He'd tried his hair short. He'd tried it long. He'd tried all kinds of hats. Eventually he'd grown the moustache as a kind of diversionary tactic, and he'd kept it.

(*The Idea of Perfection*—Kate Grenville)

4 Her grandmother was small and thin, with tiny hands and feet—**fast-moving** feet the size of a child's—and **washed-out** red frizzy hair that she dyed the color of Red Delicious apples. She had disappearing lips, painted large, twice their size, the color of plums. All her life, she'd been a dancer, every kind of dancer. Even now, at seventy-seven, she'd put on tights and a leotard and tutu, and do her ballet exercises in front of the long mirror on Alyssa's bedroom door.

(*Blister*—Susan Shreve)

5 He was just a **hot-headed**, twenty-year-old kid at the time, but he was greasy-fast with a gun. The problem was that he was spoiling for a fight and got it. At over six feet and one hundred and ninety pounds, he was a big boy and he had set out to prove to everyone that he was a man to reckon with.

(*Slade*—Robert Dyer)

7 **Group Work** Read the excerpts again and answer the questions.

1. What type of person is being described in each excerpt?
2. What physical details are included? Do they show the person's character?
3. What actions are shown? How do these reveal character?
4. What type of book do you think each excerpt is from (funny, serious, etc.)?
5. Would you like to read any of the books?

Grammar | compound adjectives

8 Read the Active Grammar box and answer the questions after each rule.

> ## Active Grammar
>
> 1. We often use compound adjectives, such as *kind-hearted*, to describe people. Which compound adjectives in the book excerpts on page 36
>   a) describe someone's character?
>   b) describe something physical?
>
> 2. Compound adjectives frequently use a hyphen (-) between the words. Often the second word is a present or past participle.
>
> 3. Sometimes we can guess the meaning of compound adjectives. What is the compound adjective for a person who works hard? keeps an open mind? looks good? thinks freely? loves fun?

See Reference page 129

9 **Pair Work** Read the sentences. Try to explain in your own words what the compound adjectives in bold mean.

1. He's very **single-minded**. It took him ten years to learn the violin, but he never gave up!
2. She's very **self-sufficient** for a child. She makes her own food and entertains herself for hours.
3. Writers have to be **thick-skinned**. Lots of people criticize their work, but they try not to get upset.
4. He's so **kind-hearted**. He's always helpful, even if he's busy.
5. They can be a little **stand-offish**. They didn't talk to anybody at the party.
6. He's very **career-oriented**. He even brings work on vacation.
7. They're really **level-headed**. Even when they won all that money, they didn't get too excited.
8. I'm a little bit **absent-minded**. I keep forgetting where I put my glasses.

Writing

10a Read the How To box and write a short description of someone you know well. Describe the following: first impressions, physical details, and character. Use at least two compound adjectives.

How To:	
Describe people	
First impressions	• She **comes across as** (adjective), but once you **get to know** her, she's (adjective). • **The thing that strikes you about** him is that . . .
Character—good things and bad things	• **The thing I (don't) like about** her is . . . • **What I (don't) really like about** him is . . . • She's **so** (adjective) • He's **such a** (adjective) person • She **can be a bit** (negative adjective)

b **Group Work** Share your descriptions. Ask questions.

> *Paul seems shy at first, but once you get to know him, he's very friendly.*

> *What makes him appear shy?*

LESSON **3** **Tell a joke**
GRAMMAR phrases with participles and gerunds
CAN DO ✔

Reading

1 **Pair Work** Who are your favorite comedians? What makes them funny?

2 Read about Groucho Marx. Guess the answer to the question at the end of each section.

KING OF THE JOKERS

1 Julius Henry Marx was born in New York on October 2, 1890. His father was a tailor and his mother, Minnie, was a promoter for her brother, comedian Al Shean. Growing up with a comedian in the family would be important later. But, as a child, Groucho's first love was reading. He was also an extremely good singer.

What happened next?
a. He became a singer.
b. He wrote a book.
c. He started performing with his uncle.

Go to 4 to find out. ➡

2 Groucho became host of a radio show called *You Bet Your Life.* It was so popular that they moved it to TV. Groucho would interview the contestants and ad-lib jokes. Some of the more memorable questions included: "What color is the White House?" and "Who is buried in Grant's Tomb?" Returned now to national prominence, Groucho embarked on his solo film career, with a string of films throughout the '50s and '60s. But by now he was entering his 70s.

What happened next?
a. Groucho went to live in the Bahamas, for health reasons.
b. Groucho started writing fiction.
c. Groucho returned to fame in the 1970s.

Go to 8 to find out. ➡

3 Desperately attempting to win some money, Groucho met Irving Thalberg, a big name in Hollywood, during a card game. Thalberg, impressed with his new friend's act, helped the Marx Brothers to get established in the movie business. In the 1930s, the brothers made their most famous movies: *A Night at the Opera* (1935) and *A Day at the Races* (1937).

What happened next?
a. Groucho got sick and then retired.
b. The Marx Brothers disbanded.
c. The brothers set up their own production company, which made them rich.

Go to 5 to find out. ➡

4 At the age of 14, he began singing with the LeRoy Trio. His first tour wasn't a great experience—the trio abandoned him in Colorado. Having been left behind, Groucho had to work his way back home. At this stage he wanted to become a doctor, but his mother had other plans for him.

What happened next?
a. He ran away to study medicine.
b. Groucho and his brothers formed a musical act.
c. Groucho won a TV competition.

Go to 7 to find out. ➡

5 Following a movie called *The Big Store* (1941), the Marx Brothers disbanded. It seemed as though Groucho was going to fade into obscurity, when suddenly another opportunity arose.

What happened?
a. He started a radio show.
b. He became a politician.
c. He went to medical school.

Go to 2 to find out. ➡

6 After suffering a severe stroke, Minnie died. Then the stock market crashed, signaling the beginning of the Great Depression. After hitting the heights of fame and fortune, suddenly Groucho and his brothers lost everything. Depressed by the situation, Groucho began to suffer from insomnia.

How did the Marx Brothers recover in the 1930s?
a. They invested in property.
b. They toured the world, playing in small theaters.
c. They started making movies.

Go to 3 to find out. ➡

7 Groucho and his brothers, encouraged by their ambitious mother, formed a group called The Six Mascots, which lasted only a short time. Having been no more than a moderate success, one day they suddenly started cracking jokes on stage. The audience loved it. Being funny came naturally to them. Soon the Marx Brothers were performing all over the country. Groucho, with his fast-talking characters, chicken-walk, painted-on mustache, big glasses, and a cigar that he never smoked, was the star. Then everything changed in 1929.

What happened in 1929?
a. The brothers' mother died and Groucho lost all his money.
b. Groucho went to live on a Pacific island.
c. The brothers argued about money and split up their act.

Go to 6 to find out. ➡

8 Groucho made a comeback in the 1970s with a live one-man show. But with his health failing, he retired. He died of pneumonia in 1977, at the age of 86. Voted the fifth greatest comedy act ever by his fellow comedians in a 2005 poll, Groucho lives on, at least in memory. Everyone recognizes those famous glasses with the fake nose and mustache.

THE END

3 ▶ **1.13** **Pair Work** Listen to someone describing Groucho Marx's life. Find the speaker's mistakes.

> *They didn't start telling jokes during a radio show. They started . . .*

Grammar | phrases with participles and gerunds

4 Complete the task after each rule in the Active Grammar box.

Active Grammar

Exercise 2 contains several examples of participles and gerunds.

There are two types of participle: past participles (*-ed* forms for regular verbs) and present participles (*-ing* forms).

A gerund is a verb + *-ing* that functions as a noun.

1. We often use participles to add extra information to the idea in the sentence. The past participle sometimes acts as an adjective. The present participle sometimes gives background information.

   Returned now to national prominence, Groucho embarked on his solo film career . . . (section 2)

   Find an example with a past participle and one with a present participle in section 3.

   _____

   _____

2. *Having* + past participle shows the cause of a second action (or a sequence of actions).

   Having been left behind, Groucho had to work his way back home. (section 4)

   Find another example in section 7.

   _____

3. We often use a present participle after conjunctions (*after, before, when*).

   After suffering a severe stroke, Minnie died. (section 6)

   Find another example in section 6.

   _____

4. We can use a gerund as the subject of the sentence.

   Being funny came naturally to them. (section 7)

   Find another example in section 1.

   _____

See Reference page 129

5 Complete the sentences, using a participle or gerund of the verb in the parentheses.

1. When _____ (tell) a joke, timing is very important.

2. _____ (work) as a comedian must be a great job, because you make people laugh.

3. _____ (make) to look out of date by modern comics, comedians from the past aren't fully appreciated.

4. _____ (tell) jokes in a foreign language is extremely difficult.

5. On _____ (be) told a joke, you should laugh even if you don't think it's funny.

6. After _____ (watch) Chaplin, I think physical humor can be very funny.

CHARLIE CHAPLIN
(CHARLOT)

6 **Pair Work** Do you agree with the statements in Exercise 5? Compare your views.

Vocabulary | humor

7 Match the types of humor to the correct definitions. Use your dictionary to check any words you don't understand.

_____ 1. bizarre (very strange) humor

_____ 2. light, humorous play or movie with an unrealistic plot and exaggerated characters

_____ 3. humor conveyed by pictures or animation

_____ 4. jokes about death and other serious issues

_____ 5. word play

_____ 6. not saying exactly what you mean, or saying the opposite of what you mean

_____ 7. saying something is much more than it is

_____ 8. laughing at politicians and famous people

a. farce

b. puns

c. cartoons

d. black humor

e. surreal humor

f. irony

g. exaggeration

h. satire

8 **Pair Work** Discuss.

1. Do you know any famous actors, comedians, writers, or movies associated with the types of humor from Exercise 7?

2. Which types of humor do you like best?

Listening

9a ▶1.14 Cover the reading below and listen to a joke. Do you think it is funny?

b Why do you think the speaker pauses at certain moments? Listen again and read the joke. Mark the pauses. The first one has been done for you.

Three colleagues, a photographer, a journalist and an editor are covering a political convention. | One day, during their lunch break, they walk along a beach and one of them sees a lamp. He picks it up and rubs it, and a magic genie suddenly appears. The genie says, "You can each have one wish." So the photographer says, "I want to spend the rest of my life in a big house in the mountains with a beautiful view, where I can take photographs." Poof! Suddenly the photographer is gone to his home in the mountains. Then it's the journalist's turn. "I want to live in a big house in the countryside with an enormous garden where I can sit and write for the rest of my life." Poof! The journalist is gone. Finally, the genie says to the editor, "And what about you? What's your wish?" So the editor says, "I want those two back before lunch. We've got a deadline at 6:00 tonight."

Speaking

10a Speaking Exchange Work in groups of three. You are going to tell a joke. Student A: turn to page 139. Student B: turn to page 141. Student C: turn to page 142. Read your joke two or three times and try to memorize it.

b Tell the joke to the other students in your group. Whose joke was the funniest? Who told it best?

Review

1 Circle the correct choices to complete the paragraph.

> In April 2000, journalists at *Esquire* magazine (**1.** *decided/were deciding*) that life at the magazine was getting a little bit boring. So they published an article about FreeWheelz, an Internet company that gave customers free cars covered in advertising. The article (**2.** *had claimed/claimed*) that FreeWheelz "will transform the auto industry more than Henry Ford did." The company (**3.** *hadn't/didn't*) yet become famous but it would "on April 1, when FreeWheelz launches on the web for real." Readers who (**4.** *were seeing/saw*) the website, which had been created by the author of the article, were impressed. Within days, the site had (**5.** *received/been receiving*) over a thousand hits and messages from other entrepreneurs who claimed that they had been planning similar businesses. The website contained a questionnaire for potential clients that (**6.** *included/was including*) strange questions such as "Does hair loss concern you?" In the next edition, the magazine owned up, explaining that the article had been an April Fools' hoax. The magazine (**7.** *had forgotten/forgot*) all about it when suddenly an offer for the domain name FreeWheelz came in. The author of the article sold the name for $25,000, splitting the profits with the owners of the magazine. The conclusion? Never trust a strange story containing the date April 1.

2 Rewrite the sentences without changing the meaning. Use participial phrases or gerunds. Use the verb in parentheses.

> **Ex:** Because we couldn't find our way, we had to turn back. (lose)
> *Lost, we had to turn back.*
>
> Robbie ate all the cherries, and then he was sick. (have/eat)
> *Having eaten all the cherries, Robbie was sick.*

1. Life's biggest pleasure is when you do things for other people. (do)

2. Anyone who wishes to take the exam must register in June. (wish)

3. Most of the jewelry that thieves stole from the store has been recovered by the police. (steal)

4. Because she felt sleepy, Luisa went to bed. (feel)

5. When you swim, you must wear a bathing cap. (swim)

6. He had been famous for years, and he finally wanted some peace and quiet. (have/be)

7. Because they were censored in their own country, they decided to publish their book overseas. (censor)

8. David woke up early and went for a run. (wake up)

3 Put the letters in parentheses in the correct order to complete the web posts.

Posted by Nico

I am a complete ___*bookworm*___ (**Ex:** bmrooowk), and I'm an _____ (**1.** ivda) reader of Spike Davies's fiction. His latest book, *Charms*, is a real _____ (**2.** eapg-eutnrr). It's full of _____ (**3.** albkc uhrom), which made me laugh aloud. I was absolutely _____ (**4.** odehko).

[posted 04:41 PM, viewed 10 times]

Posted by Nina J

I'd say that *Charms* is very _____ (**5.** rbadlaee), but I thought that the characters were a bit _____ (**6.** oen-idsilanomne) compared to his other books. His previous book, which was _____ (**7.** edbsa) on a true story, was very _____ (**8.** ggniprpi)—in fact I _____ (**9.** ulcdno't tup ti dnow). I wasn't surprised it became a _____ (**10.** sebt-lelres). But *Charms* has too many weak _____ (**11.** sunp), and it lacks the clever _____ (**12.** ynior) of his best work.

[posted 05:22 PM, viewed 8 times]

Communication | tell a story

4a **Group Work** Read the opening sentences to some pieces of fiction and discuss the questions.

1. Is there anything unusual about the situation described?
2. Where and when do you think each book is set? What makes you think this?
3. What can you guess about each story? What type of story might it be?
4. Which excerpts make you want to read more? Why?

b Choose one of the story openings and discuss how the story could continue. Decide who will tell each part of the story, and practice telling it together.

> *. . . Parker kicked the door in. Inside, he found a man sitting in a . . .*

c Tell your story to another group. Which group has the most interesting or unusual story?

1. Milena boiled things. She was frightened of disease. She would boil other people's knives and forks before using them.
   (*The Child Garden*—Geoff Ryman)

2. I'm often asked what it's like to be married to a genius. The question used to please me . . .
   (*The Mind-Body Problem*—Rebecca Goldstein)

3. It was a bright cold day in April, and the clocks were striking thirteen.
   (*1984*—George Orwell)

4. If I am out of my mind, it's all right with me, thought Moses Herzog.
   (*Herzog*—Saul Bellow)

5. Rose Pickles knew something bad was going to happen. Something really bad this time.
   (*Cloudstreet*—Tim Winton)

6. When he didn't get any answer the second time he knocked, Parker kicked the door in.
   (*The Split*—Richard Stark)

7. As Gregor Samsa awoke one morning from uneasy dreams, he found himself transformed in his bed into a gigantic insect.
   (*Metamorphosis*—Franz Kafka)

8. All children, except one, grow up.
   (*Peter Pan*—J.M. Barrie)

9. It was a wrong number that started it, the telephone ringing three times in the dead of night, and the voice on the other end asking for someone he was not.
   (*The New York Trilogy*—Paul Auster)

UNIT 4
Moving forward

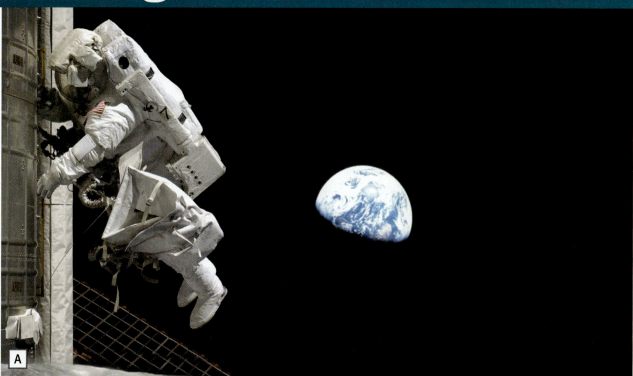

A

B

C

D

Warm Up

1 **Pair Work** Discuss. What types of progress are shown in the photos? What developments have there been recently? What developments might there be in the future?

2a Match the news headlines to the photos.

_____ 1. Resistance to antibiotics on the increase

_____ 2. New virus destroys global computer systems

_____ 3. Genetic engineering breakthrough provides hope for many

_____ 4. Space mission in danger as budget crisis grows

b ▶1.15 Listen to the news stories.

3 **Pair Work** Check the meaning of the words in bold and then answer the questions.

1. Would you describe yourself as a **"computer nerd"** or a **"technophobe"**?

2. Are you **up-to-date** with the **latest technology**? Are there any new **gadgets** that you would like to buy?

3. Do you enjoy reading scientific **journals** or watching **documentaries**? Which scientific areas interest you most? Why?

Speaking

1   **Pair Work** Discuss. Do you (or did you ever) enjoy movies or comic books featuring superheroes? Who are your favorite characters?

2a   **Group Work** You have four minutes to test your knowledge of superheroes. Write down:

   1. the names of four different superheroes
   2. the color of the Incredible Hulk
   3. four of Spider Man's five special powers
   4. the name of the planet where Superman was born
   5. the name of the superhero movie released in 2002 that broke all box-office records on its very first weekend
   6. the name of the female character who has super-strength, bullet-proof bracelets, and a lasso that makes people tell the truth

   b   ▶ 1.16   Listen and check your answers.

Reading

3   Read the article about research into real-life super powers.

HOW TO BE A SUPERHERO

Got what it takes to become a superhero? For most of us the answer is a resounding *no*. But that hasn't stopped scientists from trying to recreate super powers artificially. And you might be surprised at how successful they have been.

Wall climbing

Gecko lizards are so good at this that they can hang upside down from a glass surface by a single toe. The secret lies in the millions of tiny hairs, called *setae*, which are on the gecko's skin. Now scientists at Manchester University are developing a material covered with similar nanoscopic hairs that would enable a person to walk on a ceiling or up a wall. One square centimeter of the tape holds 100 million artificial setae and could support a kilogram of weight. There is a fairly good chance that this system could allow people to walk up walls.

Teleportation

Just as superhero Nightcrawler can teleport, scientists in Australia have discovered how to teleport matter for real—albeit on the atomic scale, for the time being. The researchers have succeeded in transmitting information about quantum particles across space and then using it to reassemble exact copies of the original particles. It is unlikely that the process will be used for larger objects.

Regeneration

Both Superman and the X-men's Wolverine can regenerate tissue instantly—they can be hit by a bullet and recover in seconds. Doctors at a children's hospital in Boston have pioneered a similar way of helping terminally ill patients to re-grow healthy organs. There is every likelihood that the procedure could eventually be commonly used to grow organs for transplants.

Super-strength

No matter how many steroids you take, you don't stand a chance of achieving the strength of the Incredible Hulk. However, there is a distinct possibility that genetics could help those seeking a Hulk-like physique. Johns Hopkins University scientists have created Mighty Mouse—a rodent that has been genetically modified so that a protein that limits muscle-growth is blocked. "They are normal in every respect, except their muscles are two to three times larger than normal," says molecular biologist Se Jin-Lee. "They look like Schwarzenegger mice." Presumably, it will also help scientists to better understand muscle-wasting diseases.

Force field

Superman's hideaway, the Fortress of Solitude, is protected by a force field. The Defense Science and Technology Laboratory run by the UK Ministry of Defense has developed a similar force field to protect tanks from rocket-propelled grenades. Once shielded by the force field, there is very little chance that the tanks can be destroyed.

Web-shooter

The US army has developed a device for the New York police that acts like Spider Man's webshooter. The nets are designed to restrain people without causing serious injury and are shot from a kind of stun gun. The victim caught in the net stands no chance of escape, as the nets come in three varieties: a regular net, one that can give an electric shock, and—most fittingly of all, one that becomes sticky on contact with air. These crime-stopping devices are bound to cause some sticky problems for New York criminals!

X-ray vision

Everyone would love to have Superman's ability to see through walls. But the odds are against the general use of X-rays, as they are dangerous, and repeated exposure to them isn't good for your health. The solution could be "terahertz imaging." Terahertz radiation lies between the infrared and microwave regions of the spectrum, so these low-energy rays can penetrate matter just like X-rays but without the harmful effects. Researchers are developing them for defense and medical imaging.

Flying

Superman has the ability to fly without the aid of wings or rockets. Researchers have looked into the possibility of using spinning discs to defy gravity. The original research was carried out by a Russian researcher working in Finland in 1996, but so far no other researchers have managed to verify his claim. It is doubtful that we will be able to achieve this in the foreseeable future.

Invisibility

The Invisible Woman is part of the Fantastic Four. Now a virtual reality expert in Japan has created a "see-through" coat, which appears to make the wearer's body disappear. The material is coated with microscopic reflectors that work like a movie screen. A tiny video camera is then attached to the back of the coat. The image from the back of the coat is projected onto the front of the coat, which makes observers think that they can see through it.

---

4 **Group Work** Discuss. Which research described in the article do you think is important? Which do you think is less important? Does any of the research worry you?

> *Actually, the research into terahertz imaging worries me a little bit. What if . . .*

Grammar | future probability

5 Complete the task and fill in the chart in the Active Grammar box.

Active Grammar

To talk about future probability, we can use modal verbs *will*, *could*, *may*, and *might*. We can also use phrases such as those in the chart. Which phrases are used to talk about future probability in the article on pages 44–45? Underline them and then add them to the chart.	1. Will almost definitely happen	• *It will presumably . . .*
	2. Likely to happen	• *The chances are that . . .* • *There is a strong possibility . . .* • *It may/might well . . .*
	3. Unlikely to happen	• *There's a slight/remote possibility that . . .* • *I doubt whether . . .* • *It probably won't . . .* • *The chances are slim that . . .*
	4. Impossible	• *It is inconceivable that . . .*

See Reference page 130

6 Rewrite the sentences, using the words in parentheses, keeping the meaning the same.

> **Ex:** There is no chance that she's borrowing my laptop. (stand)
>
> *She doesn't stand a chance of borrowing my laptop.*

1. It's highly unlikely that they will make a breakthrough in the near future. (doubtful)
2. It isn't possible that we'll be able to travel to Mars by 2050. (inconceivable)
3. I'm sure they'll notice it's missing. (bound)
4. We can't be entirely confident that the information is secure. (chance)
5. We're being met at the airport, so we don't need train tickets. (presumably)
6. China has a good chance of winning the space race. (distinct)
7. There doesn't seem to be much hope that the relationship will improve. (doubt)

Speaking

7 **Pair Work** Discuss. What are the chances of the following happening in the next 20 years?

1. We will be able to go on vacation in space.
2. There will be a cure for cancer or AIDS.
3. Nuclear energy will have been abolished.
4. Parents will be able to choose the gender, hair color, and eye color of their babies.
5. All foods will be genetically modified.

Listening

8 ▶ 1·17 Listen to an interview with Stan Lee, the creator of Spider Man. In what order does he answer the questions below? What are his answers?

____ **a.** Will there ever be real superheroes?

____ **b.** Why did he make Spider Man a scientist?

____ **c.** How did you think of Spider Man?

____ **d.** Are you at all scientific?

Vocabulary | arrangements

1 **Pair Work** Discuss.

1. How do you keep in touch with your family and friends?

2. Read the quotation.

"Modern communications technology is designed to keep us too busy to actually see anyone."
(*Paul Mendez, psychologist*)

Do you agree with Mendez? Do you think communications technology has made our lives better or worse?

2a Read the emails below. What is Tom trying to do? What happens in the end?

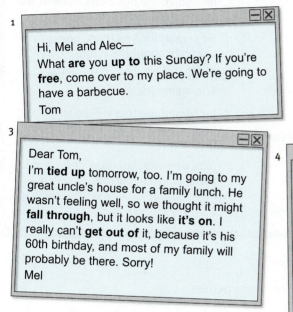

1

Hi, Mel and Alec—
What **are** you **up to** this Sunday? If you're **free**, come over to my place. We're going to have a barbecue.
Tom

2

Hi, Tom—
Thanks for the offer, but I'm completely **swamped** right now. I have to write an essay by Monday afternoon, so I'll be working all weekend. I don't have anything **lined up** for next weekend though, so maybe we can get together then? I'll call you later.
Alec

3

Dear Tom,
I'm **tied up** tomorrow, too. I'm going to my great uncle's house for a family lunch. He wasn't feeling well, so we thought it might **fall through**, but it looks like **it's on**. I really can't **get out of** it, because it's his 60th birthday, and most of my family will probably be there. Sorry!
Mel

4

OK you guys,
I'm **calling off** the barbecue. According to the weather forecast, it's going to rain all weekend anyway.
Maybe you'll have finished what you have to do by 9:00 or so, and we can go out instead! If you want to **wind down**, I'll be at Paola's, a restaurant on King Street. Gloria and I are meeting there at about 8:30, as long as nothing else **comes up**! Don't forget it closes at 11 on Sundays.
Talk to you soon,
Tom

b Read the emails again and match the words or phrases in bold to the definitions below.

1. _____ : be engaged in activity
2. _____ : arrive unexpectedly
3. _____ : busy/not free
4. _____ : planned/arranged
5. _____ : avoid doing something
6. _____ : cancel
7. _____ : extremely busy
8. _____ : not happen or take place (a plan)
9. _____ : proceed as expected (a plan)
10. _____ : have no plans/available
11. _____ : become relaxed

3 Add the missing word to each sentence.

1. The tennis match was called due to rain.
2. If you aren't to anything this afternoon, why don't you come over?
3. I'm sorry—I won't be able to make it at 5:30. Something has come.
4. I'm tied all of January, but I'll have some free time in February.
5. There's a great new band lined for tonight.
6. I need to wind after this lousy week.
7. Despite the rain, the festival is still.
8. She can't come tomorrow, because she's with work.
9. I have to clean the house today. I can't get out it.
10. The picnic plans fell when the forecast called for rain.

Grammar | future forms: review

4   Read the emails in Exercise 2a again. Which verb forms are used for talking about the future? Complete the tasks in the Active Grammar box.

Active Grammar

Complete each rule with the correct ending.

1. Use the **simple present** ___e___
   *Don't forget it **closes** at 11 on Sundays.*

2. Use **will** _____
   *I'**ll call** you later.*

3. Use **will** _____
   *Most of my family **will probably be** there.*

4. Use **be going to** or the present continuous _____
   *We'**re going to have** a barbecue.*

   *Gloria and I **are meeting** there at about 8:30.*

5. Use **be going to** _____
   *According to the weather forecast, it'**s going to rain** anyway.*

6. Use the **future continuous** _____
   *I'**ll be working** all weekend.*

7. Use the **future perfect** _____
   *Maybe you'**ll have finished** what you have to do by 9:00 or so.*

a. for predictions you make because of present evidence.

b. for something that will be finished before a time in the future.

c. for immediate decisions made at the same time as you speak or write.

d. for something you think, guess or calculate about the future.

e. for fixed timetables, schedules, and arrangements.

f. for something that will be in progress during a period of time in the future.

g. for a personal intention or for fixed plans or arrangements.

See Reference page 130

5a Make questions, using *will,* the future continuous, or the future perfect.

In one year:

1. Do you think you _____ (still study) English?

2. Do you think you _____ (have) the same lifestyle?

3. Do you think you _____ (live) in the same place?

4. Do you think your country _____ (have) a different government?

In ten years:

5. Do you think you _____ (change) much?

6. Do you think you _____ (have) the same interests?

7. Do you think you _____ (have) the same close friends?

8. Do you think you _____ (see) more of the world?

b ▶1.18 Listen to check your work. Which words are contracted? Repeat the questions, paying attention to contractions.

6   **Pair Work** Ask each other the questions from Exercise 5a. Tell the class two things you learned about your partner.

> *Do you think you'll still be studying English a year from now?*

> *I'm not sure. I think . . .*

Listening

7 ▶1.19 Listen to two telephone conversations. What are the speakers' relationships? What plans are they trying to make?

8 We use vague or imprecise expressions when we don't want to (or can't) give details. Listen to the conversations again and listen for the expressions in the How To box.

How To:	
Generalize	
Give imprecise information about how often something happens	• *once in a while* • *every so often*
Give imprecise information about quantity, time, and/or numbers	• *pretty much (all day)* • *tons of mistakes* • *about eight-ish* • *in an hour or so*
Give imprecise information about things you do/have been doing	• *that kind of thing* • *the usual*
Give imprecise answers to direct questions	• *sort of* or *kind of*

9 Put the words in the correct order to make sentences. Start with the underlined word.

1. <u>We</u> go so every to that still often café.
2. <u>I'm</u> busy weekend sort this of.
3. <u>Her</u> job solving thing that kind and involves problems of.
4. <u>I'll</u> working much be pretty evening all.
5. <u>Because</u> I'm a in busy, I while so see my sister once only.
6. <u>By</u> time tons next new I'll have this of met year, people.
7. <u>We're</u> at about hoping meet four-ish to.
8. <u>I'll</u> at or arriving so ten be.

10 **Pair Work** Ask and answer the questions. Try to include generalizations in your answers.

1. How many phone calls do you make each day?
2. How many times do you check email each week?
3. How many close friends do you have?
4. How often do you write letters?
5. What do you do in the evening?
6. How many hours do you study English each day?

Speaking

11 **Pair Work** Play *Twenty Questions*. Follow the instructions in the box.

> *Does your person appear on TV?*   *Yes, every so often.*

> **Twenty Questions**
> • Think of a famous person. Don't tell your partner who it is.
> • Try to find out who your partner is thinking of. Ask only *yes/no* questions.
> • You can ask up to 20 questions. You can generalize in your answers if you like.

Vocabulary | special abilities

1 Pair Work What are some things that most children can do by the time they are two years old? Five years old? Ten years old? Do you know of any children who developed special talents at an early age?

2 Match the words or phrases on the left to those with a similar meaning on the right.

____ 1. gifted   a. for the future

____ 2. in the making   b. difficult

____ 3. a prodigy   c. someone who is abnormal

____ 4. adulation   d. extremely talented

____ 5. peers   e. admiration

____ 6. demanding   f. a young genius

____ 7. a freak   g. contemporaries

3 Read the article and answer the questions that follow.

HOW TO MAKE YOUR CHILD A GENIUS

1 Nguyen Ngoc Truong Son grew up watching his mother and father playing chess in their home in Kien Giang Province in Vietnam. When he was three years old, he asked them to let him play, too. Expecting him to strew the pieces around the room, they gave in. Not for one minute had they imagined that their son would be able to play. Not only did Son know how to set up the chessboard, but he had also learned many rules of the game by watching them. It took Son about a month to surpass his parents. By the time he was four, Son was competing in national tournaments against children who were much older. By the age of seven, he was winning tournaments. In 2004, Son became Vietnam's youngest grandmaster ever, and one of the youngest grandmasters in the history of chess.

2 Son's parents, who are teachers, are at a loss to explain their son's talents. "It's an inborn gift," says his father. "You couldn't train an ordinary three-year-old to play like that." For Son, there is nothing unusual about his skill. The strategies and logic of chess come naturally to him. "I just see things on the board and know what to do," he says. "It's just always made sense to me."

3 Scientists have never been able to understand how child prodigies like Son acquire their talents. Prodigies have been celebrated throughout history. Rarely, however, have they been understood. As often is the case with something not

easily understood, they have also been objects of suspicion and superstition. They often must deal with teasing by other children, attention from the press, and pressure and high expectations from their parents.

4 The eternal question regarding prodigies is that of nature vs. nurture. In other words, are prodigies born with their special talents, or are their environment and upbringing responsible? Only recently has science begun to investigate the cultural and biological factors that contribute to the making of child prodigies. Unfortunately, there are still no easy answers. Studies have shown that raw intelligence, as measured through IQ tests, is very heritable, that is, tends to be inherited from one's parents and grandparents. But there is not always a connection between high intelligence and the skills of prodigies. Prodigies master very specific skills. Nowhere is this illustrated more clearly than in the case of Indian prodigy Tathagat Avatar Tulsi. At the age of six, when given any date in history, he was able to immediately calculate which day of the week it was. The press nicknamed him "Computer Brain." Tulsi's talent is a type of intelligence that cannot be inherited.

5 However, there is one point on which the experts can agree: a child's upbringing has an enormous impact on whether a gift is developed or not. As Wu Wu-tien, a Taiwanese education specialist puts it, "Prodigies are half born, half made." Parents provide environments conducive to learning. They read to their children from an early age. They stimulate their brains, engage them in discussion, and foster their talents.

1. Why were Son's parents surprised?

2. What does Son think of his gift?

3. According to the article, what problems do child prodigies face?

4. What is "the big question" about child prodigies?

5. What answer does the article suggest?

4   **Pair Work** Discuss.

1. Think about other child geniuses. How do you think society treats them?
2. What might be some benefits and drawbacks of having a child prodigy in the family?
3. Do you know any children who have a special gift for something?
4. Do you think child prodigies are "born" or "made"?

Grammar | subject/verb inversion

5   Complete the tasks in the Active Grammar box.

Active Grammar

1. Inversion is used to emphasize the adverbial phrase in a sentence and to add variety to a text. Inversion is usually used in more formal writing.

   Place a negative or adverbial expression at the start of a sentence (*never, nowhere, not only*, etc.) followed by auxiliary verb + subject + verb.

   He plays football and tennis. → *Not only does he play football, but he also plays tennis.*

   He arrived and we left immediately. → *No sooner did he arrive than we left.*

2. The article on page 50 contains the following examples of inversion. Find two other examples.

   *Not for one minute **had they imagined** that their son would be able to play.*

   *Not only **did Son know** how to set up the chessboard, but he had also learned many rules of the game.*

   *Rarely, however, **have they been** understood.*

3. Do not use auxiliary verbs when the main verb is the verb *be* or a modal verb.

   *He is a great singer and can also dance. **Not only is he** a great singer, **but** he can also dance.*

Match the rules with the sentences a–d below:

____ 1. We use inversion after phrases that use *not*.

____ 2. We use inversion after negative adverbs that emphasize a time relationship.

____ 3. We use inversion for general emphasis with phrases that use *only*.

____ 4. We use inversion with *no way* in informal speech.

a. ***No way*** *am I going to sing in public!*

b. ***Only if*** *we start to play more intelligently will we win this game.*

c. ***Not since*** *I was a child have I enjoyed myself so much.*

d. ***No sooner*** *had I arrived than I had to go out again.*

See Reference page 130

6   Circle the letter of the correct sentence in each pair.

1. a. Not since Mozart there has been a greater genius.
   b. Not since Mozart has there been a greater genius.
2. a. Only after the age of three did she begin to show her gift.
   b. Only after the age of three she did begin to show her gift.
3. a. Nowhere do the rules say you can't teach advanced subjects to children.
   b. Nowhere the rules say you can't teach advanced subjects to children.
4. a. Only later did we understand the truth about our gifted child.
   b. Only later we understood the truth about our gifted child.
5. a. Not only he was able to write poetry when he was five years old; he also played the violin well.
   b. Not only was he able to write poetry when he was five years old; he also played the violin well.
6. a. No sooner had we given her a paintbrush than she produced a masterpiece.
   b. No sooner had we given her a paintbrush, she produced a masterpiece.

Speaking

7a **SPEAKING EXCHANGE** Student A: read the paragraph on page 141. Student B: read the paragraph on page 142. Complete the paragraphs, and then make notes on the following:

- name
- special talent
- what others think of him or her

b Tell your partner about the person.

Listening

8a You are going to listen to a description of two very gifted children. Before listening, read the notes below.

People

1. The case involved twins named _____.
2. They were _____ and wore thick glasses.
3. At school, people _____ at them.

Their gifts

4. They could tell you _____ in the past and future 40,000 years.
5. They could remember long sequences of _____.
6. If you asked them about a day in their lives, they could remember _____.

Conclusions

7. Their ability is mathematical and _____.
8. When asked how they do it, they reply, "_____."

b ▶1.20 Listen and complete the sentences.

9 **Group Work** Discuss.

1. In which jobs would the twins' abilities be useful?
2. How else could they use their abilities?
3. If you could have one special mental ability (memorizing numbers or words, having a photographic memory, being able to read extremely quickly, being able to learn many foreign languages quickly, etc.), what would it be? Why?

> *If I could have one special mental ability, I would like to be able to read extremely quickly. That way I could . . .*

Writing

10 Write a summary of John and Michael's story.

Extra Vocabulary Study and
Extra Listening Activity

in *ACTIVEBOOK*

Review

1 Rewrite the sentences in three different ways, using the words in parentheses.

  1. We expect the weather to improve in the coming months. (chance/distinct/well)
  2. I doubt if they will contact us. (remote/probably/slim)
  3. We will almost certainly move in the spring. (likelihood/chance/bound)
  4. I don't believe they will offer him the job. (doubt/chance/distinct)
  5. The organizers are confident that attendance will be high this year. (presumably/bound/strong)

2 Circle the correct words.

  1. Max *will retire/is retired/will retiring* soon, so we *'ll be looking/look/will be look* for a new manager.
  2. Wait a minute. I'm *coming/will come/will be coming*.
  3. By this time next year, he *'s going to be/'ll be/is* in college.
  4. Will you *going to see/have seen/be seeing* Jade this week?
  5. Don't worry if you haven't finished. I *'m working/'m going to work/work* on it later.
  6. I'm sure he *'ll be getting/will have gotten/is getting* a job by the end of the year.

3 Circle the correct choice.

  1. No sooner ____ left the airport than I realized I had picked up the wrong suitcase.
     a. did I   **b.** had I   **c.** would I
  2. No ____ should you be made to pay the difference.
     a. means   **b.** cases   **c.** way
  3. Not ____ did they think it would be possible.
     a. for once   **b.** for one minute   **c.** for ever
  4. Only if you practice ____.
     a. you will get better   **b.** would you get better   **c.** will you get better
  5. It is not often ____ such a difficult question.
     a. that am I asked   **b.** that I am asked   **c.** do I ask

4 Use the cues in parentheses and the phrases in the box to complete the sentences.

> pretty much   in a while   every so often   came up
> fell through   up to   swamped   free

  1. I see her once _____. (very occasionally)
  2. I'm _____. (have nothing to do)
  3. What are you _____ tomorrow? (doing)
  4. I'm _____ finished. (nearly)
  5. A few problems _____ yesterday. (appeared)
  6. I still go to that restaurant _____. (not regularly)
  7. I am totally _____ right now. (very busy)
  8. The dinner _____. (was cancelled)

Communication | make an argument for research funding

5 ▶ 1.21 Listen to four speakers talking about important discoveries and inventions. Answer the questions.

1. What technologies do they mention, and what do they say about them?
2. What other important discoveries or inventions can you think of?
3. How have they changed our lives or made the world a better place?

6 **Pair Work** Read the paragraphs and answer the following questions.

1. Is each area of research likely to affect your life?
2. Would you contribute money to research in this area?

Space travel/exploration

NASA has spent billions of dollars every year to send astronauts into space. Now Virgin Galactic is offering to take private citizens into space. They have already collected $6 million in deposits. For $200,000, the paying public will fly 70 miles above the Earth, see the planet's curvature, and experience weightlessness for at least six minutes.

Robots

Various domestic robots are available to do your ironing, mow the lawn, vacuum, etc. Now, some hospitals are experimenting with robo-docs so that doctors can "visit" patients from a distance (another ward, or even specialists from another country). Also, scientists are improving robots for space exploration.

Genetic engineering

Using DNA, scientists can now manipulate the development of life. In 2001 a cloned cat named "Little Nicky" was sold to a Texan woman for $50,000. Now scientists are researching the use of DNA to predict hereditary illnesses in unborn babies. The scientists could then potentially alter the babies' genes to prevent the illnesses. Many people worry that the techniques will be used commercially, for example, to manufacture "superchildren" with unnatural physical advantages.

7a **Group Work** Prepare a case for research funding. Group A: prepare a case for research into space travel; Group B: prepare a case for research into how robots can help mankind; Group C: prepare a case for research into genetic engineering. First, discuss the questions below:

1. What important discoveries do you think might be made in this area in the future?
2. What do you think is needed to make this research possible?
3. How do you think the research should be funded?
4. How will the research affect people's lives?

b Present your ideas to the rest of the class. Discuss which arguments you found persuasive.

UNIT 5
Making money

A

B

C

D

Warm Up

1 **Pair Work** Discuss the meaning of the words and phrases in bold in the sentences below. Can any of them be used to describe the photos?

1. She **came into a fortune** when she turned 18.
2. They **haggled** to get a good deal.
3. The **stock market** is often unpredictable.
4. The employees have asked for a **raise**.
5. The taxes will affect **high-income** families.
6. John Singer Sargent's paintings are **priceless**.
7. The sales force is **paid on commission**.
8. Unfortunately, his business **went bankrupt** last year.

2 **Pair Work** Do you agree with the statements below? Give reasons for your answers.

1. Art belongs to everyone. Priceless paintings should be available for all to see.
2. It's rude to haggle when you buy something. You should pay the asking price.
3. Paying people on a commission basis makes them work hard.
4. High-income families should pay higher taxes.
5. Gambling on the stock market is a sure way to go bankrupt.
6. The best way to get a raise is to be nice to your boss.

Reading

1 **Pair Work** Discuss.

1. How important do you think it is for an employer to make sure that his or her employees are happy? Why?

2. What kinds of things do you think employers can reasonably do to increase employee satisfaction?

2 Read the article and answer the questions that follow.

Zingerman's Community of Businesses

1 Sink your teeth into a Zingerman's Reuben Sandwich—corned beef, Swiss cheese, sauerkraut, and Russian dressing on grilled rye bread—and you will get a new appreciation for the word *sandwich*. Zingerman's Deli in Ann Arbor, Michigan, has over 100 varieties of delicious sandwiches, all made on homemade breads and packed with the freshest local ingredients. It's no wonder it's been called the best deli in the world! But it's not only the menu at Zingerman's that is exceptional. The Zingerman's business model is also something to learn from.

2 Founded in 1982 by Paul Saginaw and Ari Weinzweig, Zingerman's began as a unique little delicatessen serving a modest number of traditional deli dishes and sandwiches. It rapidly grew in popularity, with customers often waiting in long lines to sample one of the infamous sandwiches. The potential for bigger success was clear. It was Saginaw who suggested franchising nationwide. But Weinzweig was not the least bit interested in expanding geographically and compromising the uniqueness and purpose of the original deli. He also preferred that they stay in their own neighborhood. So they chose a different, more unusual route. They started building other businesses around Zingerman's Deli, all located in the Ann Arbor area: a bake house, a creamery, a mail order, a coffee company, among others. Each business is run by one or more managing partners who share ownership and oversee the daily operations. All the businesses fall under the umbrella of Zingerman's Community of Businesses (ZCoB).

3 What is unique about ZCoB is that anyone can pitch an idea for a business and potentially become a member of the Zingerman's community. Several of the businesses were founded by Zingerman's employees. In general, at Zingerman's input from employees is highly encouraged and valued. And they are generously rewarded for their efforts. It's a work environment where people truly thrive. Zingerman's employees really do love coming to work. "It actually doesn't feel like work at all," shares one employee. ZCoB also provides excellent compensation and benefits, including generous vacation time, health and dental benefits, food discounts, and various incentive plans for full-time employees. But everyone agrees that it's the Zingerman's environment that is priceless. Many talented employees have left much higher paying jobs to be part of the unique Zingerman's experience.

4 So what's the secret? Zingerman's business model measures success based on great food, great service, and financial results. But this is by no means a secret. Quite on the contrary, ZingTrain, the training branch of the company, offers business training and consulting to share Zingerman's philosophies and their people-friendly management approach. So managers from grocery chains, banks, hospitals, and garden shops from across the country gather regularly in Ann Arbor for seminars on how to improve their businesses. Those who can't travel to Michigan can read about the Zingerman's culture and structure in Ari Weinzweig's book *A Lapsed Anarchist's Approach to Building a Great Business.* He readily shares the ingredients for making a unique, successful, and lasting business.

5 That in itself is perhaps what makes Zingerman's such a success—the readiness to share their wealth. And just as they don't keep their business model a secret, they don't keep the recipe for their Reuben Sandwich under lock and key. You can go to the Zingerman's mail order at zingerman's.com and find detailed step-by-step instructions for making the sandwich. And if you want to splurge, you can actually order a Reuben Sandwich Kit. It includes every single ingredient for the sandwich, from the thick slices of homemade bread to the Russian dressing—just like you would get at Zingerman's deli. Now that's great food and great service!

1. What kind of business is Zingerman's?

2. How has the company changed since 1982?

3. What are some of the things that make Zingerman's different from more traditional businesses?

4. How does Zingerman's measure success?

5. Why do managers from other companies come to Zingerman's for training?

3 **Pair Work** Discuss the meaning of the words and phrases from the reading in bold.

1. The **potential** for bigger success was clear. (paragraph 2)
2. Weinzweig was not interested in **compromising** the uniqueness of the original deli. (paragraph 2)
3. Anyone can **pitch an idea** for a business. (paragraph 3)
4. It's a work environment where people truly **thrive**. (paragraph 3)
5. ZCoB provides excellent **compensation and benefits,** including generous vacation time, health and dental benefits, food discounts, and various **incentive plans**. (paragraph 3)
6. ZingTrain offers business training and consulting to share Zingerman's **philosophies**. (paragraph 4)

Grammar | emphasis

4 Complete the task after each rule in the Active Grammar box.

> ### Active Grammar
>
> We can add emphasis by including certain words, for example:
>
> 1. *own*—to intensify possessive adjectives
>   Find an example in paragraph 2.
>
> 2. emphasizing negatives: *the least bit/at all*
>   Find examples in paragraphs 2 and 3.
>
> 3. adjectives/adverbs to add emphasis: *actually, by no means, even*
>   Find examples in paragraphs 3, 4, and 5.
>
> 4. auxiliary verbs: *do/did*
>   Find an example in paragraph 3.
>
> We can use cleft sentences for emphasis. Two important cleft constructions are:
>
> 5. *it* clauses
>   *It was Scott who asked . . .*
>   Find examples in paragraphs 2 and 3.
>
> 6. *what* clauses
>   *What you need is a cup of coffee . . .*
>   Find an example in paragraph 3.

See Reference page 131

5a Rewrite the sentences to add emphasis using the words in parentheses.

1. He can't complain. It's his fault he didn't get a raise. (own)
2. We're not certain that it is the same man committing the crimes. (by)
3. I really miss having enough time to spend with friends. (what)
4. They didn't understand what we wanted. (all)
5. The employees love coming to work. (actually)
6. Sammy always got into trouble. (it)
7. Keith wasn't annoyed when we cancelled the meeting. (least)

American English	British English
a raise	a rise

b ▶1.22 Listen to the answers. Mark the words that are stressed. Practice saying the sentences with the same stress and intonation.

Speaking

6 **Pair Work** Discuss. Use emphasis where possible.

1. What do you think the three most important elements of a successful business are?
2. Would you consider starting your own business? Why or why not?
3. Who would or wouldn't you choose for a business partner? Why?

Listening

7 ▶**1.23** Listen and complete the sentences.

1. The speaker warns against doing business with _____ .

2. The only way to get rid of a bad business partner legally is to _____ .

3. Successful partnerships will combine two types of people: _____ and _____ .

4. It's a good idea if partners have complementary _____ .

5. If your business is lacking in a particular skill area, you may need to _____ .

6. Good _____ is essential to ensure that arguments do not interfere with the success of the business.

7. Ideally, your business partner will be committed to the _____ success of the business.

8a ▶**1.24** Listen again in sections. As you listen, notice how the speaker uses the following phrases:

Section 1	50-50 partners, family-owned business, make someone a partner, buy someone out of the business, an expensive proposition
Section 2	a strategic "big picture" thinker, business model, plan, roll up their sleeves, execute the strategy, strike the right balance, strategy and tactics
Section 3	make the business work, product design, marketing background, crunch the numbers, contract negotiation, bookkeeping, hire a consultant
Section 4	communicate directly and honestly, business may suffer, hold back information, jeopardize the friendship
Section 5	start-up phase, an attractive job offer, a life-changing event, the going gets tough

b **Pair Work** Check that you understand the meaning of the phrases from Exercise 8a. Then reconstruct the speaker's advice, using those phrases and the information from Exercise 7.

9 **Group Work** Discuss.

1. Do you agree with what the speaker says? Do you know people in successful or unsuccessful business partnerships? Why do you think the relationship does or doesn't work?

2. Are you a "visionary" or an "operations" person? What skills, experience and qualities would you bring to a business partnership? In which areas are you lacking? Would you work well with the other students in your group?

> *I guess I'm a "visionary." I'm really good at coming up with ideas, but I'm not great at organizing . . .*

Discuss financial decisions and regrets

GRAMMAR conditionals: review

Reading

1 **Pair Work** Read the quotes below. Which do you agree or disagree with?

"There are a million ways to make money and a billion ways to lose it."

"Money is only a tool. It will take you wherever you wish, but it will not replace you as the driver."

2a **SPEAKING EXCHANGE** Work in pairs. Student A: read about Leon Spinks on this page. Student B: read about William Post on page 143. Make notes about the following as you read:

1. How did he win his money? How much was it?
2. How did he lose his money?
3. What does he do now?
4. What kind of relationship does or did he have with his family?
5. What "philosophy" does each man express at the end of the article?

Reading A

RICHES TO RAGS

Leon Spinks, the former heavyweight boxing champion who famously beat Muhammad Ali in a 1978 fight, has had a hard fall from glory. Once known for his wild partying and extravagant lifestyle, Spinks now works at a McDonald's and volunteers at an after-school program for kids in the small town of Columbus, Nebraska. "I love helping the kids," he says. To many of them, he is still a hero.

Spinks was at the height of his fame in the late 1970s. In 1976, both he and his younger brother Michael won gold medals at the Olympics in Montreal. "That will always be my greatest achievement," Spinks says. But he is best known for his win over Ali in 1978.

The good times did not last long, however. In the seven months between his victory and his next match with Ali, Spinks lost the self-control that had propelled him to the championship. He partied and neglected his training. He lost his next bout with Ali, and his life spiraled downward from there. He continued to box until 1995, but never again at the same level.

Spinks made millions from boxing, but the common perception is that he partied away all of his money. Spinks says the truth is that he trusted the wrong people. He gave power of attorney to his lawyers and says that he never saw a penny of the $3.25 million that he made from Ali-Spinks 2. Eventually the money was gone, and for a brief period he was homeless. Spinks lived for a while in Chicago and from there moved to Columbus, where he works for minimum wage and lives quietly.

Spinks's brother Michael did not make the same mistakes as Leon. When Michael beat Larry Holmes in 1985, the Spinks boys became the first brothers to become world heavyweight champions. But unlike his brother, Michael held on to his money. "My brother and I are close," Leon says. But he will not ask for financial help. "I can make it myself."

Spinks still carries himself with dignity, though he does worry about the future and whether he will have enough money to live comfortably. "You do the best you can," he says. "I'm still trying. I'm not giving up on life."

b Tell your partner about the person in your reading.

3a Find words and phrases in the readings from Exercise 2 that mean the following:

1. _____ : offer to work (usually for no money) (Reading A)
2. _____ : the power to make legal decisions regarding finances (Reading A)
3. _____ : didn't receive any of the money (Reading A)
4. _____ : got worse and worse (Reading A)
5. _____ : take someone to court to get money from them (Reading B)
6. _____ : new business activities (Reading B)
7. _____ : declare that you are unable to pay your debts (Reading B)

b Complete the sentences with a phrase from Exercise 3a.

1. He's made a lot of money with his new _____ _____ .
2. She said she would send a check, but I still haven't _____ _____ _____ of the money she owes us.
3. Steve has _____ to help me sort out the office.
4. The business had been failing for years before he _____ _____ .

Grammar | conditionals: review

4 Complete the sentences with the correct form of the verb in parentheses.

Ex: If you go into business with relatives, it _tends to_ (tend to) put a strain on your relationship.

1. If you happen to _____ (see) Tom, could you tell him I need some money?
2. I wish I _____ (not gamble) with the money.
3. She wouldn't have been able to pay her debts if she _____ (not come into) a lot of money.
4. They wouldn't have _____ (be able) to buy the house if it hadn't been for her father.
5. He shouldn't have to declare bankruptcy, provided the business ventures _____ (be) successful.
6. If you _____ (like) to follow me, I'll show you to your rooms.
7. We'd be rich now if we _____ (not lost) the ticket.
8. _____ (shall) you have any questions, please do not hesitate to contact me.
9. If only he _____ (stop) pestering me, I'd try to help.

5 Complete the sentences in the Active Grammar box with the correct phrase.

> ## Active Grammar
>
> a. if it hadn't been for . . .
> b. should you . . .
> c. provided (that) . . ./as long as . . .
> d. if only . . .
> e. happen to/should happen to . . .
> f. if you will/would . . .
>
> 1. ____ can be used with real conditional sentences to emphasize that something is unlikely to occur.
> 2. ____ can be used instead of *if* to show that specific conditions should be met for something to happen.
> 3. ____ is often used to show that a negative result would have occurred without a certain person or event.
> 4. ____ can be used to express a wish or regret.
> 5. ____ is often used in formal business communication.
> 6. ____ can be used as a polite form.

See Reference page 131

6 Use the prompts in parentheses to rewrite the sentences so the meaning stays the same.

Ex: I'll renew the contract if the conditions stay the same. (provided)
I'll renew the contract provided the conditions stay the same.

1. I failed the exam because the last question was so difficult. (if it . . . passed the exam)
2. I didn't have my credit card with me so I didn't buy any presents. (I would . . .)
3. The business isn't doing well because there is so much competition. (if only . . . better)
4. Thanks to Dr. Crane, I recovered quickly. (if it . . . might not)
5. They argued about money, and their partnership broke up. (if they . . . business partners now.)

Speaking

7 **Group Work** Discuss, using conditionals.

1. What would you do if only you had more time?
2. If you happened to win $1,000, what would you do with it?
3. Is there anything that you wish you had done when you were younger?

Reading

8 Read the article and circle the correct choices.

GREAT PHILANTHROPISTS

Can you imagine becoming the richest person in the world, and then giving all your money away? That's exactly what Andrew Carnegie did. Carnegie made millions of dollars during his highly successful business career. As a result, when he retired in 1901, at the age of 66, he was the world's richest man. But Carnegie outlined his beliefs about wealth in an essay, "The Gospel of Wealth."

Andrew Carnegie

In the essay, he describes how wealthy men ought to live without (**1.** *greedy/charity/money/extravagance*), provide moderately (**2.** *of/for/on/to*) their families, and consider the rest of their wealth as extra money that should be distributed to promote the (**3.** *welfare/farewell/sickness/richness*) and happiness of other people. "The Gospel of Wealth" was read all over the world, and Carnegie's worthy intentions were praised. Very wealthy people of that period lived (**4.** *greatly/lavishly/hugely/cheaply*) and spent huge amounts of money on their own personal needs and wishes, but Andrew Carnegie was not one of them. In his lifetime, he gave away more than $350 million or almost 90 percent of his (**5.** *treasure/fortune/collection/account*) for what he considered to be the improvement of all mankind.

But he wasn't the only generous American of his time. John D. Rockefeller once said, "Giving away money intelligently is more difficult than making it." Having given away $530 million to (**6.** *care/help/charity/cause*), he should know.

Rockefeller's entrepreneurial skills started when he was young. When he was just 12 years old, he lent $50 to a farmer. The following year, he got the money back and (**7.** *charged/asked/insisted/paid*) interest! But his philanthropic journey was inspired by the tragic death of his three-year-old grandson. When the boy died of scarlet fever, Rockefeller began putting his money (**8.** *onto/in/into/to*) medical research. He (**9.** *foundation/founded/found/foundered*) the Rockefeller Institute in 1901, and later his doctors became famous for flying around the world providing vaccines for children.

Helping children is a (**10.** *mission/missive/work/problem*) close to the heart of another pair of famous philanthropists, Bill and Melinda Gates. Gates not only earns but also gives away more money than anyone else in the world. The Bill and Melinda Gates Foundation has saved 700,000 children's lives through its health programs. Gates (**11.** *puts/spends/dedicates/creates*) billions to fighting diseases like malaria, which are still killers in the developing world. Closer to home, he has set up education programs and scholarship funds designed to have a major (**12.** *change/affect/result/impact*) on children growing up in the US.

While we can (**13.** *inspire/admire/cope/afford*) the generosity and (**14.** *idea/visual/ambitious/vision*) of all these people, perhaps we should leave the last word to Rockefeller's colleague, Raymond Fosdick. He wrote that it's a mistake to think "that money can create ideas, and that a great (**15.** *amounts/sum/deal/lot*) of money can create better ideas. You cannot buy scientists or poets."

Bill and Melinda Gates

9 **Pair Work** Discuss the questions.

1. Which charities do you/would you support, and why?
2. "Tragedy often inspires generosity." Would you agree?
3. "You cannot buy scientists or poets." Do you agree? Why or why not?

> *I volunteer for a local charity that delivers food to the homeless. It . . .*

Speaking

1 **Pair Work** Think about what is important in a job. Then discuss which items in the box are priorities for you. Try to use some of the expressions from the How To box.

opportunity for promotion	401K
flexible working hours	benefits
convenient location	good salary
professional development	job satisfaction
working environment	freedom/autonomy
supportive colleagues/manager	challenging work

How To:

Express priorities

Saying it's very important	• *My first priority is . . .* • *The essential thing for me is . . .* • *____ is vital.* • *I couldn't do without . . .*
Saying it's not important	• *I'm not really concerned about . . .* • *It isn't a major priority.* • *I could do without . . .*

American English	British English
flexible working hours	*flexitime*

Reading

2 Read the article and answer the questions that follow.

TOP COMPANIES

Every year since 1998, *Fortune* Magazine has published a list of the "100 Best Companies to Work For." How does the magazine choose the companies? First, it uses a survey: 350 employees answer 57 questions about their company. Second, it looks at important features of companies; for example, pay, benefits, and communication between workers and management.

To a certain extent, the results are guesswork, but the companies on the list, by and large, have many things in common: they pay their employees well, they allow workers to make decisions, and they offer a comfortable workplace. Broadly speaking, however, the winners tend to offer something above and beyond the norm. J. M. Smucker, a jam and jelly company, gives its workers free muffins and bagels for breakfast; at Griffin Hospital, employees get free massages; a bank called First Horizon National gives its employees time off to visit their children's classrooms. Wegmans Food Markets sent one worker on a ten-day trip to London, Paris, and Italy to learn about cheese. This is not unusual for the New York-based company, which is well-known for the scholarships it gives its employees to further their education. At W. L. Gore, workers decide on their colleagues' salaries. Surprisingly enough, the most important thing for the majority of employees is not money. It is the freedom to develop ideas. Timberland offers a six-month paid sabbatical for employees who have "a personal dream that benefits the community."

Let's not forget that all these companies are businesses whose priority is making money. They have to make a profit.

And do they? Seemingly, the answer is a big "yes." The number three company on *Fortune's* 2011 list, Wegmans, makes a fortune. The company, which has a motto, "Employees first, customers second," is one of the 50 largest private companies in the US, with annual sales of $3.6 billion, according to *Forbes* magazine. Apparently, being good to your employees is no obstacle to making money.

How much of Wegmans' success is due to the company's policies? "Up to a point, the success is because of the freedom they give us," says one employee. "On the other hand, no company gets rich just by being nice. Wegmans has great marketing strategies, and it's well-positioned within the community. I've been here for 15 years. Looking back, I'd say that the company's innovations for customers, such as the Shoppers' Club electronic discount program in the '90s, have been just as important as the benefits to staff."

But the employee benefits are striking. Fundamentally, Wegmans believes in professional development. In addition to scholarships, the company gives its employees business opportunities. For years, one employee made delicious cookies for her colleagues. Eventually, she started selling the cookies in Wegmans. "I just asked the manager," she says. "In hindsight, I should have asked earlier. I could have made more money!"

The staff's freedom to make decisions is another thing you won't find everywhere. Essentially, Wegmans wants its workers to do almost anything to keep its customers happy. Believe it or not, an employee once cooked a Thanksgiving turkey in the store for a customer because the woman's turkey, bought at Wegmans, was too big for her oven. One manager says, "We're a $3 billion company run by 16-year-old cashiers."

1. How does *Fortune* Magazine get the results for its annual list?

2. What makes the winners special?

3. What is Wegmans' philosophy?

4. Why does a manager say that the company is run by 16-year-old cashiers?

Grammar | sentence adverbials

3 Read the article on page 62 again. What purpose do the underlined words and phrases serve? Complete the tasks in the Active Grammar box.

Active Grammar

Circle the correct choice to complete the rules below.

1. Sentence adverbials show how the sentence fits in with the rest of the text, and frequently go at the beginning / middle / end of a sentence.

2. Sentence adverbials show the speaker's attitude and feelings, and are usually separated from the rest of the sentence by a period / comma.

Complete the chart using the underlined examples in the article on page 62.

Adverbial Functions	Examples
Basic ideas	*fundamentally, essentially*
Generalizations	
How something appears	
Contrast	
Reflection on the past	
Partial agreement	

Add any other adverbial phrases that you can think of to the chart.

See Reference page 131

4 Circle the two sentence adverbials that fit the context of each sentence.

Ex: *We want our workers to be happy. ____, this means helping them foster a sense of pride in their work.*
   a. Fundamentally   b. Essentially   c. With hindsight

1. We believe in giving our employees as much autonomy as possible. ____, we try not to interfere unless really necessary.

   a. Broadly speaking   b. Apparently   c. By and large

2. Our employees don't complain if they have to work on weekends. ____, they do expect to be paid overtime for it.

   a. On the other hand   b. Seemingly   c. However

3. We believe in second chances, because employees learn from their mistakes. ____, our company has never fired an employee.

   a. Believe it or not   b. Surprisingly enough   c. Broadly speaking

4. Employees help set salaries ____, but they are not allowed to pay themselves unreasonable amounts.

   a. up to a point   b. apparently   c. to a certain extent

5. Some employees' salaries were getting too high. ____, we should have introduced a pay cap earlier.

   a. Believe it or not   b. Looking back   c. In hindsight

Speaking

5 **Group Work** Discuss whether you agree or disagree with the statements.

1. It's a good idea for employees to set their own salaries.
2. Employees shouldn't have to wear uniforms.
3. Employees should be allowed to evaluate their managers.
4. In the future, everyone will have flexible work schedules.

> I don't think it's a good idea for employees to set their own salaries, unless there's some way to control how high they get . . .

> I'm not so sure. I think employees might be more invested in the success of the company if they're part of the decision-making process.

Listening

6a **Pair Work** Discuss. Do you know of any companies with particularly good or bad working conditions? What effect do the conditions have on the employees and on the company's success?

b ▶1.25 Listen to an interview. Then discuss the questions.

1. What do you think of the ideas introduced at Blue Skies Recruitment? Would you like to work for the company? Why or why not?

2. If you were the director of a new company, what ideas would you introduce to help retain your staff?

Vocabulary | expressing quantity

| handful | plenty | most | few | bit |
| majority | many | much | deal | |

7a Complete the phrases from the listening, using the words in the box.

1. as _____ as (a surprisingly large number)
2. a little _____ more (a little more)
3. a great _____ of energy (a lot of energy)
4. _____ of benefits (a lot of benefits)
5. not _____ of an expert (not really an expert)
6. for the _____ part (generally)
7. the vast _____ (most of)
8. quite a _____ employees (a large number)
9. only a _____ of people (very few people)

b ▶1.26 Listen to check your answers.

8 Rewrite the sentences using the words in parentheses.

1. The government spends a lot of money on defense.
   The government . . . (great)
2. The customers generally appreciate our top-quality service.
   For . . . (most)
3. There's more than enough room.
   There . . . (plenty)
4. It isn't a huge fee if you consider the amount of work involved.
   It . . . (much)
5. Three or four people asked questions.
   Only . . . (handful)
6. Most of the workers joined the strike.
   The . . . (vast)

9a Complete the sentences using phrases from Exercise 7.

Ex: I think the government wastes . . . on . . .   *I think the government wastes a great deal of money on inefficient projects.*

1. There are . . . women in top management positions because . . .
2. . . . of people in this country . . .
3. I spend . . . my time . . .
4. . . . of road accidents could be avoided if . . .
5. There are not . . . as there used to be.

b **Pair Work** Discuss your sentences with a partner. Do you agree with your partner's opinions?

Writing

10 Choose one of the sentences in Exercise 9a and write a paragraph on the topic.

Review

1   Rewrite the sentences using the correct option in parentheses. There may be more than one possibility.

1. He was offered the job, but he didn't accept it. (*surprisingly enough/broadly speaking*)
2. They explained how the project would be too difficult to manage, and I agree. (*on the other hand/ to a certain extent*)
3. They didn't know who I was talking about. Georgia left the company years ago. (*Principally/Apparently*)
4. I decided to change careers. I'm not sure that I made the right decision. (*Essentially/In hindsight*)
5. The new arrangements have worked out well. (*By and large/Primarily*)
6. The new president was faced with an impossible task. (*however/seemingly*)

2   Cross out the clause that <u>cannot</u> be used to complete each sentence.

1. If he'd planned to give the money back, why ____
   a. didn't he contact the police?
   b. hadn't he contact the police?
   c. would he contact the police?

2. If you lost your job tomorrow, ____
   a. what are you going to do?
   b. what would you do?
   c. you could call me.

3. He can come with us provided that ____
   a. he pays for his own meals.
   b. he would pay for his room.
   c. he doesn't drive the car.

4. If you happen to find my bag, ____
   a. could you call this number?
   b. just give it to Sue.
   c. I'd be really surprised.

5. If it hadn't been for Mary, ____
   a. you will still be waiting.
   b. we would never have found you.
   c. everything would have been fine.

3   Rewrite the sentences using the words in parentheses for emphasis.

1. We weren't at all surprised to hear that she got the part. (bit)
2. I think it is surprisingly warm here. (actually)
3. She makes a lot of her clothes. (own)
4. It is not certain that the game will take place. (means)
5. Rachel had the courage to complain about the service. (it)
6. They have done nothing to fix the problem. (all)

4   Complete the paragraph using the words in the box.

founded	lavishly	wealthy	vision	mind
volunteer	venture	fortune	impact	charity

Anita Cuello, who _____ (**1.**) a highly successful chain of eco-conscious clothing stores, says she plans to give away her entire _____ (**2.**) to _____ (**3.**). Ms. Cuello started her business _____ (**4.**) in 1999 with her husband. Their _____ (**5.**) was to create a line of clothing that was beautiful and stylish and that could be produced with minimal _____ (**6.**) on the environment. They succeeded beyond their wildest dreams. Now Cuello says that she has had enough of business life and hopes to achieve peace of _____ (**7.**) by sharing her good fortune with those who have not been so lucky. "I don't understand greed," she says. "I do not know why extremely _____ (**8.**) people choose to live so _____ (**9.**)." Cuello and her family live modestly and _____ (**10.**) at local charities. "Money is best when you use it to help others," she says.

Communication | negotiate

5 ▶1.27 Listen to two people discussing what they would do if their company suddenly had $1 million to spend. What ideas do they have? How are the speakers different?

6 **Group Work** What would you suggest if your company or school suddenly had $1 million to spend? Compare your ideas with other groups.

7 Read the profile of Fortune Foods and answer the questions.
1. What are the company's main strengths?
2. What are the main problems for employees?

Company Profile

Company: Fortune Foods

Product: Quality food for parties

Strengths:
- Company has an excellent reputation and is growing.
- Clients are high-end businesses.

Problems:
- Employees often stay late at night to finish preparing food.
- Employees have a high level of stress.
- Factory is in a part of the city with bad roads and heavy traffic. It is difficult to drive there.

Financial Situation: Fortune Foods made a profit last year.

8 **SPEAKING EXCHANGE** Fortune Foods has just received an investment of $2 million. Read the instructions below, and decide what the company should do with the money.
1. Work in two groups (one group represents the employees and the other represents management). Group A (employees): read page 139. Group B (management): read page 141.
2. Spend some time preparing your arguments, and then begin a negotiation with the other group.
3. Discuss. How did the negotiations go? What did you decide? Was everyone happy with the decision?

UNIT 6
Understanding power

A

B

C

D

Warm Up

1 What types of "power" are represented in the photos? Create phrases by combining the words in the box with *power* or *powerful*. Then use five of your phrases in sentences.

> **Ex:** *powerful speech   The president gave a powerful speech last night.*

medicine	nuclear	speech	spending	argument	world	tool	army
influence	political	people	consumer	economic	reasons	brain	wind

2 **Pair Work** Check that you understand the phrases in bold. Discuss the questions.
1. Do you think people **have** enough **power over** the decisions that affect their lives?
2. Should more women be **in positions of power**?
3. Can you think of any countries that are growing in **economic power**?
4. In what circumstances should police be given **special powers**?
5. What political changes often occur when a new leader **comes to power**?

Describe an important building or structure

GRAMMAR articles

CAN DO ✔

The Pentagon

The Eiffel Tower

The Forbidden City

Reading

1 **Pair Work** Discuss.

1. What is the most impressive building you have ever seen?

2. Do you generally prefer modern or traditional architecture? Give examples.

3. What is the most beautiful or ugliest building in your town or city? Are there any that you think should be torn down or restored?

2 Read the article.

The Architecture of Power

No one knew better than the Romans how to gain political influence through the use of engineering and architecture. The Romans built roads, bridges, aqueducts, forums, amphitheaters, and baths in order to win over the minds of the cultures they were conquering. It's hard not to be impressed by a power that provides you with clean water, a road to the capital city, a way to travel across previously impassable rivers, and incredible public buildings.

Architecture has played an important part in public life throughout history, whether as homage to an individual or as a monument to an institution or ideology.

Architecture has always been a potent symbol of wealth, status, and power. From castles to cathedrals, from the pyramids to skyscrapers, architecture has always served to glorify the ideal of the time.

Vocabulary | power

3 Use the words in the box to complete the definitions and example sentences. You may need to change the verb tenses.

| win | gain | impressed | part | by | play | over | important | be |

1. _____ : to obtain or achieve something

   We are hoping to _____ a better understanding of the process.

2. _____ _____ : to get someone's support or friendship by being nice to them

   The party worked hard to _____ _____ undecided voters.

3. _____ _____ _____ : feel admiration and respect for

   The CEO _____ _____ _____ your presentation.

4. _____ an _____ _____ in: to have a big effect or influence

   Everyone from the cleaners to the management _____ an _____ _____ in this year's financial success.

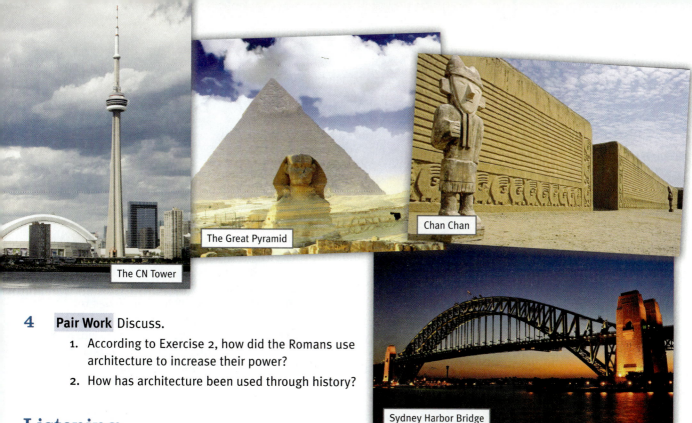

The CN Tower

The Great Pyramid

Chan Chan

Sydney Harbor Bridge

4 **Pair Work** Discuss.

1. According to Exercise 2, how did the Romans use architecture to increase their power?

2. How has architecture been used through history?

Listening

5a Look at the photos and guess which structure:

1. allows visitors to see up to 120 kilometers away?

2. had a sophisticated irrigation system?

3. was constructed by 400,000 men?

4. is known as the "coathanger"?

5. takes 20 minutes to walk around?

6. is one of the largest palaces in the world?

7. was built in 1889?

b ▶1.28 Listen and check your answers.

6 **Pair Work** Which structures sound the most impressive or interesting to you? Which have you visited or would you like to visit?

Grammar | articles

7 Circle the correct choice to complete the rules in the Active Grammar box.

Active Grammar

1. Use _a_ / _an_ / _the_ / no article to introduce something new or unexpected. It indicates that the reader or listener does not know what is being talked about.
   I just bumped into ____ old friend.

2. Use _a_ / _an_ / _the_ / no article to indicate "common ground." It may refer the reader or listener to a shared experience or general knowledge. The context will be important to establish exactly which noun is being referred to.
   I went to see ____ house this morning. (I told you about this house. Shared experience.)

3. Use _a_ / _an_ / _the_ / no article to refer to something in general.
   I enjoy talking to taxi drivers. (taxi drivers in general)

See Reference page 132

8 Write *a*, *an*, or *the* in each space or leave the space blank.

The Sagrada Familia in _____ (**1.**) Barcelona is one of _____ (**2.**) Antoni Gaudí's most impressive works. This enormous church, as yet unfinished, is in some respects _____ (**3.**) summary of everything that Gaudí designed before. _____ (**4.**) architectural style of the Sagrada Familia has been called "warped Gothic," and it's easy to see why. The contours of _____ (**5.**) stone façade make it look as though the Sagrada Familia is melting in _____ (**6.**) sun, while _____ (**7.**) towers are topped with brightly colored mosaics that look like _____ (**8.**) bowls of fruit. Gaudí believed that _____ (**9.**) color is life, and, knowing that he would not live to see _____ (**10.**) completion of his masterpiece, he left colored drawings of his vision for future architects to follow.

For nearly 30 years, Gaudí worked on the Sagrada Familia and other projects simultaneously, until 1911, when he decided to devote himself exclusively to _____ (**11.**) church. During _____ (**12.**) last year of his life, Gaudí lived in _____ (**13.**) studio at the Sagrada Familia.

Tragically, in June 1926, Gaudí was run over by _____ (**14.**) tram. Because he was poorly dressed, he was not recognized, and _____ (**15.**) taxi drivers refused to take a "bum" to the hospital (they were later fined by _____ (**16.**) police). Gaudí died five days later and was buried in the crypt of the building to which he had devoted 44 years of his life, _____ (**17.**) as yet unfinished Sagrada Familia.

Speaking

9 **Pair Work** Think of three more important buildings or structures. What do you know about them? Make notes. Then share your choices with the class and explain why you chose them.

> *I think the Great Wall of China is one of the most amazing structures in the world. It was built . . .*

Writing

10a Choose two important buildings or structures that you know about. If possible, do some research to find out more information about them.

b Write a paragraph about each of the structures you have chosen, using phrases from the How To box, as appropriate.

c **Group Work** Read your paragraphs to other students. Which buildings or structures do you think have been most influential? Why?

How To:	
Describe important architecture	
Use superlatives	• The Great Pyramid is **arguably the most** . . . , • It is **one of** Australia's **best known,** and **most photographed** . . . • It is **the world's largest** . . .
Use fronting for dramatic effect	• **Built to house the body of a pharaoh,** the base of the Great Pyramid . . . • **Fondly known as the "coathanger,"** Sydney Harbor Bridge . . .
Provide details (size, description, etc.)	• It is **built from** iron/stones . . . • **Occupying/Covering an area of more than** . . . square meters • **Standing** 134 meters **high/above** . . .
Describe reason for building/purpose	• It was **built to commemorate** the anniversary • It was **built in order to** . . .

Take notes from fluent connected speech

GRAMMAR clauses with *whatever, whoever, whenever*

Listening

1a **Pair Work** Discuss.

1. Which technologies are the people in the photos using? Why do you think they are so popular?

2. Where do you think big companies go to find out how teenagers use technology?

3. How do you think technology development has been influenced by teens and young adults?

b ▶**1.29** Listen.

2a Complete the sentences with information from the listening.

1. Kids drive technology because ____ .

2. Kids want technology that can be ____ .

3. Text messaging caught on because ____ .

4. Facebook developed as ____ .

5. Converse sent its market researchers to ____ .

b Listen again to check your answers.

Vocabulary | fashions and fads

3a Match the phrases in bold to the definitions.

____ 1. Using teenagers to find out **what's in** and what isn't.

____ 2. They experiment and they automatically **home in on** the new.

____ 3. Anything bigger than a few inches **is out**.

____ 4. Text messaging **caught on** because kids wanted to pass notes to each other during class.

____ 5. All of these things **came about** because of the needs of kids.

____ 6. If you want to **keep up with** the latest style, who do you ask?

a. know the most recent developments

b. focus or direct their attention toward something

c. is fashionable at the moment

d. became popular and fashionable

e. is unfashionable at the moment

f. happened

b Which two phrases in Exercise 3a are exact opposites? Are they formal or informal?

4 **Pair Work** Discuss.

1. What's the best way to keep up with developments in your profession or hobby?

2. What trends have caught on recently in fashion, music, food, and other areas where you live?

3. How do you think global trends come about? Can you think of any examples?

4. Think of one piece of technology or clothing that used to be "in" but is now "out."

> *Well, I think the Internet is a great way to keep up with what's happening. I regularly go to several sites related to my profession . . .*

Speaking

5 **Group Work** Discuss whether teenagers should be allowed to do the following:

1. watch however much TV they want
2. stay up late whenever they want
3. decorate their room in whatever way they want
4. go wherever they want at night
5. socialize with whomever they want
6. wear whatever they want

Listening

6a ▶ 1.30 Listen to the conversations. Which questions from Exercise 5 do they discuss?

Conversation 1: ____

Conversation 2: ____

Conversation 3: ____

Conversation 4: ____

b Listen again. What were their opinions?

Grammar | clauses with *whatever, whoever, whenever*

7 Read the Active Grammar box and answer questions a and b at the bottom.

Active Grammar

1. We use *whenever, whatever, whoever*, etc. when it doesn't make any difference *when, what, who*, etc., or when we don't have to be specific. They also mean "we don't know the exact details of *when, what, who*, etc."

   Teenagers shouldn't be allowed to watch however much TV they want. (We don't know how much TV they want to watch.)

   Teenagers should be able to socialize with whomever they want. (We don't know who they want to socialize with.)

2. *What, who, when* are a little different from *whatever, whoever, whenever*. Compare the example sentences below:

   a. *Stop what you are doing now.*

   b. *Stop whatever you are doing now.*

   c. *Whatever you are doing, stop it now.*

   NOT: ~~*What you are doing, stop it now.*~~

3. We often use *however* with an adjective or adverb. It means *No matter how . . .*

   However intelligent you are, eventually you'll meet someone more intelligent.

   However hard he works, he'll never get promoted.

   Note: *However* is also a conjunction that means *but* or *on the other hand*.

---

a. Which sentence(s) in item 2 mean(s), "I know what you are doing and I want you to stop"? _____

b. Which sentence(s) in item 2 mean(s) "I don't care what you are doing, but I want you to stop"? _____

See Reference page 132

8 Complete the sentences with *whenever, however, whatever, whoever,* or *wherever.*

1. _____ you do, don't lose these keys!
2. Send me an email _____ you have time.
3. Carry your passport with you _____ you go.
4. _____ is at the door, tell them I'm busy.
5. _____ you travel—by train, car, or bus—the trip will take at least three hours.

9a Complete the second sentence in each pair so that it has the same meaning as the first. Use *whenever, however, whatever, whoever,* or *wherever.*

Ex: If it's the last thing you do, make sure you turn off the power.

   Whatever you do , don't forget to turn off the power.

1. Call me if you feel down.

   _____ down, give me a call.

2. It doesn't matter where we go; they always follow us.

   _____, they're always close behind.

3. I'll see her as soon as I can.

   _____, I'll see her.

4. It doesn't matter who we hire; he'll have to be a genius.

   _____, he'll have to work miracles.

5. Those children can do anything, and it turns out successful.

   _____ do, they make a success of it.

b ▶ 1.31 Listen to check your answers.

10a Complete *The Teenagers' Manifesto* with *whoever, whenever, whatever, however,* and *wherever.*

THE TEENAGERS' MANIFESTO

1. Allowance—We can spend our allowance on _____ we like, including clothes, video games, and other things that our parents consider to be a waste of money.
2. TV—We can watch _____ we want on TV, _____ we want, including late at night.
3. Clothes—We can wear _____ we like.
4. Friends—We can go out with _____ we want.
5. Privacy—_____ we want to be alone, we have the right to be in our rooms undisturbed.
6. Noise/Music—we can listen to _____ type of music we choose. If others are trying to work, we will turn down the volume.
7. Cell phone use—We can talk to _____ we wish, _____ it's necessary.

b **Pair Work** Would you change anything about *The Teenagers' Manifesto?* If so, what and why?

Write an autobiographical statement ✓

Reading

1 **Pair Work** Read the definition of *charisma* below. Then discuss the questions.

> **charisma** /kəˈrɪzmə/ *n* [U] the natural ability to attract and influence other people

1. Who is the most charismatic person you know or know of? In what ways are they charismatic?
2. Is charisma something you can learn, or do you have to be born with it?

Mahatma Gandhi

Madonna

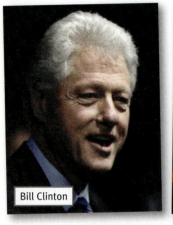

Bill Clinton

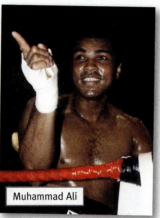

Muhammad Ali

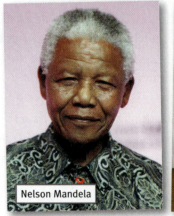

Nelson Mandela

Richard Feynman

2 Read the article.

1 According to Joan Collins, Bill Clinton "eats you up with his eyes. I don't know whether it's magic or a trick, but it's the best act I've ever seen." Of course, Bill Clinton and John F. Kennedy had it. Madonna and Muhammad Ali have it, too. It's questionable whether any of the British Royal family have it, <u>although</u> Diana, Princess of Wales, tried to develop it. Charisma. <u>Hard as we try</u> to understand it, the formula remains elusive. All we can do is watch the masters at work and learn from them.

2 Colleen Dawson's grandson was in the same class as Nelson Mandela's grandson. **During** one parents' night, the adults were talking to the teachers. The evening was progressing as usual, **at which point** Mandela suddenly walked in. "Normally we would have asked about homework and other details," says Dawson, "but no one spoke. So he just started talking in a quiet authoritative way about the important job of teaching. **While** the parents and teachers in the room were struck dumb with reverence, **on finding** himself suddenly the center of attention, Mandela found common ground for everyone present—education. Mandela's charisma shone through.

3 <u>Even though</u> charisma is usually associated with politicians, businesspeople, and celebrities, Richard Feynman proved that people in other fields can have it.

People **had no sooner begun** a conversation with Feynman than they'd be struck by his love of the subject. <u>Despite</u> the fact that Feynman's field was theoretical physics—not exactly a crowd-pleaser—he had such enthusiasm for the mysteries of the universe that he infected everyone within earshot. The Nobel Prize–winning scientist was a larger-than-life figure and very charismatic. One ex-student recalls, "**He'd hardly have started** a lecture, and you'd notice the whole audience on the edge of their seat."

4 Most of the great leaders in history possessed a star quality that drew others to them and helped them gain power and success. Winston Churchill, Mahatma Gandhi, and Martin Luther King Jr. had a magnetism that is easier to identify with than to explain. Broadcaster and confidence tutor Jeremy Milnes says, "There are some people who are just naturally charismatic, like Johnny Depp, David Bowie, and Marilyn Monroe. But I believe that there are techniques and skills that can be learned and practiced." Milnes says that, <u>much as</u> charisma can be learned, it can't be faked. "Whatever skills and techniques you have are rooted in your own personality." His thoughts are echoed by other experts in the field, who estimate that charisma is 50 percent innate and 50 percent learned.

3 Answer the questions about the reading.

1. Does the writer believe there's a simple way to become charismatic?
2. What did Mandela discuss during parents' night? Why?
3. Does the writer believe charismatic people are associated with particular professions?
4. Why did people want to listen to Feynman?
5. Why does Milnes think there's hope for normal, uncharismatic people?

Grammar | logical connectors of time and contrast

4 Complete the tasks in the Active Grammar box.

Active Grammar

There are many words and phrases used to link ideas in sentences.

Time	Contrast
1. There are six connectors relating to time **in bold** in the reading. Put them in the correct place in the chart. The first one has been done for you.	**2.** There are five expressions of contrast underlined in the reading. Put them in the correct place in the chart.

Time	Contrast
It happened soon after another thing. *on finding*	Expressions that begin a clause (with a subject and a verb).
It happened at the same time as something else.	Expressions that can be followed by a noun phrase or gerund.
It comes at the end of a long, continuous sequence of action. It often introduces a moment of change in the sequence or is the result of this sequence.	Expressions that use adjective/adverb + *as* + subject + verb to emphasize the contrast.

Add the following words and phrases to the chart above: when   by which time

Add the following words and phrases to the chart: in spite of   while   difficult as it was

---

See Reference page 132

5 Complete the paragraph using the words and phrases from the box. You will not use all of the phrases.

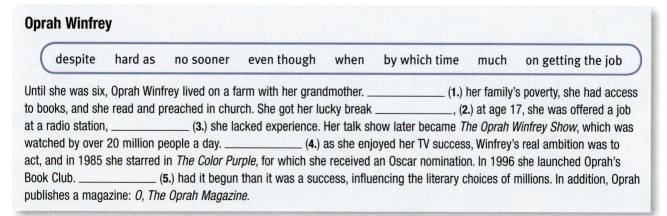

Oprah Winfrey

(despite   hard as   no sooner   even though   when   by which time   much   on getting the job)

Until she was six, Oprah Winfrey lived on a farm with her grandmother. _____ (**1.**) her family's poverty, she had access to books, and she read and preached in church. She got her lucky break _____, (**2.**) at age 17, she was offered a job at a radio station, _____ (**3.**) she lacked experience. Her talk show later became *The Oprah Winfrey Show*, which was watched by over 20 million people a day. _____ (**4.**) as she enjoyed her TV success, Winfrey's real ambition was to act, and in 1985 she starred in *The Color Purple*, for which she received an Oscar nomination. In 1996 she launched Oprah's Book Club. _____ (**5.**) had it begun than it was a success, influencing the literary choices of millions. In addition, Oprah publishes a magazine: *O, The Oprah Magazine*.

Vocabulary | personal characteristics

6   Match the adjectives on the left to the words or phrases in bold that have the <u>opposite</u> meaning. Check the meaning of any phrases you do not understand.

____ 1. charismatic	a.	She **doesn't have much drive or energy**.
____ 2. inspirational	b.	He **wavers in the face of problems**.
____ 3. dignified	c.	He's very **approachable**. He always has time to talk to people.
____ 4. aloof	d.	He's **corrupt**.
____ 5. idealistic	e.	She's fairly **nondescript**.
____ 6. tireless	f.	She's very **down-to-earth** and practical.
____ 7. trustworthy	g.	She's **not very inspiring**.
____ 8. resolute	h.	She **lacks *gravitas***.

7a   ▶1.32   Listen to the way the words and expressions above are pronounced. Mark the stresses.

b   Listen again. What is the pronunciation of *gn* in *sign*? of *gn* in *dignified*? of *ch* in *much*? of *ch* in *charismatic*?

8   **Pair Work**   Discuss.

1. What do you know about the people in the photos? Which adjectives would you use to describe them?

2. Can you think of any other famous people who could be described using the adjectives or the phrases above?

> *I would say that Hillary Clinton is resolute. For example . . .*

Pelé

Hillary Clinton

Bruce Lee

Christiane Amanpour

Writing

9a   Read the autobiographical statement in the Writing Bank on page 145 and do the exercises.

b   Read the ad below and follow the instructions.

> # SCHOLARSHIP AWARD – $5,000
>
> Piaget Educational Consultants is offering a scholarship award to study for one year at a university in Australia. The winner will be given lodging, tuition, and $5,000 spending money. Write an autobiographical statement (150–200 words) describing your character and your relationships with colleagues, teachers, and professors. Mention one colleague, teacher, or professor who has influenced you.

Review

1   Add articles to the paragraph where necessary. Change the punctuation accordingly.

> ### The Shanghai World Financial Center
>
> This 1,614-foot (492-meter) high building consists of two elements that correspond to Chinese concept of Earth as square and sky as circle. Hole in top also has practical use—to relieve pressure of wind on building. Glassy Tower is just blocks away from 1,378-foot (420-meter) Jinmao Tower in district of Shanghai that has been designated Asian center for international banking. Tower's lower levels are used for offices, and its upper levels for hotel, art museum, and restaurants.

2   Complete the conversations with *whatever, whoever, whenever, however,* or *wherever.*

1. **A:** Why do you like Italy?

   B: Because _____ you go in Italy, you can find amazing architecture.

2. **A:** What's so different about that school?

   B: There are no required subjects. You can study _____ you want.

3. **A:** What time should I come to your house?

   B: Come _____ you can make it.

4. **A:** Will you be able to get time off from work?

   B: Yes—they're flexible. I'll talk to _____ is on duty.

5. **A:** Will it be faster if we take the bus or the train?

   B: _____ you travel, it takes over two hours.

3   Choose words from each box to complete the sentences. Change the verb tense where necessary.

| come   be   home   catch   keep | | in (x2)   up   on (x2)   about   with |

1. We _____ _____ _____ the latest developments by reading magazines.

2. I don't think that new type of phone will ever _____ _____. It's too ugly.

3. I've lost touch with the music scene. I don't have any idea what _____ _____ any more.

4. This extraordinary situation _____ _____ because our marketing department had a great idea.

5. Hi-tech companies are increasingly _____ _____ _____ teenagers as their number one consumer.

4   Find and delete any unnecessary words in the text.

> An hour with the Body Earth Power Group was enough for me. No sooner but had Carin Brook entered than everyone became silent. Much as I tried to keep my mind open—and despite of the fact that I have been known to do a bit of tree-hugging myself—I couldn't help thinking that this was going to be a waste of time. Brook, even and though she is tiny, had a strong personality. We started stretching in order to "feel the Earth's rhythm," but it didn't last long. I'd hardly but lifted my hands up when she told us all to sit down, close our eyes and "re-visualize ourselves from above." Hard as though I tried, I just couldn't imagine what the top of my head looked like, and in the spite of her promptings to "relax," the hard floor was getting very uncomfortable. Thankfully, 4:00 came, by which the time I was desperate for a nice soft chair and a good meal.

Communication | evaluate personal characteristics

5 **Pair Work** Look at the picture and read the following information about the passengers: One of these people is a spy (a), one is a criminal (b), one used to be famous (c), one will be famous (d), one is a doctor (e), one is a lawyer (f), one has a dark secret (g), one is a journalist (h), and one is a soldier (i). Who is who? Guess the identity of the people and label the picture.

6 Imagine you are one of the people. Complete the short profile below.

My name is _____

I work as a _____

I am _____

I believe in _____

My strengths are _____

_____

My weaknesses are _____

_____

I will always _____

_____

7 Imagine that the plane crashes. Everyone survives, and you all find yourselves on a desert island. You decide to start a new community. Your character wants to be the leader. Think about the following questions.

1. What are your ideas for leading the community?

2. How will you persuade the others that you should be in charge?

3. What experiences do you have that will be useful?

8a **Group Work** Present your ideas and argue your case for becoming the leader of the new community.

b Elect a leader and explain your choice to other groups.

UNIT 7
The natural world

A

B

C

D

Warm Up

1   **Pair Work** Discuss. Where are the animals in the photos? Which are being used by people? How? Do you approve of the way they are being used? Why or why not?

2   **Pair Work** Discuss.

   1. Name two or more animals for each category:

   > mammal   endangered species
   > reptile   exotic animal
   > carnivore   predator

   2. Name two or more animals that live in the following places:

   > in a sanctuary or nature preserve
   > in the wild
   > in a cage

   3. What do you know about the following issues?

   > the fur trade   animal testing
   > animal rights   over-hunting and over-fishing

Reading

1 Look at the two titles in the reading. What do you think the article will be about? Read and check your prediction.

How watching animals will save us

Becoming better observers of animal behavior may be the key to surviving natural disasters in the future. During the tsunami disaster of 2004, over 300,000 people died. No one has counted the number of animals killed, but we know that it wasn't many. All over the region, before the disaster struck, animals were behaving strangely.

Shortly before the tsunami, in Khaolak, Thailand, 12 elephants that were giving tourists rides became agitated. They suddenly left their usual habitat, carrying four surprised Japanese tourists to safety. On the eastern coast of India, flamingos, which should have been breeding at that time of year, suddenly flew to higher ground. Of the 2,000 wild pigs that inhabit an Indian nature reserve, only one was found dead after the tsunami.

The idea that animals are able to predict disasters is nothing new. In fact, it has been well documented over the years. Twelve hours before Hurricane Charlie hit Florida in 2004, 14 electronically tagged sharks left their natural habitat and stayed in deeper waters for two weeks. The sharks, which were being observed by US biologists, had never done that before. They escaped the hurricane. In the winter of 1975 in Haicheng, China, snakes that would normally have been hibernating were seen on the ground. Days later, there was an earthquake that measured 7.3 on the Richter Scale.

Unlike human beings, wild animals perceive a great deal of information about the world around them. Their senses are sharper, and they can feel even the smallest changes in the environment. In other words, they see natural warnings that are invisible to the human eye. Ancient people probably had similar "animal instincts," which they needed to survive but which have been lost to us as modern technology leads us further away from the dangers that nature poses.

The real question is, can we use the reactions of animals to save ourselves from natural disasters? Animal behavior expert Rupesh Kaneira believes we have no choice. "The technology that we rely on isn't always perfect, and in poorer countries it isn't even available. Animals know the environment better than any of us. When they run for their lives, we must follow."

And how rats will rescue us . . .

In the earthquake capitals of the world—Japan, Los Angeles, Turkey—rats will soon be man's new best friend.

In the aftermath of an earthquake, rescue teams send in dogs that are trained to smell people. No one knows how many lives they have saved, but there are, of course, drawbacks: dogs are big, and they can't get into small spaces. Now a new research project is using a smaller animal to save lives: the rat.

How does it work? First, the rat is trained to smell people. When it does, the rat's brain gives off a signal, similar to what happens when a dog smells a bomb. The trained rats are sent into the wreckage. On their back is a very small radio, which is connected to the rat's brain. The rescuers, at a safe distance, monitor the radio signals. When the rat's brain activity jumps, the rescuers know that someone is alive.

Of course, there are already robots that can do this job, one of which looks and moves like a snake, but rats are better because they can smell more efficiently than robots, whose noses don't work well when there are other smells around. Rats also crawl efficiently in destroyed buildings—something that robots are not as good at—and they don't need electricity. What's more, rats have a survival instinct: they get out when it isn't safe.

2 Answer the questions.

1. What did the animals do before the natural disasters occurred?
2. How do we know what the sharks did before Hurricane Charlie?
3. What specific ability allows animals to "predict" natural disasters?
4. How do rescue teams know that a rescue rat has found someone?

3 Pair Work Discuss.

1. What differences between humans and animals does the article describe?
2. Do you believe in a "sixth sense" or "animal instincts"?
3. Do you think these ideas for using animals will be successful? What problems might there be?

Grammar | relative clauses

4 Read the sentences from the reading in the Active Grammar box and underline the adjective clauses. Then answer the questions.

Active Grammar

Defining relative clauses	**Nondefining relative clauses**
Twelve elephants that were giving tourists rides became agitated.	*Flamingos, which should have been breeding at that time of year, suddenly flew to higher ground.*
Of the 2,000 wild pigs that inhabit an Indian nature reserve, only one was found dead.	*The sharks, which were being observed by US biologists, had never done that before.*
There are already robots that can do this job.	*Rats are better because they can smell more efficiently than robots, whose noses don't work well.*
The technology that we rely on isn't always perfect.	

1. Which clauses identify a person or thing and cannot be deleted without changing the meaning of the sentence?

2. Which clauses add extra information and can be deleted without changing the meaning of the sentence?

See Reference page 133

5 Answer the questions.

1. In which type of relative clause (defining or nondefining) can we use *that* instead of *who* or *which*?

2. When do we use commas with adjective clauses?

3. Which clause ends with a preposition? Find another example in the final paragraph of the reading and underline it. Where does the preposition go in formal English?

4. Find the sentence in the final paragraph of the reading that contains the structure *one of which*.

6 **Pair Work** Do the pairs of sentences have the same meaning? If not, how are they different? Which sentences are incorrect?

1. a. Monkeys whose DNA is similar to that of humans are often used in research into the brain.
   b. Monkeys, whose DNA is similar to that of humans, are often used in research into the brain.

2. a. Guide dogs were first used by soldiers who had been blinded during World War One.
   b. Guide dogs were first used by soldiers, who had been blinded during World War One.

3. a. The funnel spider's web, which is extremely fine, was used to cover wounds.
   b. The funnel spider's web, that is extremely fine, was used to cover wounds.

4. a. Homing pigeons are able to return, weeks later, to the place which they came from.
   b. Homing pigeons are able to return, weeks later, to the place from which they came.

7a Rewrite the questions, including the phrases in the box. Add commas where necessary.

1. Should hunting be allowed?
2. Should zoos be banned?
3. Should the Amazon rainforest be protected? If so, how?
4. Should the use of fur for clothing be banned?

- that take animals from their natural habitat
- that is done only for sport and not for food
- about which there has been much debate in the fashion industry
- which is being destroyed

b **Pair Work** Discuss the questions. Think of arguments for both sides of each issue.

Listening

8 ▶2.02 Listen. Mark the sentences true (*T*), false (*F*), or doesn't say (*?*).
Then listen again to check answers.

____ 1. You need to do some planning before you buy your rabbits.

____ 2. Rabbits eat almost any type of food.

____ 3. You should be vaccinated.

____ 4. You should have at least two rabbits in a hutch.

____ 5. Lots of people choose a dog because it looks cute.

____ 6. The speaker thinks it's a bad idea to keep a dog outside.

____ 7. The owner's lifestyle is an important consideration in choosing the breed of dog.

____ 8. The speaker knows a lot of dog-owners.

Pronunciation | unstressed prepositions

9a How is *to* pronounced in these phrases and sentences from the listening?

1. The first thing you need to do . . .

2. You just need to do a little planning.

3. You have to make sure to get food that they like.

4. You have to clean out the hutch once a week or more . . .

b ▶2.03 Listen to check.

c ▶2.04 Identify the unstressed prepositions in the following sentences. How are they pronounced? Listen and check.

1. A lot of people, for example, just go for the cutest dog they can find.

2. The first thing you need to do is ask yourself a few questions.

3. . . . the next thing to think about is what type of dog would be best for you.

4. . . . if you spend most of your time at home watching TV, get a less active dog.

10 **Pair Work** Think of something that you know how to do well. Make notes on the steps involved. Then tell your partner how to get started. Use some of the language from the How To box.

> *Learning how to windsurf is hard at first, but it's worth the trouble. The first thing you should do is find a good teacher. You'll probably need to rent the equipment at first . . .*

How To:	
Explain procedures	
Prefacing with a general statement	• *It can be a little tricky at first.* • *It's pretty straightforward.* • *It's really easy./It's a piece of cake.*
Sequencing	• *First . . ./The first thing you have to do is . . .* • *Then/Second/The next step is to . . .* • *Finally,*
Checking understanding	• *OK?/Got it?/Any questions?*

Writing

11 A friend is going to stay in your home while you are away. Write three notes explaining how to use your washing machine, feed your pet, water your plants, etc.

Make inferences based on extended prose

GRAMMAR verbs followed by infinitives or gerunds: meaning

Speaking

1 **Pair Work** Discuss. What's the hottest place you have been to? What problems could you have visiting a very hot place? Think about things such as animals, places to stay, health.

Listening

2a ▶2.05 Listen to the first part of David Clark's story. Answer the questions.

1. What does David need from the bureaucrat?
2. What is the bureaucrat's attitude toward David's trip? How do we know?
3. The bureaucrat has a sense of humor. What does he say that shows this?

b **Pair Work** Discuss. What do you think the journey will be like? What do you think the Danakil Depression looks like? How do you think David will feel when he arrives?

> *I don't think David knows what he's getting into. I bet he is going to be surprised . . .*

c ▶2.06 Listen to the second part of the story. Were your predictions correct?

3 **Group Work** Discuss.

1. Why do you think David wanted to make this journey?
2. Why do you think explorers go to extreme places?
3. Why do you think David is disappointed with the Danakil Depression?
4. Would you like to go there? Why or why not?
5. "It is better to travel than to arrive." Do you agree with this proverb?

Vocabulary | descriptive language

4a Listen to the story on page 83 again. Match the words and phrases on the left with the words on the right to make common collocations.

    ____ 1. spectacular   **a.** level

    ____ 2. permanent   **b.** town

    ____ 3. tourist   **c.** settlement

    ____ 4. below sea   **d.** landscape

    ____ 5. active   **e.** volcano

    ____ 6. ghost   **f.** site

b Which of the collocations could be used to describe the photos below?

1   2   3

5 Complete the sentences with collocations from Exercise 4a.

1. The world's most popular _____ is the area around the Eiffel Tower, in Paris.

2. Mount Etna in Sicily, Italy, is the world's most _____ .

3. Antarctica is the only continent on which there is no _____ . It is too cold!

4. The Dead Sea is the lowest point on Earth. It is 1,371 feet (418 meters) _____ .

5. Walhalla, Australia, is a rare example of a _____ that came back to life. Originally a gold mining town, it was abandoned when the gold ran out, but is now popular with tourists.

6. Some of the world's most _____ can be found in Cappadocia, Turkey.

6a Read Audioscripts 2.05 and 2.06 on page 155. What things and people do the words in the box describe? Look up the definitions of any words that you don't know.

> **Ex:** *"Drone" describes the noise of a fan.*

Verbs	Adjectives
drone	warped
zig-zag	vibrant
loom	hunched
trespass	drenched
	parched

b **Pair Work** Now think of other things you can describe using the adjectives.

Vibrant—the colors were vibrant

Barcelona has a vibrant nightlife. She has a vibrant personality.

Grammar | verbs followed by infinitives or gerunds: meaning

7 Complete the tasks in the Active Grammar box.

Active Grammar

Some verbs can be followed by an infinitive or a gerund. Sometimes the meaning changes. Compare the sentences and answer the questions.

Mean

1. Which verb phrase means **a)** intended, **b)** involves?

   ____ *Going to the Danakil Depression **means walking** into hell on Earth.*

   ____ *David **meant to write** a book after his trips.*

Remember

2. Which verb phrase describes **a)** a responsibility or something that you need to do, **b)** a memory of the past?

   ____ *He **remembers experiencing** a feeling of emptiness when he arrived.*

   ____ *They tell you . . . to **remember to drink** even when you're not thirsty.*

Regret

3. Which verb phrase means **a)** a feeling of sadness about something in the past, **b)** a formal apology?

   ____ *I **regret to inform you** that your application for a visa has been turned down.*

   ____ *I didn't **regret going** to the Danakil Depression.*

Stop

4. Which verb phrase means **a)** paused in order to do something, **b)** completely finished something?

   ____ *We **stopped to visit** a ghost town.*

   ____ *David **stopped looking** for vegetation and wildlife once he realized nothing survived in the Danakil Depression.*

Try

5. Which verb phrase describes **a)** an experiment to see what will happen (as a solution to a problem), **b)** an effort to do something difficult?

   ____ *They had **tried to build** a railway.*

   ____ *He **tried drinking** more water but he still felt terrible.*

Go on

6. Which verb phrase means **a)** continued an action, **b)** did something after finishing something else?

   ____ *They waved and **went on riding**.*

   ____ *David Clark **went on to write** a book about his experiences.*

See Reference page 133

---

8 Using patterns from the Active Grammar box, add two words to complete each sentence.

   Ex: I don't remember ⌄ photo, but it turned out really well. *(taking the)*

1. After six hours of driving, we take a break by the roadside.
2. We visit the cathedral, but it was closed that day.
3. Even after I told her to be quiet, she went loudly.
4. She regrets so early this morning. Now she's really tired.
5. I remembered traveler's checks this time. Last time, I forgot and lost all my money.
6. After leaving school with a law degree, she to become a famous lawyer.

Speaking

9a Circle the correct choice.

1. For me, a vacation means *to lie/lying* on a beach.
2. I try *spending/to spend* time outside whenever I can.
3. I'll never stop *traveling/to travel*, even when I'm old.
4. I've never regretted *to go/going* anywhere.

b **Pair Work** Are the sentences true or false for you? Expand on your answer.

> *I prefer doing something active when I'm on vacation, like hiking or skiing. . .*

Listening

1a Pair Work Can you think of any jobs that involve animals? What skills do you think are required?

b ▶ 2.07 Listen and discuss the questions. What are Sharon's job responsibilities? How does Sharon feel about her job? What qualities do you think are necessary for a job like this? Would you like Sharon's job? Why or why not?

Reading

2 Read the article and then circle the correct choice to complete each statement.

ANIMALS ONLINE

1 Can you really buy anything on the Internet? Believe it or not, some of the items marketed on the Internet as gifts for children or as prestige items for the home are actually live animals, many of them endangered species.

2 Despite international laws against the sale of endangered species, animals such as gorillas, tigers, chimpanzees, and leopard cubs are bought and sold on the Internet, some for as little as a few hundred dollars. According to a report by the IFAW (the International Fund for Animal Welfare), well over 1,400 live, exotic animals were being sold online in just one 6-week period. "That's an astonishing number," says one IFAW employee involved in the study. Of these 1,400 animals, most of the online ads were for birds, though in the US alone, 13 primates, 5 big cats, and 2 rhinos were for sale.

3 So what exactly would it cost, and what would you have to do to buy a wild animal? The researchers found chimpanzees dressed as dolls for $60,000 each. What about proof that you can look after and house an animal adequately? None needed. Although gorillas require space and very specialized care, the researchers also found a gorilla for sale for $8,100. For those with a little more head room, giraffes can also be bought. Got-PetsOnline.com offered a young giraffe for $15,000.

4 Though the vast majority of animals for sale are birds, monkeys make up a large portion of Internet sales, and experts are particularly concerned by the way they are marketed and traded on the Internet. A number of websites describe them as if they are little more than large, hairy dolls. They offer "accessories, such as diapers, bottles, and clothes." The traders even have a cute name for themselves: "monkey moms." They call the animals themselves "monkids." Virtually none of these websites explains how to take care of the animals.

5 When the IFAW undercover investigators contacted some of the US traders, they were told that it would be possible to export them to European countries—a blatant breach of EU law. There is also concern that demand for monkeys and chimps is fueling the illegal trapping and trading of wild species. Although there were approximately 2 million chimpanzees in the wild a century ago, there are as few as 150,000 left, and one research project says that by 2020 there will be a maximum of 100,000.

6 The effort to stamp out the live animal trade is made more difficult by the number of websites involved and by the fact that it is sometimes almost impossible to track sales made offline once sellers and buyers have made initial contact on the Internet. The IFAW's message to online shoppers is straightforward: "Buying wildlife online is as damaging as killing it yourself."

1. The animals are marketed as if they are _useful around the home/dangerous/toys_.
2. The IFAW was surprised _at the size of the illegal market for wild animals/to find endangered species for sale/at the way the traders treat the animals_.
3. The online animal trade is one cause of _economic problems in poor countries/violent crime/illegal hunting_.

3 Pair Work Discuss.
1. Should people have wild animals as pets? Give reasons.
2. What can be done to stop the illegal trade? Is it possible to stop illegal Internet sales in general?

Grammar | *as . . . as*; describing quantity

4 Complete the tasks in the Active Grammar box.

Active Grammar

1. *as* + adjective + *as* is used to:
   - show that two things are equal
   - describe quantity

   Find three examples in the article (paragraphs 2, 5, and 6). Which meanings does *as* + adjective + *as* have in these cases?

2. There are other phrases commonly used to describe quantity. Look at the phrases below and find their <u>opposites</u> in the article.

   paragraph
   2   *as much as* → _____
   2   *well under* → _____
   4   *a tiny minority of* → _____
   4   *virtually all (of)* → _____
   5   *precisely* → _____
   5   *as many as* → _____
   5   *a minimum of* → _____

a. Which phrases use numbers? *(For example, **as much as 20**)*

b. Which two phrases <u>can't</u> be used with count nouns?

See Reference page 133

Pronunciation

5a ▶2.08 Listen to how *as* is pronounced in the sentences.

b **Pair Work** Now create sentences with some of the phrases from the Active Grammar box. Practice saying them.

> *The vast majority of my friends have pets.*

6 Put the words in order. Begin and end each sentence with the <u>underlined</u> words.

1. <u>Hamsters</u> many birth to as offspring can as give eight <u>at a time</u>.
2. <u>The</u> to able majority domestic repeat of parrots are vast <u>human speech</u>.
3. <u>The life</u> as housefly of 17 is short as a <u>days</u>.
4. <u>Koalas</u> lives their virtually of spend all asleep: <u>22 hours per day</u>.
5. <u>Tortoises</u> years, well longer a over 100 live deal can great <u>than humans</u>.

Speaking

7 **Pair Work** Discuss.

1. Do you own or have you ever owned a pet? What type of animal?
2. Would you ever consider buying an animal on the Internet? In what circumstances?

> *I might consider buying a common pet online. I'd still prefer to "meet" it in person, though.*

Vocabulary | buying and selling

8a Match each phrase on the left with an expression with a similar meaning on the right.

____ 1. It's in excellent condition.	a. It's one of a kind.
____ 2. It's the latest model.	b. It's used.
____ 3. It's second hand.	c. It's on the market.
____ 4. It's available now.	d. It's not in perfect condition (it's been used a lot).
____ 5. It's handcrafted.	e. You can choose from a selection of . . .
____ 6. It's brand new.	f. It's made by hand.
____ 7. It features . . .	g. It's still in its packaging.
____ 8. It has some wear and tear.	h. It's as good as new.
____ 9. It's unique.	i. It includes . . .
____ 10. It comes in a wide range of . . .	j. It's state of the art.

b **Pair Work** Say a sentence using a phrase from the Vocabulary. Without looking at the book, your partner rephrases the sentence, using his or her own words. Take turns creating and rephrasing more sentences.

Speaking

9 **Pair Work** Which phrases from the Vocabulary could you use to describe the things in the photos? Were any animals used to make these things?

Writing

10a Read the ads on an Internet auction site. Find five spelling mistakes and five preposition mistakes.

b Choose something that you would like to sell (for example—furniture, books, toys, clothes) and write an ad describing the object, price, condition, etc.

c **Group Work** Show your ads to each other. Ask and answer questions about the different items, and try to find something you would like to buy.

d Tell the class about the item you decided to buy and explain why you chose it.

Sellit.com *the **BEST** auction site!*

Animal Instincts by well-known psychologist Paul Marrow. The book is slitely damaged on the spine and has a few highlighted passages in the first chapter, but otherwise on excellent condition. — bids (0)

Children's T-shirt and shorts combo, feeturing *Animal Magic* design. You can chose for red, green, or blue. All are brand new and hand designed. *Animal Magic* hats also availlable. — bids (2)

Dog kennel for sale. Some wear and tare on the door. Made by hand in Mumbai, this is one in a kind. — bids (3)

State in the art fish tank. 1 yard long, 24 inches wide, 30 inches deep. Includes large oxygen tube and plants. Bought just two weeks ago, it's as good of new. — bids (11)

Extra Vocabulary Study and
Extra Listening Activity
in *ACTIVEBOOK*

Review

1 Complete the paragraphs by inserting the phrases in the box in the correct places.

that trains	when they	that will
who spend	who work	that has
who trained		

2 Combine the two sentences into one sentence, using relative clauses.

> **Ex:** The animals escaped to higher ground. The animals sensed the tsunami approaching.
>
> *The animals, which sensed the tsunami approaching, escaped to higher ground.*

1. I got a new dog at the animal shelter. The shelter rescues homeless animals.
2. Rats can smell more efficiently than robots. The rats are sent into damaged buildings.
3. The explorer was amazed by the view. She had hiked for hours up the mountain.
4. The volcano erupted last night. The volcano hadn't been active for years.
5. Many animals are sold illegally. The animals are sold on the Internet.
6. Zoos can help save endangered species. The species might otherwise become extinct.

One problem that faces many prison inmates, most of their time locked up, is how to develop self-esteem and do something useful. One idea been piloted at a prison in Washington is to get the inmates to train dogs eventually help disabled people. The project has been a great success. The relationship between the inmates and the guards at the prison has improved considerably. Many of the inmates, leave the prison, go on to work with animals.

In another scheme, Pilot Dogs, a company dogs for the blind in Ohio put five dogs in the hands of prison inmates, the dogs successfully.

3 Circle the correct choice to complete each sentence.

1. I meant *to say/saying* something to you earlier, but now I've forgotten what it was.
2. She's such a crazy dresser. I hate *to think/thinking* what she's wearing tonight!
3. He remembered *to lock/locking* the door this time. Last time, we got robbed!
4. We regret *to tell/telling* you that your application was turned down.
5. Please stop *to talk/talking*. I can't hear the movie.
6. She tried *to drink/drinking* warm milk before bedtime, but she still couldn't sleep.
7. Despite a difficult childhood, he went on *to become/becoming* the world's greatest athlete.

4 Use the words in the box to complete the sentences.

maximum	none	well
virtually	vast	as
approximately	much	

1. Apparently you can buy a leopard for _____ little as $10,000 on the Internet.
2. A _____ majority of the public—nearly 90 percent—voted to keep the old currency.
3. There are _____ 6,000 in the hall, but we don't know the exact number.
4. I spent _____ all my money on the entrance fee. I only have $5 left for food.
5. This elevator holds a _____ of eight people.
6. He's huge! He must be _____ over 6 feet tall.
7. You can earn as _____ as $200,000 a year, if you work hard enough.
8. Virtually _____ of the team members had ever played there before.

Communication | reach a compromise on a plan

Paradise Island has 31 square miles (50 square kilometers) of land that can be developed.
The land has some hilly areas and a little forest.
The land and climate are good for growing vegetables, fruit, etc.
There is a lot of wildlife on the island.
There are two natural springs on the island. The spring water is very good for people's health.
The island nearby has recently become more popular with tourists.

5   Look at the photo and read the notes about Paradise Island.

6   **Pair Work** Make a list of all the things you could do with the island if it belonged to you. Compare your ideas with other students.

7   ▶2.09 Listen to the discussion. Are any of their ideas the same as or similar to yours?

8   **SPEAKING EXCHANGE** Work in groups. Student A: read the role on page 138. Student B: read the role on page 141. Student C: read the role on page 142. Then discuss what to do with the land. You must agree to do something with it; if you can't agree on one thing, you can combine some of your ideas.

9   Report back to the class. What did you decide to do with the land?

UNIT 8
Problems and issues

A

B

C

D

Warm Up

1 **Pair Work** Discuss. What is happening in the photos? What issues are represented? Do you think they are important? Why or why not?

2 Which photos can be associated with the words and phrases in the box?

> giant corporations   global warming   identity theft   cloning   oil spill
> cost and safety issues   multiculturalism   pollution   energy

3 **Group Work** Discuss.

1. What issues have been in the news recently? Do any of them affect you personally? Which issues do you think are the most important?
2. Which issues do you think will become more important in the future? Why?

LESSON 1
Stall for time when asked a difficult question
GRAMMAR reporting verbs
CAN DO ✓

Speaking

1a Match each photo to *two* sentences below.

A B C D

____ 1. **It's a waste of space.** Most of it is either reruns or ads, and it ruins your eyes.

____ 2. **It's overrated.** You can't trust the information on it, because anyone can publish things on it.

____ 3. **They've been disastrous for humanity.** If they're poisonous for insects, they're poisonous for humans.

____ 4. **We can do without them.** No one really needs to have a conversation every five minutes.

____ 5. **It's underrated.** It lets us find information quickly and keep in touch with people.

____ 6. **We can't do without them.** They're essential for talking to people no matter where you are.

____ 7. **It's indispensable.** It gives us up-to-date news, movies, and many other kinds of programs.

____ 8. **They've had big benefits for humanity.** They make it possible to grow more food with less work.

b **Pair Work** Discuss your opinions on the issues in Exercise 1a.

> *I agree that pesticides are bad for our health. On the other hand, . . .*

Reading

2 **Pair Work** Discuss. What do you think are some of the most important problems facing the world today? Can you think of any possible inventions that can solve them?

3 Read the article.

FUTURE INVENTIONS

The editors of Future World Magazine *look at the inventions we will need for a brighter future.*

1 Everyone has their favorite invention. Some of us even make lists of them. One survey recently named the toilet as the greatest invention ever. Another survey named the bicycle, which received twice as many votes as the World Wide Web. That's the past, but what about the future? What inventions will shape our lives? J.B.S. Haldane, a scientist, once made his prediction for the future. He said that whatever hadn't happened would happen and no one would be safe from it. Whether you agree or not, one thing is beyond doubt: human beings need to invent a few things pretty quickly. Here is our own list:

2 Number one is a new source of power. Oil is running out. A teenager, in a recent letter to a newspaper, wrote that it would take over a hundred years to produce fresh oil. He was wrong by a few million years. Once our oil is gone, it's gone forever. We have about fifty years' worth left, less if rates of industrialization accelerate. A hundred million new cars will need a lot of oil. At a recent conference about the world's future, scientist Hilary Craft said we had already found the answer: solar power. She believes that we will eventually have enormous mirrors in the sky that will provide the world's electricity.

3 Number two on our list is a plan to deal with waste. Many societies bury their waste underground or dump it into the sea. Now we're running out of space. If we want to avoid choking the Earth, we'd better find a way to recycle more effectively. According to inventor Ray Kurzweill, tiny self-replicating microscopic robots will convert trash into new sources of energy. Another inventor, Clara Petrovic, said she was working on a prototype that would convert waste into bricks and other building material.

4 Number three on our list is biological ID. Criminal investigator Alexis Smithson said that in the past, thieves had always taken objects. Now they steal identities. ID theft is the fastest-growing type of crime. So how will we stop it? You can expect to have tiny microchips injected into your body; scanners will read your genetic

continued on page 93

information to check your ID. Or worse, you may need to provide skin cells whenever you go shopping. Imagine scratching yourself in the checkout line every time you buy the groceries. Supermarkets will never be the same.

5   Finally, medicine. In the past, a cold could kill you. Now we are examining people's genes for signs of future illness. Find the disease early enough, and you can prevent it. Glen Hiemstra of Futurist.com recently claimed that somewhere on planet Earth there is a young child who will be the first person to live forever. If that happens, we'll need another invention: a new retirement system.

4 Circle the correct choice to complete each sentence.

1. The writers of the article ____ .
   a. think that the bicycle is the greatest invention
   b. are interested in things that haven't been invented yet

2. Two inventors are trying to find ways to ____ .
   a. use our trash productively
   b. reduce waste

3. Protection against ID theft will involve ____ .
   a. microchips in every object we own
   b. technology "reading" the human body

4. According to the article, the main invention in medicine will be ____ .
   a. a way to predict the illnesses a person is vulnerable to
   b. a pill that will enable people to live forever

Grammar | reporting verbs

5 Find one example of reported speech in each paragraph of the text. What happens to verb tenses when we report speech? Which example from the text <u>doesn't</u> shift the tenses back?

6 Read the rules and complete the task in the Active Grammar box.

Active Grammar

Often we use a reporting verb to *paraphrase* the meaning:

"Let's go home." → *She **thinks** we should leave.*

"Why don't we discuss it with everyone?" → *He **suggested** that we talk about it with everyone.*

"It was my mistake." → *He **admitted** that it was his fault.*

Match reporting verbs with similar meanings. Are there any differences in meaning or formality?

A	B
____ 1. admit	a. maintain
____ 2. remember	b. imply
____ 3. tell	c. respond
____ 4. answer	d. confess
____ 5. suggest	e. recollect
____ 6. threaten	f. inform
____ 7. insist	g. warn

See Reference page 134

7 Cross out the incorrect choice in each sentence.

1. I *warned/informed/threatened* them that ID theft was common.
2. He *suggested that they discuss/suggested discussing/implied discussing* immigration at the meeting.
3. She *insisted/maintained/informed* that technology would solve the problem.
4. He *admitted/told/confessed* that he knew nothing about developments in biotechnology.
5. We must *tell/inform/suggest* the audience about the research into global warming.

8 **Pair Work** Report the conversation using the verbs from the box.

~~admit~~	suggest	remember
warn	confess	

Mike: I never recycle anything, because I'm too lazy.

Mike admitted that he never recycles anything because he's too lazy.

Sarah: If we don't start recycling, the consequences will be serious for the planet.

David: So why don't we start a recycling group in the community?

Sarah: Wait a minute. There already is one.

Mike: Well, there was. I started one, but then it became too much work, so we stopped.

Listening

9 Look at the pictures. Can you guess what these new inventions do?

10 ▶ **2.10** Listen to seven people answering the question: "Which new invention would you most like to see?" Write the number of the speaker next to the pictures.

☐ d.

☐ a.

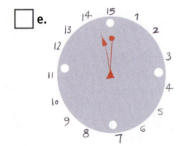

☐ b.

☐ c.

☐ g.

☐ e.

☐ f.

11a **Pair Work** Discuss. Try to use the expressions from the How To box.

1. Which inventions in Exercise 10 do you think are a good idea? Why?
2. What other invention(s) do you think might help the world?
3. What other invention(s) do you think might help you at work or at home?
4. What invention could you not do without?
5. Are there any modern inventions that you think are overrated?

How To:

Stall for time (when you're asked a difficult question)

That's a good question.	Let me see.
That's tricky.	I'll have to think about that.
That's a difficult question.	Well, . . .

b Work with another partner. Report your original partner's opinions.

Tara told me that she would like to have a robot to do the housework. She also . . .

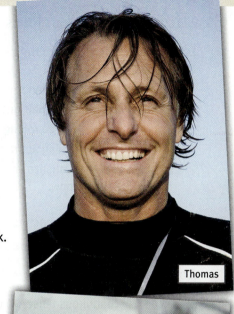

Thomas

Listening

1 Pair Work Look at the photos. What types of people do you think Thomas and Elise are?

2 ▶2.11 Listen to Thomas and Elise. How do their opinions and lifestyles differ?

3a Choose the best answer.

1. What made Thomas change his lifestyle?
   a. He received an important email.
   b. He couldn't enjoy Rome because he was obsessed with work.
   c. He went to the beach and fell in love with the sea.

2. Why does he think people carry technology around with them?
   a. Because they wish they were in the office.
   b. Because it helps them feel less stressed.
   c. Because they are worried they will miss important pieces of information.

3. What has Thomas learned from living near the ocean?
   a. That human actions and money aren't so important.
   b. That you can't make much money there.
   c. That he should have left his city job much earlier.

4. What do Elise's friends think of her working life?
   a. They think it's making her sick.
   b. They think she's too competitive.
   c. They think Elise never has enough time.

5. Why does Elise carry around so much technology?
   a. Because she doesn't have an office.
   b. Because she travels a lot and doesn't want an office.
   c. Because she travels a lot, and the technology gives her confidence.

Elise

b Listen again to check your answers.

Vocabulary | lifestyles

4 Listen again and read the Audioscript on page 156. Match the expressions with the correct definitions.

____ 1. tearing my hair out   a. the excitement
____ 2. the be-all and end-all   b. be too exhausted to continue a long-term action (usually a job)
____ 3. security blanket   c. something that makes you feel safe and confident
____ 4. burn out   d. the most important thing
____ 5. the buzz   e. getting into a panic because of frustration

5 Pair Work Discuss.

1. Do you agree that "the world is one stressed-out place"? What are the main causes of this stress?

2. What do you think are the symptoms of "running out of time syndrome"? Do you—or does anyone you know—suffer from these?

> *I agree that many people are stressed. Some of the causes of stress are technology . . .*

Grammar | continuous forms

6 Look at the sentences from the listening on page 95. Match each sentence to the correct continuous form.

___ 1. I'd been having dinner with a client all evening.

___ 2. I was tearing my hair out trying to get access to a computer.

___ 3. The waves will be rolling in every morning long after we're gone.

___ 4. I've been working at an investment company for about four years.

___ 5. In fact, the statistics are getting worse – I think it's under three years now.

a. present continuous

b. past continuous

c. present perfect continuous

d. past perfect continuous

e. future continuous

7 Complete the tasks after each rule in the Active Grammar box.

Active Grammar

1. We can use continuous tenses to describe activities. Match the sentences from Exercise 6 to the uses below.

   a. Actions that are background events (possibly finished) before another event (*sentences 1 and* ___).

   b. Actions that are temporary or incomplete, or we want to stress the duration (usually a long time) (*sentence* ___).

   c. Actions that are repeated (*sentence* ___).

   d. Actions that are in the process of changing (*sentence* ___).

2. The continuous forms (especially the past continuous) can also be used to sound more tentative and less direct in suggestions, offers, and inquiries.

   I was wondering if . . . ?

   Can you think of any examples?

3. Stative verbs are usually not used in the continuous. Write four more common stative verbs for each category below.

Verbs of personal feeling:
like

Verbs of thought:
know

Verbs of the senses:
appear

See Reference page 134

8a Rewrite the sentences using a continuous form of the verb. How does the meaning change?

1. I've read that book.
2. I'll work until about 8:00 tonight.
3. She hit me.
4. The first chapter is written.
5. What music do you listen to?
6. He had lost his hair.
7. We go to work at 8:00.

b Write responses to the sentences in Exercise 8a— both the original sentences and your sentences in the continuous.

   Ex: I've read that book.   *Was it good?*

   I'm reading that book.   *Are you enjoying it?*

9 Use the verbs in the box to complete the paragraphs below. Change the verb tense where necessary. Use the continuous if possible.

> urge   go back   grow   begin   drive   seem   advocate   question   quote

At the beginning of last month I looked out of my window and saw the telltale signs: increased traffic, early-morning crowds, glum faces. Yes, that's right, the children _____ (**1.**) to school and parents _____ (**2.**) a new work year. And I asked myself an old question: do we have the work/life balance right?

A new generation of economists _____ (**3.**) the century-long assumption of economics: that men and women are motivated by more—more profit, more possessions, more work. Is a hectic pace of life what we really want? And will it make us happy?

The number of people in mid-career who _____ (**4.**) ready to abandon the desperate climb up the corporate ladder _____ (**5.**). And now, several journalists and social commentators _____ (**6.**) us to go slower and enjoy life.

Tom Hodgkinson, in *How to Be Idle*, says that prominent literary figures _____ (**7.**) the idle life for centuries. He _____ (**8.**) Bertrand Russell, Samuel Johnson and others. Carl Honoré's *In Praise of Slow* also suggests that slowing down may be the best way, and he provides a telling anecdote. He recalls a time recently when he _____ (**9.**) extremely fast in Italy because he was late for a Slow Food meal. The irony of it!

Speaking

10 Read the profile of Dana Kolansky. Would you say she has a busy life?

Profile of Dana Kolansky
- Dana is a store clerk and part-time anthropology student.
- Before getting a job as a store clerk, she had been working in a bar.
- After finishing work she usually goes jogging.
- Right now she's reading a book on anthropology.
- In the last few days she has been studying for a test.
- Recently she's been learning German as a hobby.
- This weekend she'll be working on a paper for her master's degree, playing tennis with a friend, and going to a movie with her boyfriend.

11a Look at the profile outline below. What questions will you need to ask to complete it?

Profile of _____ (name)
- _____ is a _____.
- Before _____, _____ had been _____.
- After finishing work or school, _____ usually _____.
- Right now _____ is reading _____.
- In the last few days _____ has been _____ _____.
- Recently _____ has been _____.
- This weekend _____ will be _____.

b **Pair Work** Interview your partner. Choose one or two pieces of information about your partner to tell the class.

Reading

1   **Pair Work** Discuss. What is happening in the photo? Have you ever been in a situation like this? What happened?

2a   Read the two letters to an advice column. What advice can you think of?

```
◄ ► ↻ ⊘   http://www.advice.com
```

Problem A

My friend's kids are too spoiled!

My closest friend has two children. The trouble is, they are really spoiled. Every time they come to visit, they jump on the furniture and break things. When I try to say something to my friend, she gives me a dirty look and says, "That's kids for you!" What really irritates me is the fact that my friend just can't see it. I don't know what to do.

Silvia

Problem B

Too much exaggeration?

I recently got a job at a very good company. During the application process, I exaggerated a few details on my resumé. The thing is, I really wanted the job. I knew I could do it and felt that adding a few things to my resumé would give me a better chance. Recently, a colleague of mine who had done the same thing got caught. They fired him. What really worries me is that my company is now promising to check up on all the employees. I am seriously nervous, even though I am doing a good job and my boss likes me. What should I do?

Jake

b   Read the advice to Silvia and Jake's problems. Do you agree with the suggestions?

Comments

1 Dear Silvia,

What you need to do is to put yourself in your friend's shoes. She's used to their behavior. You're not. The fact remains that you need to find a solution. One thing you could try is giving the children rewards for good behavior. What might also work is having some games available for them. Maybe there's not enough for the children to do at your house. Good luck!

Faisal

2 Dear Silvia,

There's not much you can do. They're her kids, not yours. But you don't have to put up with that kind of behavior in your house. Why don't you arrange to visit them in her house? That way, if the kids start acting up, you can leave at any time. The point is, she was your friend before the kids, and she can still be your friend now.

Karen

Comments

3 Dear Jake,

I can understand why you fooled the company (you wanted the job). Why you insist on fooling yourself I really don't know. You didn't "exaggerate." You lied. The first thing you must do is go straight to your boss and explain exactly what you did and why you did it. The truth is, if your boss values you and your work, you may get away with it.

Ava

4 Dear Jake,

The fact of the matter is that 19 percent of all job applicants claim skills they don't have, and 28 percent exaggerate the pay from their former jobs. Don't worry about it. Look at it from the company's point of view. Do they really want to go to the trouble of firing you and finding a replacement when they don't really need to? What they really care about is your ability to do the job. Relax, man! You're safe.

Anthony

Grammar | fronting

3 Complete the tasks after the rules in the Active Grammar box.

Active Grammar

1 **Fronting** is rephrasing sentences by moving the object, verb, or adverb to the front of the sentence (before the subject). We sometimes add *what* (or another question word). In Problem A:

   The fact that my friend just can't see it really irritates me ... →
   What really irritates me is *the fact that my friend just can't see it ...*

   Fronting is used:
   a. to emphasize the subject (for example, ***the fact*** *that my friend just can't see it*).
   b. sometimes to provide a clear link with the previous sentence: *She told us to go quickly.* ***This we did***.
       Find other examples in Comments 1, 3, and 4.

2. We often use **fronting phrases** (*the trouble is, the question is, the fact of the matter is, the fact remains that*) to emphasize the importance of what we are going to say:

   The trouble is, *they are really spoiled.* (Problem A)
   The thing is, *I really wanted the job.* (Problem B)
   Find other examples of **fronting phrases** in Comments 1–4.

American English	British English
spoiled	spoilt

See Reference page 134

---

4 Rewrite the sentences, keeping the meaning the same. Start with the underlined word.

   1. Their bad behavior bothers me. <u>What</u>
   2. I'm not sure how long he hoped to get away with the lie. <u>How</u>
   3. I don't know how she manages with those kids. <u>How</u>
   4. She didn't discipline them. That was the problem. <u>The</u>
   5. My colleague lost his job. It worries me. <u>What</u>

5 **SPEAKING EXCHANGE** Work in groups of three. Student A: read page 139, Student B: read page 141, and Student C: read page 142. Explain your problems to each other and give advice. Try to use fronting expressions.

> *What you need to do is encourage your friend to have some fun. Maybe you can ...*

Listening

6a **Pair Work** Tell your partner about problems you have had with everyday machines.

b ▶2.12 Listen. What problems are the people having with their machines?

7 **Pair Work** Imagine there is a problem with an item of technology in your home. Describe it (without mentioning the name of the item), using phrases from the How To box. Your partner guesses what you are talking about and gives advice.

How To:

Describe problems

It keeps (getting jammed).
I can't get it to (make copies).
I don't know how to make it (shut down).
I'm having a problem (turning it on).
This seems to (be stuck).
It won't (turn).

Vocabulary | cause and effect

8 Complete the statements with words and phrases from the box. Then match the problems with each piece of advice.

> resulted   source   bring   from   influence   origins   gives   consequence

____ 1. My father was a great _____ on me, and I've always followed in his footsteps, but now nothing I do is good enough for him. He criticizes me all the time.

____ 2. My obsessive work ethic has _____ in several problems. I can't sleep or relax, and I get headaches.

____ 3. I dropped out of college. The _____ of my actions is that my parents won't talk to me now.

____ 4. Most of my problems stem _____ my laziness. I just can't get motivated to do anything.

a. Overwork _____ rise to many health problems. You need to get some balance back in your life. Take some time out every day and take up a relaxing hobby.

b. Personal happiness has its _____ in our achievements. Do something small every day, and you will feel happier and motivated to do more. Take that first step.

c. A child's uncertain future is a major _____ of stress for parents. They probably can't understand why you have dropped out. Try explaining the whole story from beginning to end.

d. You should try to _____ about small changes in your relationship with him. Explain that you are an adult now and you need to find your own path in life.

9 **Group Work** Complete the sentences so they are true for you. Compare your answers with other students.

1. _____ is sometimes a source of stress for me.

2. _____ influenced me a lot, because _____.

3. _____ resulted in my learning English.

4. The consequence of _____ was _____.

5. I hope to have an influence on _____.

Writing

10a Read the essay in the Writing Bank on page 146 and do the exercises.

b Think of a problem or issue, for example—stress, noisy neighbors, unemployment, unhealthy lifestyles, annoying emails, pollution. Make notes about the causes of the problem and the effects it has had on you or others. Try to come up with some solutions.

c Write an essay of 200–250 words about the problem or issue.

Review

1 Find eight mistakes and correct them.

We propose to adopt a new measurement of people's lives. Recently it was explained us that the kingdom of Bhutan measures its citizens' well-being by Gross National Happiness instead of Gross National Product. The country encourages people think about their quality of life, not just money. In many countries, tourism is blamed for destroy the local culture. While the Bhutanese are not accusing anyone of deliberately harm the environment, in Bhutan, tourism is strictly limited.

We suggest to adopt this same idea. We urge people to considering spiritual wealth, as well as money. This approach is guaranteed to opening our eyes to a better way of life.

2 Complete the questions.

1. _____ (plan) on getting your PhD?

   Yes, I was. It seemed like a good idea, but I didn't have enough money.

2. _____ (wear) those weird clothes?

   Because I'm supposed to be at a costume party in ten minutes.

3. _____ (go) when I saw you this afternoon?

   To the bank. But it was closed by the time I got there.

4. _____ (play) basketball?

   For about ten years. But I only play once a week nowadays.

5. _____ (live) there long before they kicked him out?

   Yes, he had. Almost 20 years.

6. _____ (see) what I mean?

   Not exactly. Can you explain it again?

3 Put the words in the box in the correct place in the paragraphs.

would	problem	is
matter	surprises	why

My family is going to visit my mother-in-law next week. The is, we can't stand her cooking! I want to be culturally sensitive—she is from another country—but the fact of the is that the kids and I just can't eat her meals.

Marlene

What me is her cultural insensitivity. The thing, she has to adapt to you, too. Why not take her out to a nice restaurant instead?

Veronica

You're complaining about this I really don't know. All over the world, people are starving. You're lucky enough to have food, so just pretend you like it. If you're desperate, one idea be to train the kids to say "Mmm, delicious."

Ayodele

4 Complete the sentences.

1. Carl Honoré had a great _____ on the Slow Life Movement. Many people followed his ideas.

2. The modern work ethic has _____ in more stressful lifestyles.

3. Twenty-two percent of us suffer from work-related stress. The _____ of this are very serious.

4. Stress at work _____ rise to absenteeism, which is disastrous _____ business.

5. Honoré wants to _____ about a great revolution in lifestyles. His work could have big _____ for humanity.

6. Violence, job insecurity, and overwork are the major _____ of stress in the US.

7. Honoré's philosophy has its _____ in the lifestyles of our ancestors, who didn't work so hard.

5a Read the statements. Can any of them be used to describe the photos above?

_____ a. Travel is the greatest form of education.

_____ b. Marriage is an old-fashioned idea, and it's not necessary these days.

_____ c. Money can't make you happy.

_____ d. The dominance of any one culture is bad for the world.

_____ e. Modern technology has not made the world a better place.

_____ f. Rich countries should always give money to poor countries.

_____ g. Space exploration is a waste of money.

_____ h. As you become older, you become wiser.

_____ i. Nature gives us the best things in life.

_____ j. Childhood is the happiest time of life.

_____ k. For some crimes, the death penalty is appropriate.

b Read the statements again and give each a number from 1 to 5 (1 = disagree completely, 5 = agree completely).

6a **Group Work** Choose five topics from Exercise 5a to discuss. Compare the numbers you gave for each statement and exchange opinions.

> _I don't think that rich countries should automatically give money to poor countries, but I do think that they should provide aid in some situations . . ._

b Report back to the rest of the class: which issues did you talk about? What were the main views and opinions on each?

UNIT 9
People with vision

A

B

C

D

Warm Up

1 **Pair Work** What art forms are represented in the photos? What kinds of art do you prefer and why?

2 Do the words and phrases in bold refer to books, movies, theater, art, or architecture? There may be more than one answer.

1. It was a **spectacular / breathtaking / disappointing** performance.
2. It's a **masterpiece / not one of his best / his finest piece**.
3. The acting was **stereotyped / poor / over the top**.
4. It's a **fantastic / difficult / heavy** read.
5. The style is **contemporary / traditional / art deco**.
6. The special effects were **astonishing / incredible / awful**.
7. He is famous for his **landscapes / portraits / sculptures**.

3 **Group Work** Talk about paintings, movies, books, and other art forms that you like or dislike, using vocabulary from Exercise 2.

> *My favorite painting is Picasso's Guernica. I think it's a masterpiece.*

> *I didn't really enjoy King Kong. In my opinion, the special effects were pretty disappointing.*

Express a degree of certainty ✓ CAN DO

GRAMMAR collocations with prepositions

Reading

1 **Pair Work** What do you know about the people in the pictures?

2 Read the short biographies.

Leonardo da Vinci

The Yellow Emperor

Sir Isaac Newton

Leonardo da Vinci

As a painter, his legacy of work is indisputably less extensive than other master painters. As an anatomist, he failed to publish his research. As a sculptor, he left us not a single verified sculpture. As a mathematician, he had no significant input into **the development of** the theories of mathematics. As a scientist, his records are disorderly. As a musician, he left little record of his music. As an architect, he left no notable buildings for us to visit. And yet he is popularly held as one of the most important figures of the Italian Renaissance. In the words of Sigmund Freud, "Leonardo da Vinci was like a man who awoke too early in the darkness, while the others were all still asleep."

Most people recognize the *Mona Lisa* or *The Last Supper* as examples of this artist's extraordinary capabilities. However, he was not just an artistic genius. He was also a genius **in the fields of** architecture, engineering, and science. His sketchbooks, with notes often written in mirror form, were full of **ideas for** his inventions. Some were improvements on existing machines; others were new and **ranged from** a primitive tank **to** a human-powered flying machine. These books were to stun the world when they were discovered centuries after his death.

Huang Di

The first sovereign of civilized China, Huang Di, or the Yellow Emperor as he became known, is thought of as the common ancestor of the Chinese people. A semi-legendary figure who is said to have begun his reign around 2697 BC, **in a time of** constant warfare between tribes, Huang Di strove to improve the virtues of people, pacifying by strengthening his army and unifying the tribes. He introduced **the idea of** military discipline, invented the compass to improve his military strategy, and used carts in warfare.

Once he had established peace, he created civilized systems for his people. Among the many inventions **attributed to** him are the calendar, mathematics (he invented numbers and a system for measuring length and weight), music (he invented the flute using bamboo), writing (he invented Chinese characters), boats, carts, and bows and arrows.

His scientific interests also led him to author *The Inner Book of Simple Questions of the Yellow Emperor*, the founding classic of Chinese medicine. His Empress is also **famous for** having been the first to raise silkworms to make clothes with silk.

Sir Isaac Newton

Newton **made** fundamental **contributions to** every area of scientific and mathematical concern in his generation. Born in a rural English village on Christmas Day, 1642, he was so small no one thought he would survive. During his childhood he spent much of his time inventing and building toys. He was distracted at school and did not do particularly well. So his mother, unwilling to pay for his education, brought him home to look after the sheep. However, he was always so busy building gadgets that the sheep would often escape. Eventually, his uncle persuaded his mother to send him to Cambridge University, where he became so **immersed in** his studies that he often forgot to eat or sleep.

When Cambridge was closed for two years due to the plague, Newton went home to **work on** his ideas. He absorbed himself in mathematics and began developing a mathematical theory that would later become calculus. It is a popular belief that **on one occasion** he was sitting under an apple tree when an apple fell on his head, and that this helped him to understand the laws of gravity. It is now thought that perhaps he invented this story later in life in order to exemplify how he **drew** his **inspiration from** everyday events.

3 **Pair Work** Discuss. Which of the people in the reading achieved the most, in your opinion? Which person would you most like to have met? Why?

Grammar | collocations with prepositions

4 Complete the tasks in the Active Grammar box.

Active Grammar

1. Look at the examples of dependent prepositions in bold in the Reading. Write the correct prepositions in the chart.

a. verb + preposition	range _____ . . . to . . .
	work _____
	attribute _____
b. verb + object + preposition	draw inspiration _____
	made contributions _____
c. noun + preposition	in the fields _____
	idea _____ / _____
	the development _____
d. adjective + preposition	(be) famous _____
	(be) immersed _____
e. prepositional phrases (beginning with a preposition)	_____ a time of
	_____ one occasion

2. Write the letter of the correct dependent preposition form next to the phrases below.

_a_ succeed in   ___ hope for   ___ admiration for
___ improve on   ___ specialize in   ___ in recognition of
___ of all time   ___ a solution to   ___ devote your life to
___ in later life   ___ the quality of   ___ (be) obsessed with
___ make observations about

See Reference page 135

5 Find expressions in the chart that mean the following:

  a. spend your life trying to do something
  b. thought to have been achieved or accomplished by someone
  c. be worried about something all the time
  d. be completely involved in something
  e. make something better
  f. feeling of great respect or liking for something or someone

6 Circle the correct choices to complete the paragraphs. What is the name of this visionary scientist?

Widely regarded as the greatest scientist of the 20th century, or even (**1.** *of/all/in*) all time, this man devoted his life (**2.** *in/on/to*) science. He made major contributions (**3.** *from/to/for*) the development of quantum mechanics, statistical mechanics, and cosmology. In recognition (**4.** *for/of/about*) his work, he was awarded the Nobel Prize for Physics in 1921.

In 1905, while working alone in a patent laboratory, he eventually succeeded (**5.** *to/in/with*) finding a solution (**6.** *to/at/of*) a problem he had been working (**7.** *in/for/on*). He developed his own theory of relativity. He later improved (**8.** *on/to/with*) his own theories until he developed the theory which he became famous (**9.** *of/about/for*), $E=mc^2$. (**10.** *In/At/To*) later life, he realized both the positive and negative implications of his work, as nuclear energy and atomic bombs were developed.

7 **Pair Work** Think of other famous "visionaries" or inspirational people. Ask and answer questions about them, using the phrases in the Active Grammar box.

> *This person was famous for the beautiful music he wrote.*

Listening

8 ▶ **2.13** Read the headings on the post-it. Then listen to a radio interview. Make notes under the headings.

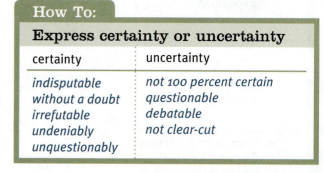

1 Discoveries made outside the laboratory

2 The psychology of high achievers

3 Can only creative people be geniuses?

9 **Pair Work** Discuss.

1. Did you find any of the information in the interview surprising?
2. Have you ever come up with the solution to a problem by "sleeping on it"?
3. Do you pursue any creative hobbies or interests?
4. What do you do to take your mind off a problem?

10 Read the words and phrases in the How To box. Then circle the correct choice to complete each statement.

1. It's *debatable/without a doubt* whether Leonardo da Vinci was a genius.
2. It's *not 100 percent certain/undeniably* what or who killed Mozart.
3. The Yellow Emperor was *not clear-cut/unquestionably* a great leader.
4. It's *not clear-cut/irrefutable* why Leonardo wrote in mirror form.
5. Mozart was *not 100 percent certain/irrefutably* exceptionally gifted.
6. The story about Newton's discovery under the apple tree is *questionable/without a doubt*.
7. The novel is *not clear-cut/indisputably* his greatest work.

How To:

Express certainty or uncertainty

certainty	uncertainty
indisputable	*not 100 percent certain*
without a doubt	*questionable*
irrefutable	*debatable*
undeniably	*not clear-cut*
unquestionably	

Speaking

11 **Group Work** Do you agree or disagree with the statements? Explain your views, using phrases from the How To box.

1. Mozart is the most talented musician to have ever lived.
2. Einstein should have kept quiet about his discovery when he realized the implications for nuclear weapons.
3. Being a "genius" generally implies being at least a little crazy. Van Gogh would never have achieved the same recognition if he hadn't suffered a psychological breakdown.
4. Given time and the right encouragement, anyone can become a genius.

LESSON 2

Use colloquial expressions to explain your tastes

GRAMMAR discourse markers

CAN DO ✔

Vocabulary | describing art

1 **Pair Work** Discuss. What sort of art do you like or dislike?

2 Match the sentences on the left with their opposites on the right. Which of the words in bold are used to show personal opinions? Which describe facts?

____ 1. This is an **abstract** painting by Mondrian.

____ 2. This painting is really **striking**. It stands out.

____ 3. I don't like **avant-garde** art. I can't understand it.

____ 4. Don't you find her work really calm and **tranquil**?

a. So you prefer more **traditional** stuff?

b. No way! I think her work is very **disturbing**.

c. Oh, I think that one's **dull**. It doesn't appeal to me.

d. He also did a lot of **figurative** work, didn't he?

3 **Pair Work** Tell your partner about a painting or photograph you like (or don't like). Use phrases from the How To box.

Listening

4a ▶ 2.14 Listen to each conversation. Answer the questions.

Conversation 1: Which statement best describes their reaction to the first painting?

a. It's abstract.   b. It's disturbing.   c. It's striking.

Conversation 2: Which statement best describes their reaction to the second painting?

a. It's disturbing.   b. It's fascinating.   c. It's dull.

Conversation 3: Which statement is true about their reaction to the third painting?

a. It's their favorite.   b. It's disappointing.

c. It's over the top.

How To:	
Say what you like/dislike	
Saying what you like	*I've always admired her work.* *I'm really into her work.* *I'm a big fan of his stuff.* *He's one of my all-time favorites.*
Saying what you don't like	*It's not my (kind of) thing.* *It's not my taste.* *It's not my cup of tea.* *I can't relate to it.*

b ▶ 2.15 Listen. Which painting won the art competition?

a. The portrait of the woman.

b. The portrait of the man.

c. The portrait of the group.

What does the man think about the winning portrait? _____

Grammar | discourse markers

5 Read the Active Grammar box and complete the chart.

Active Grammar

1. Discourse markers are words and expressions that help us organize what we are saying or writing. They also show our attitude toward the subject.

   Look at the following phrases from the Listening and put the words **in bold** in the correct place in the chart.

   *. . . **as I was saying**, it really does look like a photo . . .*   *. . . **to be honest**, it's not really my taste . . .*
   *. . . the expression on her face **is kind of** intense . . .*   *. . . **to tell you the truth**, I still wouldn't*
   *. . . **it sort of** looks like a photo . . .*   *want it hanging on my bedroom wall.*

Focusing on the main topic	Returning to the main point (what was said before didn't matter)	Returning to a previous line of discussion
Introducing a strong opinion or criticism	Softening an opinion or criticism	Making additional (often contrasting) points

2. Look at the phrases below and add them to the chart.

more or less	mind you	in fact	frankly,	as a matter of fact
at any rate	regarding	as for	anyway	as far as __ is concerned,
anyway, what I was going to say was				

See Reference page 135

6 Circle the best choice to complete each sentence.

1. **A:** *To be honest/As far as it's concerned/Regarding*, I don't like Impressionism very much.
   B: Neither do I. *As for it/What I was going to say/At any rate*, I think it's been over done.

2. **A:** Pollock's technique of dripping paint onto canvas was *as for/anyway/kind of* strange.
   B: I agree. *More or less,/ Mind you,/As regards* his work did revolutionize modern art.

3. **A:** I love performance art. *Sort of/Regarding/As a matter of fact*, David Blaine's my hero.
   B: David Blaine? The magician? *Anyway, what I was going to say was/Frankly,/As I was saying*, I think he's crazy!

4. **A:** I love Spanish art. *Kind of/In fact/As for* Picasso, I think he was the greatest of all time.
   B: Well, yes, he *more or less/as regards/to tell you the truth* invented modern art.

5. **A:** *As far as it's concerned/Regarding/Anyway,* photography, Cindy Sherman is currently the most famous artist.
   B: Really? *In fact/As I was saying/To tell you the truth*, I've never heard of her.

Speaking

7 **Pair Work** Discuss.

1. Do you ever go to art exhibitions? If so, what was the last one you went to? Did you like it?
2. Do you have a favorite artist? Why do you like his or her work?

Reading

8a Look at the picture. What is happening?

b Read the article and answer the questions that follow.

Now you see it . . .

1 No wonder the man in Munch's *The Scream* is screaming. He keeps getting stolen. The famous painting was stolen in 1994 and again ten years later, both times from museums in Norway. Apparently, security was extremely 5 poor. Officials thought the painting was so famous that it wouldn't be stolen. Wrong.

The world of art theft is not, as you might imagine, populated with stylish **aesthetes**, **masterminding** their operations from tax-free **hideouts**. Art thieves are 10 **thugs**, according to a new book by Charley Hill. Hill was an undercover policeman whose job was to **track down** stolen paintings. He says that the people who steal paintings were usually stealing wheels from cars a few years earlier. He describes priceless Vermeers being 15 **stuffed** into the back of cars, Gainsboroughs being passed around by drug dealers with dirty hands, and a particularly bad end to one of Henry Moore's huge sculptures. The bronze, *King and Queen*, a masterpiece by Moore, was too heavy for the thieves to move, so they 20 took out a chainsaw and cut off the heads, thinking they might be worth something.

Hill's is an adventure story fit for any James Bond fan. In 1986 he **cracked a case** in which 11 valuable paintings had been stolen from Russborough House 25 near Dublin. In order to rescue *The Scream*, Hill posed as a buyer for the J. Paul Getty Museum in LA: bow tie, big suit, even bigger Mercedes. He also had to learn everything about the painting, or should we say paintings: there are four versions of *The Scream*. He 30 even memorized the patterns of wax droplets left on one version of the painting when Munch blew out a candle one night.

The artworks usually turn up, sometimes many years later, though the police don't always catch the thief. Even 35 rarer is when a gentleman thief—one who steals art for personal pleasure only—is caught. In 2003, a waiter, Stephane Breitwieser from Switzerland, was found guilty of stealing 69 artworks from museums since 1995. He told the court he did it for the love of art. His **haul** was 40 worth over $1 billion—not bad for a waiter.

1. Why was *The Scream* so badly protected?
2. What are Vermeers and Gainsboroughs, and what happened to them?
3. What did Hill have to do to find *The Scream*?
4. Who is Stephane Breitwieser, and why is he unusual among art thieves?

9 **Pair Work** Discuss.

1. Would you like Charley Hill's job? Why or why not?
2. Do you think Hill's book sounds interesting?
3. What type of person do you think Stephane Breitwieser might be?
4. What type of people collect art? Do you think it would be an enjoyable hobby?

10a Answer the questions.

1. What does *thug* (line 10) mean?
2. How does the article describe the people who steal paintings? How does this help us guess the meaning of *thug*?

b Answer the same questions for the following words and phrases: *masterminding* (line 8), *aesthetes* (line 8), *hideout* (line 9), *track down* (line 11), *stuffed* (line 15), *crack a case* (line 23), *haul* (line 39).

Writing

1a Choose one of the photos. How does it make you feel? What does it remind you of? What do you think is happening? Imagine that you are in the scene. Write a paragraph about what you are feeling and doing.

  b Read your paragraph to the rest of the class. Were your impressions similar or different?

Speaking

2 **Pair Work** Discuss.

    1. Do you have a camera or a camera phone? How often do you use it?

    2. What do you think makes a good photo? Can you think of any tips for taking better photos?

Reading

3a **SPEAKING EXCHANGE** Student A: read the article on page 138. Student B: read the article on page 140. As you read, note what the article says about:

    1. the best time to do it   2. stories   3. the local culture   4. learning from professionals

  b Tell your partner about the main ideas in your article and your answers to Exercise 3a.

4 **Pair Work** Discuss.

    1. What do you think of the advice in your article? Was it interesting, obvious, or surprising?

    2. Which sounds easier—being a photographer or being a travel writer?

    3. Would you like to be a travel writer or a photographer? Why or why not?

Grammar | unreal past

5 Complete the tasks after each expression in the Active Grammar box.

Active Grammar

Wish or If only
> *If only I'd gone on that trip.*

1. Find more examples of these expressions in the introductions to your articles in Exercise 3a.

2. What verb tense follows *wish* or *if only* to talk about (**a**) the present? (**b**) the past?

It's high time or It's about time
> *It's high time we visited Tokyo.*

3. Find examples of these expressions in the introduction on page 138 and section 1 on page 140.

4. Does *It's high time* or *It's about time* mean (**a**) something should be happening now, but it isn't OR (**b**) something is happening on time?

5. What verb tense follows *It's high time* or *It's about time*?

Would rather
> *I would rather go.*
> *I would rather they left.*

6. Find examples of *would rather* in section 5 on page 138 and section 2 on page 140.

7. What verb form follows *would rather* if the person speaking and the subject are (**a**) the same? (**b**) different?

What if or Suppose
> *Suppose you had taken that job as a photographer. Would you be happier now?*

8. Find more examples of these expressions in section 1 on page 138 and section 3 on page 140.

9. What verb tense follows *what if* or *suppose* to talk about an imaginary situation in the (**a**) present? (**b**) past? (**c**) future?

See Reference page 135

6 Complete the second sentence so that it has a similar meaning to the first. Use the corrrect form of the verb in parentheses.

1. We should start our journals. (begin)

   It's high _____ writing our journals.

2. What if you had the chance to become a travel journalist? (offer)

   Suppose someone _____ a job as a travel journalist?

3. Please stop taking photos! (take)

   We'd rather _____ photos.

4. I should have sent in my story for the writing competition. (enter)

   If only _____ the competition, I might have won!

5. I'd love to be able to take good photos. (be)

   I wish _____ a good photographer.

6. We should select the photos for my new travel book together. (choose)

   I'd rather _____ photos together.

7. You should finish writing that article soon. (finish)

   It's about _____ that article.

7 **Pair Work** Complete the sentences so they are true for you. Then share them with your partner. Ask your partner questions about his or her sentences.

It's high time I ___.   It's about time ___.   I wish ___.

I'd rather ___ than ___.   Suppose ___.   If only ___.

> *It's high time I applied to graduate school.*

> *What are you going to study?*

Speaking

8a **Pair Work** Think about the situations below and discuss them. Try to use some of the expressions in the How To box. Extend the discussion for as long as possible.

> **Ex:** *A: What if you were alone in the house and it suddenly caught fire?*
>
> *B: I'd probably try to save my photos.*
>
> *A: Why? Wouldn't you rather save something valuable?*
>
> *B: No way! I'd rather save the photos because they represent a lot of happy memories.*

1. Suppose you could write great novels or paint great pictures or sing beautifully. Which would you choose?

2. What if you could travel to any one period in the past? Which would you choose?

3. What if you could be Leonardo da Vinci, Albert Einstein, or Mozart for one day? Who would you be?

4. Suppose a film director asked to make a film about your life? Would you accept? Who would you like to play you?

5. Suppose you could interview one famous person for a magazine. Who would it be?

6. What if someone asked you to participate in a reality TV show?

b Think of two more hypothetical questions to ask your partner. Start your questions with *What if . . .* or *Suppose . . . ?*

How To:	
Respond to hypothetical questions	
positively	*It's highly likely I'd agree.*
	I would probably agree to that.
	I would consider doing that.
	I suppose I might do that.
negatively	*I probably wouldn't accept.*
	It's unlikely I'd be able to do that.
	There's no way I'd do that.

Writing

9 Choose one of the situations in Exercise 8a. Imagine that it really happened. Write the story in about 150 words.

Review

1 Choose the correct phrase to complete each sentence.

____ 1. Doris Lessing won the Nobel Prize for literature in recognition

____ 2. Stephen Pinker, a well-known academic, is a master in the fields

____ 3. Many people have drawn inspiration from

____ 4. Kurosawa was one of the greatest film directors of

____ 5. Da Vinci's abilities ranged from

____ 6. Thomas Edison succeeded in

____ 7. US pilot Amelia Earhart devoted her life to

a. of her contribution to the novel.

b. the life of Helen Keller.

c. all time.

d. flying.

e. painting to designing weapons.

f. registering 1,093 patents for new inventions.

g. of both cognitive science and linguistics.

2 Complete the conversation with the words and expressions in the box.

> more or less   regarding   be honest   in fact   as far as my work is concerned   kind

A: Rachel, how are you feeling now that you've won the Turner Prize?

B: Thrilled. To _____ (1.), I never expected to win. I _____ (2.) of knew I had a chance, but it was still a big surprise.

A: How will this affect you?

B: _____ (3.), it won't affect me at all. I already have three exhibitions planned. _____ (4.) the money, it'll mean I can focus on my work.

A: We hear you'll be making videos, rather than painting. Is this true?

B: That's _____ (5.) true. I'll be making videos, but I'll still paint. _____ (6.), my next exhibition will be mainly paintings.

A: Thank you, Rachel. We're looking forward to it.

3 Circle the correct word or phrase.

1. What if we *are leaving/left/would have left* really early? Would we arrive on time?

2. I would rather *know/to know/knowing* the truth now than later.

3. I wish I *will/can/could* dance better.

4. It's high time we *had gone/went/go*.

5. She wishes she *had gotten up/got up/was getting up* earlier yesterday.

6. Suppose you *are running/run/have run* into trouble, what will you do?

7. It's about time they *learn/learned/had learned* to act like adults.

8. We wish you *didn't bring/hadn't brought/wouldn't bring* your dog yesterday.

4 Complete the sentences with suitable words and phrases with meanings similar to those in parentheses. Use the letters shown.

1. It was a disaster—a really d_____ performance! (*poor*)

2. The show is quite funny. The characters are really o_____ t_____ t_____. (*exaggerated*)

3. He does have interesting ideas, but his style makes it a pretty h_____ read. (*hard work*)

4. The decor hasn't changed since the 1980s, so it's not very c_____. (*modern* or *up-to-date*)

5. Michelangelo's *David* is without a doubt his f_____ p_____. (*best work*)

6. The i_____ special effects were what made the film such a success. (*unbelievable*)

Communication | collaborate on a proposal

Clarence Birdseye

Chester Carlson

5a ▶ 2.16 Listen and mark the statements true (*T*) or false (*F*).

_____ 1. Clarence Birdseye was the first person to put food in salt water to freeze it.

_____ 2. The equipment for his experiments was cheap.

_____ 3. Birdseye sold the first modern freezer for $22 million.

_____ 4. Chester Carlson's job was to invent a machine to make copies.

_____ 5. Carlson found his work difficult because of his own health problems.

_____ 6. The first commercial photocopier was made over 20 years after Carlson had first invented the machine.

b Listen again to check your answers.

6 **Pair Work** Discuss.

1. Would you describe frozen food as an "original" idea?

2. Can you think of any other popular products that are based on earlier inventions?

7a **Pair Work** You are planning a new business venture and need to persuade the rest of the class to invest in your idea. Choose one of the ideas on the right (or come up with an idea of your own) and plan how you are going to "sell" it to the rest of the class.

b Write the name of the product, service, or movie, and a short summary of the main ideas behind it, its main benefits, and other important features. Then present your proposal to the rest of the class. Ask and answer questions about each proposal.

A NEW PRODUCT

You have invented a jacket that can change color and _____ . Made of the latest high-tech material, and with a range of ten colors, the jacket takes five seconds to change color. It also has special _____ . . . .

A NEW SERVICE

Doitforyou.com offers to help you with _____ . Users pay a fixed monthly fee and can use the service as often as they wish. Additional benefits include _____ . . . .

A NEW MOVIE

It is 2100. The world has become _____ . Only one person can save the planet because he or she has the key to the secret _____ . The problem is that there is a terrible _____ who doesn't want the world to be saved. . . .

UNIT 10
Expressing feelings

A

B

C

D

Warm Up

1   **Pair Work** Discuss. How do you think the people in the photos are feeling? Why?

2   Check that you understand the meaning of the idioms in bold. Which idioms apply to the people in the photos? Then match the sentences on the left with the sentences on the right.

____ 1. She was **at her wits end** with worry.

____ 2. He failed his exam, so he's a bit **down in the dumps**.

____ 3. They saw the same car at a much lower price, so now they're **kicking themselves**.

____ 4. He is very **pleased with himself** for winning the game.

____ 5. I'm **of two minds** about whether to accept the invitation.

____ 6. Try not to get so **wound up**—it's only a traffic jam.

a. He deserves **a pat on the back**.

b. Just **chill out**!

c. We should try to **cheer him up**.

d. But they can't **do anything about it** now.

e. We went out to **take her mind off** the problem.

f. I just can't **make my mind up**.

Discuss how feelings affect you CAN DO ✓

GRAMMAR modals (and verbs with similar meanings)

Listening

1 **Pair Work** Discuss.

1. Do you think your outlook can affect what happens to you in life? How?

2. Do you consider yourself optimistic? Explain.

2 ▶ **2.17** Listen to the interview and choose the correct phrase to complete each sentence.

1. Optimists and pessimists are predisposed to ____.

   a. view events similarly   **b.** view events differently

2. Optimists believe that ____.

   a. they are responsible for the good things that happen

   b. good things happen by chance

3. Pessimists ____.

   a. are more depressed than optimists

   b. are more likely to be depressed than optimists

4. Positive patterns of thinking ____.

   a. are inherited   **b.** can be learned

5. Cognitive restructuring is a way to change ____.

   a. patterns of thought   **b.** a pessimist into an optimist

3 **Pair Work** Discuss.

1. Do you agree with what Dr. Bright says about optimists and pessimists?

2. Do you think that cognitive restructuring makes sense for someone who has a pessimistic outlook?

3. Do you think it's possible for someone to be both an optimist and a pessimist?

4. After listening to the interview, do you consider yourself an optimist or a pessimist? Why?

Grammar | modals (and verbs with similar meanings)

4 Look at the way the words in bold are used in the sentences below. Match them to their correct usage in the Active Grammar box on page 117.

____ 1. He **can't** see the positive in anything.

____ 2. He still **won't** let me forget that incident.

____ 3. There **must** have been some other reason for the accident.

____ 4. It was proof that more good things **will** happen to you.

____ 5. A person with a negative outlook is more **likely to** be depressed.

____ 6. See it as proof that more good things **are bound to** happen to you.

____ 7. You **might** think about whether they are due to something you did.

____ 8. You **must** guard against assuming that you are responsible.

____ 9. I **shouldn't** be too bummed about that?

____ 10. Think of extenuating circumstances that **might** have contributed to the game.

____ 11. And **can** I ask you about your name?

____ 12. We're **supposed to** think positive thoughts.

Active Grammar

1. will

  a. for predictions:
    Do you think the president will win re-election?

  b. for willingness or unwillingness:
    I'll get that for you.
    He won't pay the bills.

2. might

  c. to talk about possibility:
    Sonya might phone later.

  d. to make suggestions (polite):
    You might try asking your brother.

3. must, can't

  e. for obligation:
    You must be at the office by 8 A.M.
    You can't leave before 5 P.M.

  f. for deduction:
    There must be some kind of problem.
    That can't be the manager—he's far too young.

4. can

  g. for permission:
    Can we leave our bags here?

  h. for possibility or impossibility:
    We can't all fit in one car.

5. (be) supposed to

  i. to talk about what you have to do according to rules or regulations:
    We are supposed to be at the presentation.

6. (be) bound to

  j. for future prediction of certainty:
    She's bound to give the secret away.

7. (be) likely to

  k. for probability:
    You're not likely to pass.

8. ought to, need to, should

  l. for obligation, duty, or necessity:
    Do you think we ought to tell them?
    Do we need to make a reservation?
    You really should contact the office.

See Reference page 136

5   **Pair Work** Tell your partner about: 1) three things you should do this week; 2) what you think your best friend is likely to be doing right now; 3) how you think teachers can best motivate their students; and 4) how you think people's lives will change in the future.

Vocabulary | outlook and attitude

6a   Check you understand the phrases in bold and complete the questionnaire.

HOW OPTIMISTIC ARE YOU?

How strongly do you agree or disagree with the statements? Use the scale below.

	1 strongly disagree
	2 disagree
	3 neither agree nor disagree
	4 agree
	5 strongly agree

_____ 1. When something I have tried doesn't work, I try to think of new ways to solve the problem.

_____ 2. I rarely feel lonely, even when I am by myself.

_____ 3. When I'm **going through** a tough time, I turn to my friends and family.

_____ 4. I try to **look on the bright side**, even when things are not going my way.

_____ 5. When I meet someone new, I assume that he or she will like me.

_____ 6. I try to learn from my failures, but I don't **dwell** on them.

_____ 7. There are a lot of things that can go wrong, but **chances are** that they won't.

_____ 8. I am fairly good at relaxing after I leave work.

_____ 9. I **tend to trust** people until they give me a reason not to.

_____ 10. You shouldn't take life's problems seriously. Usually things will **work out in the long run**.

_____ 11. It's good to look at life with a sense of humor.

_____ 12. I see problems as challenges.

b   **SPEAKING EXCHANGE** Read the results of the questionnaire on page 143. Compare your answers with other students. Do you agree with the results?

Reading

7 **Pair Work** Discuss whether you agree or disagree with the following statement: You can achieve your dream if you try hard enough, no matter what your limitations are.

8 Read the article.

Flo Fox

I try to set an example by taking the negative and making it positive—both in life and in my work. —Flo Fox

Blind photographer might seem like an oxymoron. How could a person who cannot see possibly take pictures? Flo Fox is among the extraordinary people in this unique profession.

Flo Fox was born blind in one eye. She has joked that this automatically made her a photographer, since she never had to close one eye to take a picture! She bought her first 35 mm camera in 1972 and carried it everywhere she went in New York City. She became a street photographer, particularly drawn to ironic images and subjects that have historical value.

In 1975, Flo Fox lost vision in her good eye and was declared legally blind. Nonetheless, she continued to take pictures. If that weren't a challenge enough, it was right around this time that she was diagnosed with multiple sclerosis and started losing control of her limbs. She was determined not to let her physical limitations affect her career. Instead of walking the streets of New York City with a cane, she drove around in a motorized scooter and continued to seek out subjects for her art. Despite her disabilities, she also managed to travel extensively and document her experiences through her photography.

Flo Fox has taken over 100,000 photographs in her career. Her work has been published in various books and magazines. She has participated in numerous exhibits. Her work is in the permanent collections of the Brooklyn Museum and the Smithsonian Museum. She has given seminars on her photography. She has even hosted a photography show on cable television.

Today Flo Fox is confined to a wheelchair, most of her body immobilized. But she still takes a camera with her wherever she goes. Although she can't take pictures herself, she instructs her attendants and friends on what subjects to shoot and exactly how to do it.

Jimmy Dean once said, "I can't change the direction of the wind, but I can adjust my sails to always reach my destination." Flo Fox has consistently and inspirationally adjusted her sails to realize her dreams. She indeed has an outstanding talent for making negatives into positives!

9 **Pair Work** Discuss the meaning of the following statements.
1. Flo Fox has consistently and inspirationally adjusted her sails to realize her dreams.
2. She indeed has an outstanding talent for making negatives into positives.

Speaking

10a **Group Work** Think about a dream you would like to realize or a goal you would like to achieve. Make a few notes about the following:
1. What is your dream?
2. Why is it important?
3. How will you go about achieving it?
4. Who will help you?
5. What have you done in the past that could help you?
6. How will you motivate yourself?

b Tell each other about your dream or goal. Try to offer advice on how your classmates might achieve their goals.

GRAMMAR modals of deduction (past and present)

Listening

1 Pair Work What is happening in the photos? What would it be like to be there? What problems might there be?

2 ▶ **2.18** Listen to the conversations. Then listen again and answer the questions.

1. What difficulties with early flights does the speaker mention?
2. What doubts does he think the pilot had?
3. When Machu Picchu was discovered by modern explorers, how was the actual site different from now?
4. What positive and negative emotions does the speaker think Gagarin had?

Grammar | modals of deduction (past and present)

3 Look at the modals of deduction below and read the Audioscript on page 158. Can you find any examples of the modals?

must be, must have been	*couldn't be, couldn't have been*
might feel, might have felt	*could happen, could have happened*
can't have, can't have been	*may live, may have lived*

4 Answer the questions and read the rule in the Active Grammar box.

Active Grammar

1. Which three modals from Exercise 3 have similar meanings?
2. Which modals mean that something is not possible?
3. Which modal means we are sure about something (in the positive)?
4. How are the meanings of *must be* and *must have been* different?

We can also use *will be* to make a guess about the present when we are almost sure that something is true because of habit or deduction.

That'll be John on the phone. He always calls at 6:30.

See Reference page 136

5 What is the difference in meaning (if any) between the two options *in italics* in the sentences below?

1. He *can't/shouldn't* be happy about his exam result. He *normally does/could've done* better.
2. You *couldn't/can't* have stayed awake all night. You never do that.
3. He *might be/could have been* hungry—that would explain the crying.
4. They *may/might* have found the gold.

Speaking

6a SPEAKING EXCHANGE Look at the photos on page 142. Discuss what you think is happening or has happened and why.

b Read the story behind each photo on page 139. Were your speculations correct?

Reading

7 **Group Work** Read the introduction on the right. What do you think "some of the biggest highs" and "some of the worst lows" might be?

8 **Pair Work** Read the book review and discuss whether you think the statements that follow are true or false. Give reasons.

> *Esquire* magazine interviewed 61 people who had experienced some of the biggest highs and the worst lows known to humanity. The result is a book called *Esquire Presents: What It Feels Like*.

So what does it feel like . . . ?

1 As we watch James Bond jump out of a plane, shoot 28 bad guys in 5 seconds flat, mix a perfect cocktail and get the girl, most of us know that real life just isn't like this. We're never going to win the Nobel Prize, walk on the Moon, win the lottery, or get attacked by grizzly bears. And that's why *Esquire* magazine decided to find out what these things really feel like.

2 Thanks to Buzz Aldrin, we can share the thrill of walking on the Moon. He describes, "powdery dust . . . the sky velvety black . . . surreal," and his feelings of responsibility: "If we made a mistake, we would regret it for quite a while." Aldrin's account gives us just the right blend of emotion and cold, hard fact. Aldrin's story is, of course, extremely well-known. One of the strengths of *Esquire Presents: What It Feels Like* is that it also covers normal, unexceptional people who find themselves in exceptional circumstances.

3 Max Dearing tells us what it feels like to be struck by lightning: "I was absolutely frozen, just as cold as I've ever been in my entire life, but then part of me was incredibly hot, too. I saw these red flashing lights, and I kept thinking, "It's a fire truck! A fire truck!" as if I were a little kid. Then there was the most incredible noise I'd ever heard."

4 If Dearing's experience is shocking (literally and metaphorically) because of its sudden life-changing violence, Craig Strobeck's story is altogether more terrifying because it affects every minute of his life. Strobeck describes what it feels like to have an obsessive-compulsive disorder. He has to take two-and-a-half-hour showers. He runs out of hot water but doesn't stop. He cleans every inch of his body a thousand times, and sometimes he gets back in the shower because one area just doesn't feel clean enough.

5 Possibly the strangest experience described in the book, though, is that of Geoffrey Petkovich. He went over Niagara Falls, one of the world's largest waterfalls, in a barrel. He did it "for a bit of fun," though it

was a pretty bumpy ride. With him in the barrel were two cans of beer, a packet of cigarettes, and two hours' worth of oxygen in tanks, just in case the barrel sank.

6 Petkovich's story is an example of the book's humorous tone, but its editor, A. J. Jacobs, thinks *Esquire Presents: What It Feels Like* has a serious message. "The guy who was buried under 50 feet of snow in an avalanche says that nowadays he can hit his thumb with a hammer and it doesn't bother him. He's just happy to be here." The same is true for most of the people in this fascinating book.

1. The book was published so that ordinary people could read about extraordinary experiences.
2. The book is mainly about famous people's achievements.
3. Buzz Aldrin talks about his regrets.
4. Geoffrey Petkovich is probably a fun-loving person.
5. The book is a serious, academic text.

Vocabulary | strong feelings

9 Put the adjectives in bold in the correct box in the chart. Use a dictionary if necessary.

1. You've just been offered the best job in the world. You must be absolutely **thrilled**!
2. One thing that makes me **furious** is when people litter.
3. I was **taken aback** when they asked me to be the team captain. I hadn't expected it at all.
4. She was **ecstatic** when she finally passed her driving test.
5. I feel completely **indifferent** about that issue; I don't care one way or the other.
6. They split up after ten years together, and now they're both **miserable**.
7. I know math isn't your favorite subject, but do you have to look so **uninterested**?
8. She was **terrified** when she saw the spider in her bed!
9. I was **flabbergasted** when they told me I'd won the lottery.
10. When she won the award, she was **dumbstruck**. She just couldn't believe it!
11. He was **outraged** by your terrible behavior.
12. We're **delighted** that you can come.
13. When the plumber didn't show up again I was **livid**. I'd taken the day off work.
14. Walking down the dark deserted streets, they were **petrified**.
15. We were a little **upset** that you didn't call to say you'd be late.

1. happy	2. unhappy	3. neither happy nor unhappy
4. scared	5. surprised	6. angry

10 **Pair Work** How would you feel in these situations? Why? Try to use adjectives you haven't used before.

1. You won the Nobel Prize for Physics.
2. You were chosen to go to the International Space Station.
3. You were caught in the middle of a lightning storm.
4. You were offered a job as a model for a clothing company in Milan.
5. You found a large box full of gold coins under your floor.
6. Your neighbor played loud music every night and would not turn it down when asked to.
7. You saw a tiger wandering around your local supermarket.

Listening

1 **Pair Work** Discuss. Which of the topics in the box do you remember from your childhood? How did they make you feel?

> playing sports   moving
> playing games   babysitting
> making friends   taking tests
> changing schools
> summer vacation
> spending time alone
> staying with grandparents
> birth of a brother or sister
> arguing with friends or family

2 ▶ **2.19** Listen. Which of the topics does each speaker mention? Do any of the stories remind you of experiences from your own childhood?

3 Listen again and answer the questions.
  1. Did Speaker 1 find it easy to get along with other children? Why or why not?
  2. How has her experience shaped her character?
  3. What was bad about Speaker 2's experience?
  4. What smells, sensations, and colors does Speaker 3 mention?
  5. What was different about the breakfasts she had on vacation?
  6. How did playing in the woods make Speaker 4 feel?

Reading

4a Look at the picture. Where do you think the story is set? What do you think it is about? How do you think the girl is feeling?

b Read the excerpt from *The House on Mango Street*. Were your ideas correct?

5 **Pair Work** How did the story make you feel? What do you think life is going to be like in the house on Mango Street?

The House on Mango Street

We didn't always live on Mango Street. Before that we lived on Loomis on the third floor, and before that we lived on Keeler. Before Keeler it was Paulina, and before that I can't remember. But what I remember most is moving a lot. Each time it seemed there'd be one more of us. By the time we got to Mango Street we were six—Mama, Papa, Carlos, Kiki, my sister Nenny, and me.

The house on Mango Street is ours, and we don't have to pay rent to anybody, or share the yard with the people downstairs, or be careful not to make too much noise, and there isn't a landlord banging on the ceiling with a broom. But even so, it's not the house we thought we'd get.

We had to leave the flat on Loomis quick. The water pipes broke and the landlord wouldn't fix them because the house was too old. We had to leave fast. We were using the washroom next door and carrying water over in empty milk gallons. That's why Mama and Papa looked for a house, and that's why we moved into the house on Mango Street, far away, on the other side of town.

They always told us that one day we would move into a house, a real house that would be ours for always so we wouldn't have to move each year. And our house would have running water and pipes that worked. And inside it would have real stairs, not hallway stairs, but stairs inside like houses on TV. And we'd have a basement and at least three washrooms so when we took a bath we wouldn't have to tell everybody. Our house would be white with trees around it, a great big yard and grass growing without a fence. This was the house Papa talked about when he held a lottery ticket and this was the house Mama dreamed up in the stories she told us before we went to bed.

But the house on Mango Street is not the way they told it at all. It's small and red with tight steps in front and windows so small you'd think they were holding their breath. Bricks are crumbling in places, and the front door is so swollen you have to push hard to get in. There is no front yard, only four little elms the city planted by the curb. Out back is a small garage for the car we don't own yet and a small yard that looks smaller between the two buildings on either side. There are stairs in our house, but they're ordinary hallway stairs, and the house has only one washroom. Everybody has to share a bedroom—Mama and Papa, Carlos and Kiki, me and Nenny.

Once when we were living on Loomis, a nun from my school passed by and saw me playing out front. The Laundromat downstairs had been boarded up because it had been robbed two days before and the owner had painted on the wood YES WE'RE OPEN so as not to lose business.

Where do you live? She asked.

There, I said pointing up to the third floor.

You live *there*?

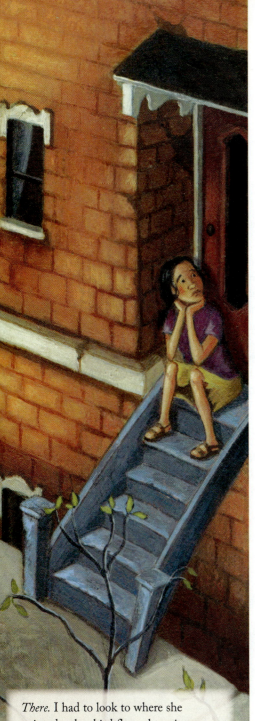

Grammar | uses of *would*

6 Match the example sentences in the Active Grammar box to the different uses of *would*.

> ### Active Grammar
>
> ____ 1. *Each time there'd be one more of us.*
>
> ____ 2. *The landlord **wouldn't** fix them.*
>
> ____ 3. *They always told us that one day we **would** move into a real house.*
>
> ____ 4. *We packed all the books in wooden boxes so that they **wouldn't** get damaged.*
>
> ____ 5. *We'd have moved to a different area if we'd been able to afford it.*
>
> ____ 6. ***Would** you shut the window, please?*
>
> ____ 7. *I wish they **wouldn't** make so much noise at night.*
>
> a. polite request
>
> b. recurring situation in the past
>
> c. past purpose or reason (often used after *so that*)
>
> d. imagined situation
>
> e. strong wish that someone would or wouldn't do something
>
> f. past intention or expectation (reported)
>
> g. refusal

American English	British English
move	move house

See Reference page 136

7 Add *would* or *wouldn't* to the following sentences (as appropriate).

1. If you like to follow me, I'll show you to your rooms.
2. I have more time for work if you took care of the kids more often.
3. When we were alone at home, we always cook for ourselves.
4. He never help me with my homework.
5. If only he answer the phone, I could explain what happened.
6. We hid the package in the cabinet so that she notice it.

8 **Pair Work** Complete the sentences and compare your ideas with other students.

Ex: When I was ten years old, I thought
    I would grow up to be a doctor .

When we were young, my friends and I would _____.

I wish people wouldn't always _____.

When I was a child my parents wouldn't _____.

Would you mind if I _____?

If I were younger (or older), I'd _____.

There. I had to look to where she pointed—the third floor, the paint peeling, wooden bars Papa had nailed on the windows so we wouldn't fall out. You live *there?* The way she said it made me feel like nothing. *There.* I lived *there.* I nodded.

I knew then I had to have a house. A real house. One I could point to. But this isn't it. The house on Mango Street isn't it. For the time being, Mama says. Temporary, says Papa. But I know how those things go.

Sandra Cisneros

Reading

9   Read the stories from a website and write a title for each one.

Stories from Childhood

We asked you to send in stories about some of your earliest childhood memories:

_____

I have a vivid recollection of walking to school when I was about ten years old. Every morning I would meet my childhood sweetheart at the corner of the street and carry her backpack all the way to the girls' school gate. In the afternoon, I would wait for her outside the same gate. We would walk home together singing "You Were Made for Me" by Freddie and the Dreamers.

_____

I'll always remember my grandfather bringing a newly born black sheep up to the house one time. He let me hold him without completely letting go because the little ball of curls was wriggling like an eel. I was five years old and had never seen a black sheep. His skull was hard as a rock. Later my grandfather told me I was like that little black sheep . . . hard-headed and very special.

_____

My earliest memory is of my dad carrying me on his shoulders. On Sundays, we would often go for an afternoon walk, and when I got tired he would carry me. I felt I could see the entire world. And I could . . . my three-year-old world, at least.

_____

One memory that sticks in my mind is of my brother and me when we were younger. We generally spent most of our time fighting. We were always chasing each other around the house hitting each other and throwing things. But one night we were staying at my aunt's house, and I was sad about something. I just remember crying into my brother's arms as we were going to bed. I can't even remember now what I was so sad about, but the important thing is that I remember knowing he was there for me, and being comforted by him. Looking back, it's hard to believe what happened that night.

_____

One of my earliest memories was of being scared to death because I thought that I'd been abandoned in the hospital ward. I had my tonsils removed when I was two and a half and had to stay overnight by myself. My parents kept telling me that they'd come to take me home "in the morning when the sun shines." The problem was that the next morning, it was raining!

10   Cover the Reading. Think of different ways to complete the phrases in the How To box. Then compare your ideas with the Reading.

Speaking

11a Choose two or three childhood memories or experiences to talk about. Write a few notes and try to use some of the expressions in the How To box.

b   **Group Work** Share your stories. Ask questions about your classmates' stories.

Writing

12   Write a paragraph describing an early childhood memory, using phrases from the How To box.

How To:

Describe a childhood memory

Introducing the story	• _I have a ____ recollection of . . ._ • _I'll ____ remember . . ._ • _One of my ____ memories is of . . ._
Background	• _We always/usually/____ spent . . ._ • _On Sundays we ____ often . . ._ • _I had never . . ._
Specific event	• _One time/But ____ night/ On this occasion . . ._ • _The problem was that . . ._
Reflecting	• _Looking back, . . ._ • _It's ____ to believe_ • _I can hardly believe . . ._

Extra Vocabulary Study and
Extra Listening Activity
in *ACTIVEBOOK*

Review

1 Rewrite each sentence so that the meaning stays the same. Use the words in bold.

1. It won't be a surprise if the manager is angry about the situation. **likely**
2. I'm sure they'll call us this morning. **bound**
3. They asked me to be there at 10:30. **supposed**
4. There must be another way out of the building. **can't**
5. Maybe we'll have time to chat before the meeting. **might**
6. They are refusing to pay the bill until the dispute has been resolved. **won't**
7. Do you want us to wait for you outside the conference hall? **should**
8. It's better if he brings his own laptop. **ought**

2 Complete each sentence with a suitable modal phrase in the past.

Ex: The mud was up to 16 feet (5 meters) deep in places.

It _must have been_ impossible to drive through.

1. Why isn't she here? She _____ understood your instructions.
2. You should have seen their reaction! They _____ been happier.
3. We were lucky to get out alive. We _____ killed.
4. They didn't come home until the early hours of the morning. The party _____ good.
5. She could see my face. She _____ realized who I was.
6. They'd had such a difficult journey. They _____ relieved when they arrived.
7. They lost the game. Sam _____ disappointed.

3 Correct any mistakes in the sentences. Not all sentences have mistakes.

1. If I'd have known, I'd have called you earlier.
2. I wish she won't always tell me what to do.
3. I wouldn't change it for the world.
4. We left the keys in the office so you will see them when you got there.
5. I'd sit on my grandfather's knee and put tobacco in his pipe.
6. Wouldn't it be easier if we went home first?
7. I told Marcella that we meet her outside the theater.
8. My parents wouldn't never have dreamed of sending me to private school.

4 Complete the paragraph with words from the box.

end	calm	aback	pleased	terrified	delighted
tends	minds	upset	thrilled	worked	

When I was about ten years old, I remember my father coming into the room, looking very _____ (1.) with himself, to tell us that we were going to have another brother or sister. It was unexpected, so we were both taken _____ (2.), but I was _____ (3.). My brother, on the other hand, was of two _____ (4.). He was younger than me, and I don't think he was too impressed with the idea. He _____ (5.) to worry about things, and I think he was _____ (6.) by the fact that he might not be the center of attention all the time. When the big day came, unfortunately there were problems, and my mother had to stay in the hospital. We weren't allowed to visit, and we were all at our wits _____ (7.) with worry. We tried to _____ (8.) each other down, but basically we were all _____ (9.) that something awful would happen. It all _____ (10.) out in the end though, and when I was finally able to see my little sister, I was _____ (11.). She was so tiny and special. We all love her so much.

Communication | express strong feelings about an issue

5 Read the dictionary definitions and discuss. When was the last time you complained about something, raved about something, or took a stand on something?

> **complain** /kəmˈpleɪn/ *v* [I] **1** *informal* to say that you are annoyed, not satisfied, or unhappy about something or someone

> **take a stand** *v* [I] to state publicly a strong opinion about an important issue

> **rave** /reɪv/ *v* [I] **1 rave about/over something** to talk in an excited way about something because you think it is very good

6 ▶2.20 Listen to the speakers. What does each speaker talk about? Are they complaining about something, raving about something, or taking a stand? What are their opinions?

7 Think about an issue or topic that you feel strongly about. Prepare to explain your feelings. Use the pictures below if you need inspiration.

8 **Group Work** Explain your position. As you are listening to other students, write down their topics and one question to ask when they have finished.

TOPIC	QUESTIONS
1	
2	
3	
4	

Unit 1 Reference

Verbs and adjectives with prepositions

There are many phrases that use fixed prepositions.

Verb + preposition: *opt for, distinguish from, succeed in, stem from, appeal to, bother about, rely on, benefit from*

Adjective + preposition: *short of, riddled with, lacking in, nervous about*

> *See page 10 for a full description of preposition use.*

Passives

Passives can be used for "distancing." This means that the speaker or writer doesn't want complete responsibility for the ideas he or she expresses. The passive is often used:

- to make a statement less personal and slightly more polite.

   *We don't allow that. → That **isn't allowed**.* (It isn't the speaker's decision; it is an impersonal rule.)

   *You must hand in the essay by Friday. → The essay **must be handed** in by Friday.*

- in formal writing when the focus is on achievements and events rather than the people who were responsible.

   *The vaccine **was discovered** by chance.*

There are some common passive expressions to show that we are not certain of a statement.

> ***It is believed that** the thief was an ex-employee.*
> ***It is said that** he was able to speak more than 20 languages, but there is no proof.*
> ***It was claimed that** the president hadn't seen the documents before the scandal broke out.*
> ***She was thought** to have come from Germany originally, but there was little evidence.*
> ***He was reported** to have been living in Brazil, but there was only one sighting of him.*

Perfect forms

Use perfect forms to refer from one point in time to another point in time before that. It shows that the speaker sees one event as 1) linked to a later event or 2) finished by a certain time.

> *She**'d lost** her ticket, so she missed the show.*
> *By 6:00, I **will have finished** my work.*

Use the present perfect to describe something that happened:

- during a period that includes past and present.

   *We**'ve been** here since 8:00 A.M.*

- in the past but when the exact time isn't relevant to this discussion or isn't known.

   *She**'s lived** in over 20 countries.*

- in the past but has a result or effect in the present.

   *Oh no! I**'ve lost** my passport.*

- in the very recent past (especially with *just*).

   *I**'ve just heard** the news.*

Use the past perfect to talk about completed actions that happened before another action in the past.

> *She wanted to go to the museum, but **we'd already been** there.*

Use the future perfect with time phrases with *by*, for example—*by that time, by this time next week, by the end of February, by the end of the day*.

> ***By June** we **will have finished** the project.*

Perfect forms are often used with *for, since*, and *just*.

> *By January, I **will have been** here **for** a year.*
> *I**'ve just been speaking** to Mickey.*
> *I thought it was time to move because I**'d been living** there **since** 1967.*

Unit Vocabulary

Challenges

have the right attitude	face challenges
rises to the challenge	set achievable goals
couldn't have done it without	

Learning languages

fluent	master	pick up	dialect
linguistic ability	cram	mother tongue
universal language		

Talking about knowledge

next to nothing	I'm pretty sure	inside out
I'm positive	I haven't a clue	by heart
I've never heard of him	I don't know offhand
I haven't the faintest idea	off the top of my head
like the back of my hand	

Achievement

pursue	deal with	an ultimate ambition
paid off	believe in	have the potential
head (straight for the top)	
continue to push someone	

Unit 2 Reference

Gerund and infinitive review

When one verb follows another, the second verb is either a gerund or an infinitive.

Some of the verbs that are followed by a gerund are related in meaning. These verbs show personal tastes: *adore, like, don't mind, detest, can't stand*

> I **adore living** here.
> I **can't stand listening** to their music all night.

Other verbs take an object + infinitive. (*I told her to come here.*) Some of these verbs are also related in meaning. These verbs show one person (or thing) influencing the actions of another:
warn, tell, advise, urge, order, persuade, encourage, force, forbid, allow

> I **persuaded her to visit** me.
> She **warned him not to go** there.

Verbs that are followed by a preposition use the gerund:

> I **look forward to meeting** her.
> He **succeeded in finding** a job.
> We **insist on paying**.

Some verbs can only be followed by the infinitive or the gerund. See page 21.

Comparisons

There are many expressions that show if the difference between two things is big or small.

For a small difference use:
slightly, a little bit, a tiny bit, etc.

> I'm **slightly taller** than Peter.
> The population is **slightly larger** than that of Ghana. *(formal)*

For a large difference use:
much, far, considerably (formal), etc.

> They're **far better** than us at football.
> The government was **considerably more** corrupt a hundred years ago. *(formal)*

As + adjective + *as* means the two things are equal.

> I'm **as intelligent as** my sister.
> It took me **as long** to drive to the city **as** it did to travel there by train.

To indicate two things aren't equal, say:

> She's **not as big as** me. *(= she's smaller)*
> The new menu **isn't as nice as** the one they had during the summer.

There are many expressions with *as* + adjective + *as* that show whether the difference is big or small.

For a small difference use:
not quite as

> This bed is**n't quite as comfortable as** the other one. *(= It's nearly as comfortable)*

For a big difference use:
nowhere near, not nearly

> He's **not nearly as good as** me at tennis.

We can use double comparatives with *the* to say that one thing causes another.

> **The longer** you take, **the less** chance we have of catching the plane.
> **The more** you write down, **the more** you'll remember.

Unit Vocabulary

Qualities of communities

cost of living	mild climate
healthcare system	freedom
standard of living	crime rate
unemployment	pollution
cultural life	nightlife

Recommending places

a must	a must-see	Don't miss . . .
overrated	overpriced	You should try . . .
If I were you, I'd go to . . .		watch out for
Make sure you go to . . .		
good value for the money		
not all it's cracked up to be		

Adjectives to describe places

unspoiled	diverse	off the beaten track
tranquil	vast	run-down
stunning	packed	magnificent
bustling		

Unit 3 Reference

Review of past forms

Past forms are often used together in order to make clear the order of events in a story.

Use the **simple past** to talk about completed actions in the past.

> We **went** to Paraguay last year.

The simple past can be used for short actions, long actions, or repeated actions.

Use the **past continuous** to talk about actions in progress at a particular time in the past.

> We **were talking** about her when she walked in.

The past continuous is often used to set the scene in a narrative.

> The sun **was shining** and the children **were playing** in the park. Suddenly . . .

Use the **past perfect** to talk about completed actions that happened before another action in the past. The past perfect is used only to refer to two actions or moments in the past.

> She took out a DVD, but I**'d already seen** it.

The past perfect is <u>not</u> needed to describe past events in chronological order.

> We **ordered** the food, **ate** and **paid**.

Use the **past perfect continuous** to talk about actions or situations that continued up to the moment in the past that is being talked about.

> Before he gave up, he**'d been smoking** for years.

The past perfect continuous is often used to show the reasons for a situation.

> He was angry because he**'d been waiting** for hours.

Compound adjectives

Compounds frequently use a hyphen (-) between the words, but there are no definite rules about this.

Often the second word is a present or past participle.

When the first word of the compound is an adjective, the stress is often on the second word.

> far-**seeing**, strong-**willed**, slow-**moving**

When the first word of the compound is a noun, the stress is often on the first word.

> **man**eating shark, **sun**tanned, **attention**-craving

Phrases with participles and gerunds

Instead of a complete adjective clause, we can use a participial phrase:

> I recognize the man **who is sitting** over there. →
> I recognize the man **sitting** over there.

A full adverbial clause can be reduced to a participial phrase to express cause, result, conditions, etc. They sound formal and are more common in writing than speech.

> **Because he was feeling hungry**, he bought a cake. →
> **Feeling hungry**, he bought a cake. (cause)

Participles can be used after many conjunctions, for example—as, after, before, since, when, once, without, in spite of.

> **Before leaving**, he gave me a present.
> He swam **in spite of having** a sore arm.

Having + past participle is a special form that shows the cause of a second action or a sequence of actions.

> **After running the marathon**, he was exhausted. →
> **Having run the marathon**, he was exhausted.

Gerunds can function as the subject of the sentence.

> **Talking** is the best therapy.

The subject of the participial phrase is usually the same as the subject in the main clause.

> Running around until they were tired, the kids had fun. (the kids ran and the kids had fun)
> NOT: ~~Waiting for hours, the day seemed to Tom as if it would never end.~~ (Tom was waiting; the day wasn't)

Unit Vocabulary

Books

I couldn't put it down	a bookworm
It's very readable	an avid reader
It's a page-turner	a best-seller
based on a true story	hooked
It was very moving/gripping	depict
the characters are one-dimensional	

Compound adjectives

single-minded	self-sufficient	thick-skinned
kind-hearted	stand-offish	career-oriented
level-headed	absent-minded	

Humor

a farce	black humor	exaggeration
a pun	surreal humor	satire
cartoons	irony	

Unit 4 Reference

Future probability

Use *will* to talk about something that is definite or a very strong probability.

Use *could*, *may*, or *might* to talk about something that is possible but not certain.

There are many other phrases for describing possibility.

Adverbs and adverbial phrases:

> *it will almost definitely, it almost definitely won't, it will presumably*

Verb phrases:

> *it may well, it might well, I doubt*

Adjectives and adjective phrases:

> *it's bound to, certain to, sure to, unlikely to*

Noun phrases:

> *the chances are that, there's a strong/slight possibility, you don't have a hope of ___-ing*

Future forms: review

For timetables:

Use the simple present to talk about timetables.

> *The plane **departs** at 2:30 from Rio.*

For decisions, plans and intentions:

Use *will* to talk about a decision made at the time of speaking (including offers and promises).

> ***I'll have** a coffee. Thanks.*

Use *going to* to talk about a plan or intention (maybe details haven't been decided yet).

> ***I'm going to work** in finance.*

Use the present continuous to talk about a future arrangement (details such as time and place have been decided).

> ***I'm playing** tennis at 4:30 with Zara.*

For predictions:

Use *will* to make predictions based on what you know or believed. We often use words like *think*, *hope*, *believe*, with *will* in this case.

> *I think Mike **will be** a good manager.*

Use *going to* to make predictions based on what you can see, hear, think, or feel now.

> *I think I**'m going to** be sick.*

Use the future continuous to talk about something that will be in progress at a definite time in the future.

> *This time next year I**'ll be living** in France.*

Use the future continuous to ask about someone's plans.

> ***Will** you **be working** late tonight?*

Use the future perfect with time phrases with *by*, for example—*by that time*, *by this time next week*, *by the end of February*, *by the end of the day*, etc.

> ***By** June we **will have finished** the project.*

Subject/verb inversion

We use inversion to emphasize the adverbial phrase in a sentence. Inversion is usually used in more formal writing.

Form: negative or adverbial expression + auxiliary verb + subject. Note: the word order is the same as the question form.

> ***Not once did she** look up from her book.*

Do not use auxiliary verbs when the main verb is the verb *be* or a modal verb.

> ***Not only is he** a great musician, but he can also teach.*

Inversion can be used after restrictive words; for example—*never*, *rarely*, *little*, *hardly*.

> ***Never before had he** seen such a beautiful vase.*

Inversion is also used with phrases beginning with *only*. These emphasize the first clause.

> ***Only** when I heard her speak **did I** remember her.*

Use *no way* + inversion to show that something is impossible or that the speaker doesn't want to do something. It is informal.

> ***No way would I** do a bungee jump!*

Unit Vocabulary

Progress

genetic engineering	virus
space mission	antibiotics

Arrangements

get out of	lined up	tied up	be free
fall through	be up to	call off	be on
wind down	swamped	come up	

Special abilities

gifted	adulation	a freak
in the making	peers	
a prodigy	demanding	

Unit 5 Reference

Emphasis

Passive constructions can be used to emphasize information at the beginning of a sentence.

*The suspect **was arrested** by police.*

Fronting

The order of clauses in a sentence can be changed to put a clause at the beginning that would not normally be there.

***What she thinks she is doing,** I don't know!*

Cleft sentences

Clauses beginning with *It is*, *It was*, or *What* can be used for emphasis.

***It was Ellen** who spotted the mistake.*

Adding words for emphasis

*She used her **own** ingredients.*

*They aren't **the least bit** scared.*

*I haven't thought about it **at all**.*

*Some people were **even** asking for discounts.*

*I **do** think we should warn them about the delay.*

Conditionals: review

To talk about something that is always true, use *if* + simple present in the *if* clause, and the simple present in the result clause.

*If you **go** into business with relatives, it **tends** to put a strain on your relationship.*

To talk about a possible real situation in the future, use *if* + present tense in the *if* clause, and *will* (*might*, *may*, *could*, *should*) in the result clause.

*If we **find** a bank, we **could change** some money.*

To talk about a hypothetical or unlikely situation in the future, use *if* + simple past in the *if* clause, and *would* (*might*, *may*, *could*, *should*) in the result clause.

*If they **asked** me to go back, I **wouldn't hesitate**.*

To talk about a hypothetical past situation, use *if* + past perfect in the *if* clause, and *would have* (*could have*, *should have*, *might have*) in the result clause.

*If he **had taken** his phone, I **could've called** him.*

To talk about past regrets, use *if only* or *I wish* + past perfect.

***If only** I **hadn't told** him about Johnny.*

*I **wish** I'd **thought** of looking it up on the Internet—it **would've saved** so much time.*

Mixed conditionals

These may express a hypothetical present result of a past action: *if* + past perfect in the *if* clause, and *would*, *could*, *may*, *might*, or *should* in the result clause.

*If we **hadn't answered** the advertisement, we **wouldn't** be here now.*

Other words and phrases can be used with, or instead of, *if* in conditional sentences, for example—*provided that*, *as long as*, *if only*, *should you happen to*, *supposing*, *if it hadn't been for*

Sentence adverbials

Sentence adverbials are adverbial phrases that modify part of a sentence. They can be used to show the speaker's attitude toward a subject, to organize information, rephrase, change the subject, summarize or generalize, etc. They are usually separated from the rest of the sentence by a comma.

***Broadly speaking,** we all agree.*

Common adverbials: *fundamentally, essentially, broadly speaking, however, surprisingly enough, seemingly, apparently, up to a point, on the other hand, looking back, in hindsight, believe it or not*

REFERENCE

Unit Vocabulary

Money, achievement, and charity

come into a fortune	high-income	haggle
stock market	go bankrupt	a raise
paid on commission	priceless	sue
philanthropist	volunteer	vision
power of attorney	provide for	
business venture	not see a penny	
declare bankruptcy	put money into research	

Expressing priorities

the essential thing	vital
couldn't do without	my first priority
not concerned about something	

Describing a job

freedom/autonomy	401K
convenient location	salary
working environment	benefits
flexible working hours	job satisfaction
opportunity for promotion	challenging work
professional development	
supportive colleagues/manager	

Unit 6 Reference

Articles

Definite article

Classes: *The arctic fox is known to inhabit the area.*

National groups: *The French are unhappy about the new policy.*

Other groups: *The Green Party has staged a protest.*

Unique objects: *The sun was setting on the horizon.*

Titles: *The president has yet to make a decision.*

Musical instruments: *She learned to play the harp.*

Geographical names: rivers (*the Amazon*), oceans (*the Pacific*), compass points (*the North Pole*), collective countries (*the EU*), mountain ranges (*the Alps*). NOT: lakes (*the Lake Erie*), single mountains (*the Mount Everest*), continents (*the Asia*)

Shared knowledge or experience: *We'll meet them in the café.* (the café by our office—shared knowledge)

Indefinite article

Jobs: *Martha is a dentist.*

Measuring: *It costs $150 a week. (per week)*

Introducing something new: *There's been an accident!*

No article

Names: *Tom Cruise is my favorite actor.*

Streets: *They live on Harvard Street.*

General countable plurals: *I love cats.* NOT: *I love the cats.*

Clauses with *whatever, whoever, whenever*

Use *whenever, whatever, whoever,* etc. when it doesn't make any difference *when, what, who,* etc., or we don't have to be specific, OR we don't know the exact details of *when, what, who,* etc.

> Come **whenever** you can. (It doesn't matter exactly when you come)

What, who, and *when* are a little different from *whatever, whoever,* and *whenever.* Compare:

> Repeat **what** you just said! ✓
> Repeat **whatever** you just said! ✓
> **Whatever** you just said, repeat it! ✓
> NOT: *What you just said, repeat it!* ✗
> **Whoever** you saw was probably the criminal. ✓
> NOT: *Who you saw was probably the criminal.* ✗

However has two meanings. Compare:

> **However** you go, by train or by car, it takes a day.
> It takes two days by car. **However,** if you go by train, it takes only a day. (contrast)

Connectors of time and contrast

There are many words and expressions that allow us to link our ideas and narratives in different ways.

To link things happening at the same time: *while, when, as, during*

> **As** the plane took off, she felt free.

To link things that happen when other longer actions are finishing or have finished: *by which time, at which point.*

> I reached the end, **by which time** I was tired.

To link things that happen immediately after the previous action: *hardly + when, on + present participle, no sooner + than*

> **On hearing** of the crash, he ran straight to the hospital.

To link things that contrast with previous information: *though, although,* and *even though* + verb phrase

> **Although he's short,** he's good at basketball.

We can also use *despite* and *in spite of* + noun phrase or gerund.

> **In spite of my poor grades,** I got a good job.

We can use adjective/adverb + *as/though* + subject + verb to add emphasis to the contrast. Typical examples are *much as* (I like), *hard though* (we tried).

> **Much as I love** television, even I can't watch for more than three or four hours a day.

Unit Vocabulary

Power

win over	be impressed by
gain	play an important part

Fashions and fads

catch on	be out	home in on
come about	be in	keep up with

Personal characteristics

inspirational	charismatic	dignified
nondescript	idealistic	tireless
gravitas	approachable	resolute
down-to-earth	trustworthy	inspiring
drive or energy	corrupt	aloof
waver in the face of problems		

Unit 7 Reference

Relative clauses

Defining relative clauses make it clear who or what is being referred to. They cannot be omitted.

> That's the town **where** I lived ten years ago.

That can replace *who* or *which*.

> They're playing the song **which** Jenny wrote =
> They're playing the song **that** Jenny wrote.

If the relative pronoun is the object of the clause, it can be omitted.

> John ate the cake (**that**/**which**) we bought yesterday.

Don't use commas before the relative pronoun in defining relative clauses.

Nondefining clauses give extra information. This information can be omitted.

> I went rock climbing last weekend, **which was fun**.

That cannot replace *who* or *which*.

The relative pronoun cannot be omitted.

Use a comma before and after nondefining relative clauses, unless they end the sentence.

Relative clauses with verb + dependent preposition usually have the preposition at the end of the clause.

> That's the company (which) I worked **for**.

In formal English, put the preposition at the beginning of the clause.

> That's the company **for which** I worked.

A common pattern is (*one*/*some*/*all*/*either*/*neither*, etc.) *of which*/*whom*. This pattern is slightly formal.

> I saw two women, **neither of whom** was tall.

Verbs followed by infinitives or gerunds

Some verbs can be followed by the infinitive or the gerund. Sometimes the meaning changes.

> Going there **means** entering a new world. = involves
> I **didn't mean** to break the door. = didn't intend

Some verbs of perception (*hear, watch, feel, observe*, etc.) don't change their meaning when followed by different verb forms. BUT compare:

> **a.** I **saw the camel eat** the leaves.
> **b.** I **saw the camel eating** the leaves.

Sentence **a** describes a finished action. Sentence **b** describes an action that may be unfinished.

As . . . as; describing quantity

Use *as . . . as* to say that two things are equal in some way.

As . . . as can be used with adjectives, adverbs, *much* and *many*.

> I'm **as strong as** an ox.
> He sang **as sweetly as** an angel.
> The motorcycle costs **as much as** a car.

A clause can be put after the second *as*.

> She doesn't talk to me **as much as she used to**.

Possible, *ever*, or *usual* is often placed after the second *as*.

> I got here as quickly **as possible**.
> You're looking as beautiful **as ever**.
> The program wasn't as interesting **as usual**.

Unit Vocabulary

Animals and their environment

endangered	sanctuary	cage
animal rights	mammal	reptile
animal testing	carnivore	fur trade
nature preserve	predator	exotic
over-hunting/fishing		

Descriptive language

active volcano	permanent settlement	
ghost town	spectacular landscape	
below sea level	tourist destination	
drenched	zig-zag	loom
trespass	warped	drone
hunched	vibrant	parched

Buying and selling

It's in excellent condition.	It's as good as new.
It's the latest model.	It's state of the art.
It's second hand.	It's used.
It's available now.	It's on the market.
It's hand crafted.	It's brand new.
It's made by hand.	It includes ____
It's still in its packaging.	It features ____
It's one of a kind.	It's unique.
It has some wear and tear.	
It comes in a wide range of ____ .	
You can choose from a selection of ____ .	
It's not in perfect condition.	

Unit 8 Reference

Reporting verbs

Reporting verbs show the function of the original piece of speech.

> *"You can't leave the office before 6:oo."* → *She* <u>*informed*</u> *him that he couldn't leave the office before 6:oo.*

Reporting verbs use different patterns. The majority use a verb + (*that*) clause. Other examples are:

Verb + *that* clause: *accept, recollect, respond, imply, insist, presume, maintain, suggest, answer, confess, remember, conclude, state, boast, repeat*

Verb + object + infinitive: *persuade, remind, tell, advise, urge, warn, expect, force, invite, order*

Verb + object + *that* clause: *inform, advise, remind, tell, warn*

Verb + infinitive: *agree, refuse, propose, decide*

Verb + gerund: *deny, regret, suggest, mention*

Verb + object + preposition + present participle: *blame* (someone) *for, congratulate* (someone) *on, thank* (someone) *for*

Continuous forms

Use continuous tenses to talk about:

- background actions that are in progress at the moment we describe:

  *When I woke up, **it was raining**.*

- actions that are temporary or incomplete:

  *She**'s working** for me right now.*

- actions that are repeated:

  *I**'ve been training** every day for the last month.*

- actions in the process of change:

  *Prices **are rising**.*

- Stative verbs are not usually used in the continuous. Some common stative verbs are:

- Verbs of personal feeling: *like, love, hate, want, prefer, dislike, wish*

- Verbs of thought: *know, believe, imagine, mean, realize, understand, doubt, feel* (have an opinion)

- Verbs of the senses: *hear, sound, appear, taste, see, smell, resemble, seem*

- Verbs of fixed situations: *depend on, contain, belong to, own, involve, include, possess*

Some stative verbs have a progressive form, but the meaning may be a little different.

> *I **feel** he should win.* (belief) *I**'m feeling** sick.* (sense)
> *I **see** your point.* (understand) *I**'m seeing** the boss tomorrow.* (plan to meet)

Fronting

Sometimes in informal English a sentence begins with the complement (object, verb, adjective, or adverb). This gives the complement more emphasis.

> *Intelligent she may be, but kind she isn't!*

What or another question word is sometimes used.

> *I don't know what she's doing here!* → ***What** she's doing here I don't know!*
> *I'll never understand why you went there.* → ***Why** you went there I'll never understand.*

Fronting can be used to provide a link to information already mentioned.

> *Her first book was bad. **Much better was her second.***

We can front verbs and adjectives with *as* and ***though***.

> ***Tired though I was,** I didn't stop running.*

There are a number of common fronting phrases that show the importance of what follows.

> ***The trouble is,** he's so lazy.*
> ***The question is,** can we get her to join us?*
> ***The fact of the matter is,** you're not strong enough.*
> ***The fact remains** that we still have no definite date.*

Unit Vocabulary

Global issues

multiculturalism	cloning	oil spill
giant corporations	pollution	energy
cost and safety issues	identity theft	
	global warming	

Positive and negative opinions

It's a waste of space.	It's overrated.
We can do without it.	It's underrated.
We can't do without it.	It's indispensable.
It's been disastrous.	It's had big benefits.

Lifestyles

tear my hair out	burn out	the buzz
a security blanket	the be-all and end-all	

Cause and effect

consequence	bring about	stem from
has its origins in	give rise to	result in
an influence on	a major source of	

Unit 9 Reference

Collocations with prepositions

Sometimes verbs are followed by a preposition: *ask for, contribute to, range from . . . (to . . .), suffer from*

The verb and preposition are sometimes separated by the object: *remind someone of, distinguish someone from, receive training in*

Sometimes nouns are followed by prepositions: *relationship with, insurance against, in the fields of*

Sometimes adjectives are followed by a preposition: *bad at, similar to, famous for, concerned about*

Sometimes prepositions can begin common phrases: *in advance, out of order, at the time, on one occasion*

Discourse markers

Discourse is a piece of language that is longer and more complex than a sentence.

We use **discourse markers** to organize our speech or writing and make clear the relationship between what we have said and what we will say. We also use discourse markers to show our attitude toward a subject. The use of discourse markers depends on the function of our speech. For example, persuading, agreeing, etc., use different markers.

Here are some common discourse markers:

- focusing on the main topic: *regarding, as far as ___ is concerned, as for*
- returning to the main point (what was said before didn't matter): *anyway, anyhow, at any rate*
- returning to a previous line of discussion: *as I was saying, anyway, what I was going to say was*
- introducing a strong opinion or criticism: *all the same, and yet, still, on the other hand*

Unreal past

Wish or If only

Use *wish* or *if only* to describe unreal or imaginary situations. These are often regrets.

Wish or *If only* + past tenses describe imaginary present or future: *If only I were stronger.*

Wish or *If only* + past perfect describes the imaginary past: *I wish I had bought that CD.*

Wish + object + *would* is used to complain: *I wish you would be quiet!*

It's time, It's high time, It's about time

Use *it's time*, etc. + past tenses to say something should be happening now but isn't. It is often used for criticizing someone or something.
    It's high time you **stopped** acting like a child.

Would rather

Use *would rather* + simple past to describe preferences: *I'd rather she gave me the cash.*

If the person who expresses the preference and the subject are the same, use *would rather* + base form. *I'd rather dance the tango than the foxtrot.*

These expressions are often used to refuse permission: *I'd rather you didn't smoke in my home.*

What if or Suppose

Use *what if* or *suppose* + past tenses to ask about an imaginary situation in the present or future:
    Suppose you **asked** the bank for a loan?

Use *what if* or *suppose* + past perfect to ask about an imaginary situation in the past:
    What if we **had arrived** earlier?

Use *what if* or *suppose* + simple present to ask about a situation that you think is probable:
    What if your plan **doesn't work**?

Unit Vocabulary

Describing art

It's not my kind of thing.	abstract
It's not my taste.	avant-garde
I can't relate to it.	traditional
It's not my cup of tea.	contemporary
I'm a big fan of his stuff.	art deco
I'm really into her work.	disturbing
I've always admired her work.	tranquil
He's one of my all-time favorites.	figurative
his/her finest piece	striking
not one of his best	dull
masterpiece	stereotyped
over the top	poor acting
breathtaking	disappointing
fantastic/difficult/heavy read	spectacular

Unit 10 Reference

Modals (and verbs with similar meanings)

don't have to
lack of obligation: *We **don't have to go** until 2:30.*

must not
obligation not to do something: *You **mustn't talk** to him like that.*

should or **ought to**
advice: *You **should see** a doctor.*

recommendation: *You **ought to see** the castle.*

polite obligation: *Guests **should not smoke** in the bedrooms.*

uncertainty: ***Should** we **lock** both the doors?*

expectation: *They **should be** here by now.*

can
permission: ***Can** I **use** the telephone?*

can't
impossibility: *This **can't be** the right place!*

can + be
criticism: *He **can be** so annoying!*

will
assumption: *They**'ll be** here in a minute.*

won't
refusal: *I **won't stop** until I get what I want.*

may or **might**
possibility: *We **might need** an umbrella.*

might as well
the last option, when the speaker is not enthusiastic: *We **might as well just pay** the bill.*

must
certainty: *They **must be** hungry by now.*

need
behaves like a normal verb: ***Do** you **need to speak** to the doctor?*

is supposed to
obligation: *They **were supposed to deliver** the package this morning.*

be bound to
prediction of certainty: *He**'s bound to get** the job.*

be likely to do or **be**
probability: *Children living in rural areas **are likely to move** to the city as adults.*

Modals of deduction (past)

must have (been)
certain: *The crash **must have been** terrifying.*

might have (been)
possibility: *I **might have left** my keys in the car.*

can't have or **couldn't have (been)**
impossibility: *He **can't have finished** already! They **couldn't have come** this far.*

could have or **may have (been)**
possibility: *We **could have been** left there for a long time. There **may have been** a good reason for the delay, but we were angry anyway.*

Uses of *would*

polite request: ***Would** you help me get the files?*

recurring situation in the past: *She **would** always have a pack of gum in her pocket.*

past purpose or reason (often used after *so that*): *We took a taxi so (that) we **wouldn't** be late.*

imagined situation: *I**'d** love to know what happened!*

strong wish that someone would or wouldn't do something: *I wish he **would** make more of an effort!*

past intention or expectation (reported): *They asked if we **would** like anything to drink.*

past refusal: *He **wouldn't** let go of my bag.*

Unit Vocabulary

Idioms and phrases for feelings

down in the dumps	at her wits end
kicking themselves	of two minds
pleased with herself	wound up

Outlook and attitude

tend to trust	go through
look on the bright side	dwell on things
work out in the long run	chances are

Strong feelings

thrilled	outraged	taken aback
ecstatic	indifferent	miserable
upset	terrified	flabbergasted
furious	delighted	dumbstruck
livid	petrified	uninterested

Speaking Exchange

Unit 1 | Page 14, Exercise 2a

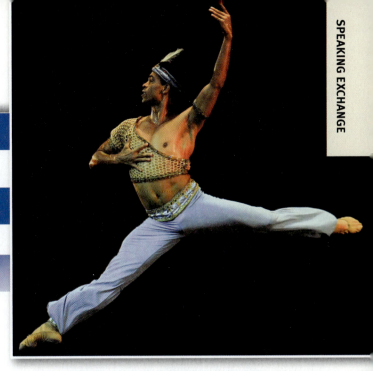

Carlos Acosta
An Artistic Superstar

Carlos Acosta is the greatest ballet dancer of his generation—a man sometimes called "Air Acosta" for his incredible jumps and leaps—and he has been setting the classical dance world on fire for over a decade and a half.

Born in 1973 in Cuba, Acosta was one of 11 children. He lived with his family in a cramped one-bedroom apartment in Havana, where he dreamed of one day being a soccer star. Acosta's childhood was one of poverty, brushes with crime, and frequent absences from school. Fearing that his son was becoming a delinquent, Acosta's strong-willed father enrolled him in ballet school at age 9. Pedro Acosta was determined that his son would escape from the poverty in which they lived.

Much, if not all of the credit for Acosta's start as a dancer goes to his father. When Acosta was expelled from his first ballet school for absences, his father went to the school and arranged a transfer. He <u>continued to push</u> his son, despite the fact that Carlos did not at first like ballet and endured much teasing and fighting for being a boy ballet dancer. Despite his mixed feelings about ballet, Carlos eventually trained at the National Ballet School of Cuba. His hard work <u>paid off</u>, and in January 1990 Acosta won the Gold Medal at the Prix de Lausanne. In November of the same year he won the Grand Prix and Gold Medal at the Paris ballet competition.

It was upon winning the Prix de Lausanne, his first competition, that Acosta realized that his talent was world-class. He was the last competitor to perform, and had entered the competition at the last minute. "My greatest hope was to reach the final," he says. "I never dreamed of winning." Of all the awards he has won, Acosta says that the Prix de Lausanne means the most to him.

After winning the Prix de Lausanne, Acosta spent a year in Turin, Italy, and then joined the English National Ballet. He returned to join the National Ballet of Cuba in 1992. After that, he danced with the Houston Ballet, and finally the Royal Ballet in England, where he has been the principal guest artist since 2003.

Acosta has performed the principal male role in nearly every classical ballet. He holds dual Cuban and British citizenship. Yet he still feels like an exile and misses his homeland. The title of his 2007 autobiography is *No Way Home*. It is ironic that, though Acosta's father is responsible for forcing his son to begin ballet, it is ballet that has caused Acosta to build a life apart from his family. "I didn't choose ballet, and for years I rebelled against it, believing it kept me from my family, from home, and from happiness," he says. "But I have come to terms with it. It has taken many years."

Though he is still a commanding force on the stage, Acosta is looking ahead to a time when he will retire from ballet. "You can only go on so long," he says. "I have done all the repertoire, all the Swan Lakes. If you are an artist and you want to keep seeking and growing and discovering things, you could get to a dead end, if you know what I mean." So what will be next for Acosta? For a start, he has begun experimenting with modern dance, including a collaboration with contemporary choreographer Russell Maliphant. "I'm searching for a transition," Acosta says. "The artistry is still in me. It's a question of finding the right vocabulary and language for your artistry." And for Acosta, that means moving into contemporary dance.

And his <u>ultimate ambition</u>? To return to Cuba, where he has bought a large house, and to create a new dance company there. "I would like to create a bridge from Cuba to the world, so that all the choreographers like Russell Maliphant can come and maybe try different things with the dancers there." In the meantime, Acosta continues to dazzle audiences around the world with his incandescent performances.

On Being a Travel Photographer

A picture is worth a thousand words—but only if it's good.

Introduction

Imagine this: early morning, the sun rising over the Swiss Alps, light glistening off fresh snow, flowers opening to greet the dawn. The scene is incredibly beautiful, and you wish you could capture the image forever. So you take a picture.

Unfortunately, on returning home, you find that the photo is blurred at the edges, and your finger takes up half the frame. "If only I'd taken a better picture!" you cry. "I wish I had a decent camera!" Actually, it's not about the camera. If you really want a good photographic record of your trip, it's high time you learned a few basics.

1. Composition

Suppose you see a beautiful landscape stretching in front of you for miles. What do you do? Don't try to fit it all in. Pick one interesting part and focus on it. Look for natural lines that draw the viewer in and give your picture depth, like a river starting in the foreground and disappearing into the distance.

2. Time of day

If traveling, the best time of day for a photo is either early morning or late afternoon. The light is softer at these times of day, unlike midday light, which can be too harsh for some subject matter. Make sure to keep the sun behind you, or you may end up with a silhouette of your intended subject. If you're shooting at night, keep your subjects no farther than 8–10 feet (3 meters) away; even the strongest flash can't illuminate more space.

3. Focus

What if you want a close-up of a person or animal? What do you focus on? The eyes. The most interesting travel photography often includes people or animals as well as beautiful environments. And much can be conveyed through people's eyes. Get as close as possible and fill the frame. There should be nothing in the picture that doesn't relate to the subject. Also, look for symmetrical subjects; it doesn't have to be a mirror image, just well-balanced.

4. Learn from others

Keep your eyes open; be aware of your surroundings. Before traveling, spend some time looking through big coffee-table picture books and magazines to see how the professionals do it. Take note of different ways in which light, perspective, and color are used. And don't be afraid to experiment: change the angle, get on your knees, climb onto a chair, find a balcony with a view.

5. Be sensitive

In many cultures, the people would rather you asked before photographing them. Take time to get to know them. Learn a few words of the language so that you can be polite. They are more likely to smile if you have addressed them in their language.

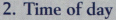

You want to build a luxury hotel with a golf course. The hotel could also serve as a conference center. It will bring lots of money and jobs to the local economy, and encourage businesses such as tourist shops, tour guides, and new restaurants.

Unit 5 | Page 66, Exercise 8

Group A

You are the employees. You want:

– to build a gym and a swimming pool for employees to use at lunch and after work.

– free buses to and from work.

– overtime pay.

– to update the kitchen equipment.

Which issues are very important, important, not so important?

Decide how you will negotiate for what you want.

Unit 3 | Page 40, Exercise 10a

Student A

An artist has been displaying his paintings in an art gallery. He asks the gallery owner if anyone has bought his work.

"I have good news and bad news," says the gallery owner. "The good news is that a man asked if your work would be worth more after your death. I told him it would, and he bought all ten of your paintings."

"That's wonderful," says the artist. "What's the bad news?"

"The man was your doctor."

Unit 8 | Page 99, Exercise 5

Student A

Your friend works too hard. He has a tough job and spends all of his time at work. He doesn't look healthy, and he isn't much fun to be with. You want to help him, but you are worried he will reject your advice.

Unit 10 | Page 119, Exercise 6b

Picture 1

Polo player Peter Koscinsky feels the pain after falling off his horse. It happened when he was attacking the ball and collided with an opposing team player. To make matters worse, the umpire awarded a free goal to the other side, which meant his team lost.

Picture 2

Chimpsky is on a beach, being filmed for a soft drink ad. Apparently, the three-and-a-half-year-old chimpanzee enjoyed the drink so much that he finished four bottles and had to be excused for numerous bathroom breaks.

Picture 3

Stuntman Todd Carter does his stuff for a forthcoming film about tornadoes. The truck, which is made of a very light metal and has no engine, was lifted into the tree by a crane, with Carter in it!

Picture 4

Actor Jack Black was the voice for the hero Po in the animated movie *Kung Fu Panda*, and Dustin Hoffman was the voice for his "co-star," Shifu. Here they goof off at the Berlin premiere of the movie.

On Being a Travel Writer

Introduction

Moving out of the shade of the high palm trees, you stroll for one last time along the sand dunes, allowing the transparent water to brush over your feet. You head for the bar, sip slowly on a cocktail, go to your beachfront hotel suite, and write 600 words. You email it the following morning to the travel magazine, before checking out with the immortal line, "Put the bill on my company's expense account."

"Ah, if only I were a travel writer!" you say. "I wish I could live like that!" Unfortunately, being a travel writer is no picnic.

1. Write often

The way to become a better writer is to write regularly. Some people say they don't have time. This isn't true. You have to *make time*. Start by keeping a journal every day. It doesn't matter what time of day you write it as long as you do it. Use it to record sights, sounds, smells, tastes. If you've always wanted to write, it's about time you started—no excuses.

2. Travel with your senses

Suppose you could have either a week on a beach or a week exploring a hot, dangerous jungle. Which would you choose? Travel writers would rather go to the jungle. Don't be a tourist; be a traveler. Keep your eyes and ears open for unusual details. Professional travel writers don't just see the normal things (the pretty sunset); they spot things that most tourists don't see (the sound of a bat's wings, the way a boat leans in the wind). Learn from them. And interact with the local culture: talk to people, try the food, haggle in the markets. You can't write well about something unless you really understand it.

3. Look for a story

Like journalists, travel writers look for stories, not just descriptions. Find something unusual that has happened and ask why it happened and what the consequences were. Look for a beginning, a middle, and an ending. Alternatively, find an original angle. Thousands upon thousands of people have written about the Grand Canyon, but what if you could interview someone who lived in it, or parachuted into it, or got lost in it . . .?

4. No cash, but a strong stomach

Only a tiny minority of travel writers get paid to do it, and it's rarely enough money to live on. You need a combination of talent, luck, and perseverance. Oh, and a strong stomach. Who knows what you'll have to eat in the name of research?

Unit 3 | Page 40, Exercise 10a
Student B

The queen is traveling through the countryside when she decides that she wants to drive. The chauffeur gets into the back of the car, and the queen gets into the front and starts driving.
She goes too fast, and a police officer stops the car. One minute later the police officer calls headquarters.
"I can't make an arrest," he says. "This person is too important."
"Who is it?" asks the police chief. "The mayor?"
"No. Someone even more important than that."
"The governor?"
"No. Someone even more important than that."
"The president?"
"No. Someone even more important than that."
"Who can possibly be more important than the president?" asks the chief.
"I don't know, chief, but he has the queen as his chauffeur."

Unit 5 | Page 66, Exercise 8
Group B
You are the managers. You want:
– to build a new cafeteria with better food. The workers want a gym and swimming pool. You think the cafeteria is more important. You can't build both.
– to arrange buses for employees to come to work, but the employees must pay for a portion of the fare.
– to install some modern art in the reception area. This is to impress clients who visit the office.
Which issues are very important, important, not so important?
Decide how you will negotiate for what you want.

Unit 4 | Page 52, Exercise 7a
Text A

Not only _____ (1.) Junichi Ono have his first exhibition when he was eight, but the young artist _____ (2.) met Junichiro Koizumi and George W. Bush, such was his fame as a young prodigy. The boy had always been artistic. Only _____ (3.) he drew his first character, "Liberty-kun," at the age of six, _____ (4.) his mother, a designer, realize he was truly gifted. The picture, based on the Statue of Liberty, made Ono famous as a Japanese pop artist. Rarely _____ (5.) a day go by when Junichi isn't producing at least one new work. _____ (6.) occasionally do people notice how different he is. "He's a little strange," says one student. "He talks to himself a lot," says another.

Unit 7 | Page 90, Exercise 8
Student B
You want to have a wildlife sanctuary. You believe there needs to be a place where wild animals are protected. You think it's fine for some paying customers to come and view the wildlife, but you don't want too many tourists to spoil the atmosphere. You will bring in a lot of wildlife for the sanctuary.

Unit 8 | Page 99, Exercise 5
Student B
You regularly go to the gym with a friend, but he spends the whole time chatting, not exercising. You don't want to go with him any more, but you are afraid of hurting his feelings.

Unit 7 | Page 90, Exercise 8

Student C

You want to start an alternative community for a maximum of 50 people. The residents will farm the land, growing all their own food and living in harmony with nature. Throughout the year there will be music festivals, as well as regular yoga, tai chi, and a school for children.

Unit 3 | Page 40, Exercise 10a

Student C

A woman goes to a doctor, complaining of pain. "Where does it hurt?" asks the doctor.

"Everywhere," says the woman.

"Can you be more specific?"

So the woman touches her knee with her finger. "Ow!" she says. Then she touches her nose. "Ow!" Then she touches her back. "Ow!" Finally, she touches her cheek. "Ow!"

The doctor tells her to sit down, takes one look at her and says, "You have a broken finger."

Unit 10 | Page 119, Exercise 6a

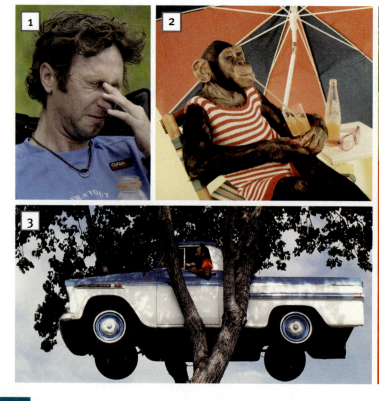

Unit 8 | Page 99, Exercise 5

Student C

Your friend is an Internet addict. She spends up to seven hours a day online. You want to help her, but you are worried that she will be offended.

Unit 4 | Page 52, Exercise 7a

Text B

Not _____ (1.) is Abigail Sin one of Singapore's greatest pianists; she is _____ (2.) a gifted mathematician, and she was able to read at the age of two. No sooner _____ (3.) Abigail Sin taken her first piano lesson at the age of five than she became hooked on the instrument. Only _____ (4.) she has completely mastered a piece of music _____ (5.) she stop for a break, sometimes practicing for 30 hours a week. Her twin brother, Josiah, is also talented, but the difference is the "fire inside." "She always practices the same stuff over and over again," complains the ten-year-old boy. _____ (6.) way would average children have the dedication to practice like this. While they are out playing with their friends, Abigail can be found in the music room, hammering away at the keys.

Unit 10 | Page 117, Exercise 6b

HOW OPTIMISTIC ARE YOU?

Add up your total score from the questionnaire on page 119. Then find your optimism rating below:

48–60: You are definitely a "glass-half-full" type of person—an eternal optimist. Almost nothing can make you feel bad. You greet life head-on, convinced that you cannot fail. And chances are that you will succeed a great deal of the time. However, it's important to take a minute every now and then to make sure that you are not being unrealistically optimistic.

30–47: You may have found a happy medium between optimism and pessimism. You know that it's important to have a positive outlook on life while at the same time being realistic about what you can and cannot achieve. If you are at the lower end of this spectrum, you may want to remember to try to ignore those negative thoughts when they begin to be more numerous than the positive ones.

12–29: Like many of us, you may think of yourself as a realist. Take care, however, not to let negative thought patterns rule your life. You may want to try cognitive restructuring—when you are aware of a negative thought, consciously replace it with a positive one. When something good happens in your life, realize that you are responsible for it, and don't assume that everything bad that happens is your fault.

Unit 5 | Page 59, Exercise, 2a

Reading B

RICHES TO RAGS

Most people who dream of winning the lottery assume that a big win would mean the end to all of their financial problems. Sometimes, however, winning a lot of money brings on an entirely new set of problems. Take, for example, William "Bud" Post, who won $16.2 million in the Pennsylvania lottery but ended up with nothing. "Everybody dreams of winning money, but nobody realizes the nightmares that come out of the woodwork, or the problems," he said just five years after winning. "I wish it'd never happened. It was a total nightmare."

Post's problems were partly of his own making and partly the result of friends and family who took advantage of him. "Promises he made to family members and his inability to control his spending led to most of the money he had won being squandered," said a lawyer who worked for Post. Post admitted that he went wild after his win. He bought expensive cars, motorcycles, houses, a sailboat, and a twin-engine plane. He even bought a car dealership for his brother and invested in a restaurant for another brother and sister. Neither business venture made any money for Post. Yet another of Post's brothers tried to hire a hit man to kill Post and his wife. The brother hoped to inherit Post's money.

Post had legal troubles, as well. A former girlfriend sued him for a share of the winnings, claiming that they had purchased the winning lottery ticket together. The court awarded her $5.3 million. In addition, Post served time in jail for firing a gun over the head of a bill collector. Within three months of receiving his first lottery payment, Post was $500,000 in debt. By the early 1990s, he had declared bankruptcy.

Post spent the last years of his life living quietly on a $450 monthly Social Security check. Once the money was gone, he was more content. "That's all I want. Just peace of mind," he declared.

Writing Bank

Unit 2 | Page 25, Exercise 11

Formal emails

1 Read the email and answer the questions.

    1. What did Mr. Reiss want?

    2. What is Ms. Du Pont offering?

    3. What can't she give Mr. Reiss?

    4. What can't she go to?

Writing skill | redrafting

2 After writing an email, you need to check it at least twice. Below are five things to check for. Match them to the examples of mistakes below.

    _____ **1.** greeting and signing off appropriately

    _____ **2.** coherence and cohesion

    _____ **3.** punctuation—do not write in capital letters or use multiple exclamations

    _____ **4.** spelling or typing mistakes

    _____ **5.** formal style

    a. Manny thanks, We have recieved the shipment.

    b. We are ABSOLUTELY DELIGHTED that Holborn Company has been able to guarantee the deal!!

    c. Dear Mrs. Winston,

    Thanks for the invitation, but I can't really go to the event because I've got tons of work to do right now.

    d. I have a number of questions concerning the contract. It is an excellent job opportunity. The salary is lower than I had expected. It also proposes that I work abroad for one month per year. It may pose a problem.

    e. Hi Mr. Kawazaka,

    Regarding your email on January 15th, 2007 . . .

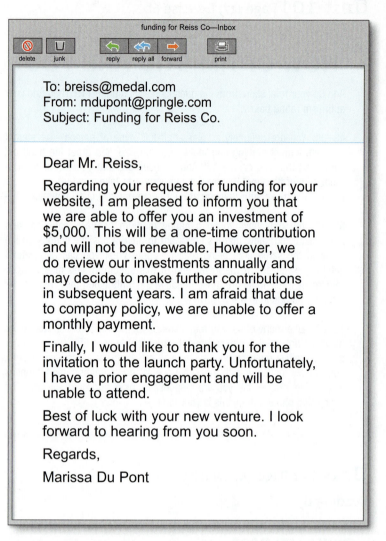

To: breiss@medal.com
From: mdupont@pringle.com
Subject: Funding for Reiss Co.

Dear Mr. Reiss,

Regarding your request for funding for your website, I am pleased to inform you that we are able to offer you an investment of $5,000. This will be a one-time contribution and will not be renewable. However, we do review our investments annually and may decide to make further contributions in subsequent years. I am afraid that due to company policy, we are unable to offer a monthly payment.

Finally, I would like to thank you for the invitation to the launch party. Unfortunately, I have a prior engagement and will be unable to attend.

Best of luck with your new venture. I look forward to hearing from you soon.

Regards,

Marissa Du Pont

Useful Phrases

Apologizing	• _I would like to apologize for the delay._
Giving good or bad news	• _I am pleased to inform you that . . ._ • _I regret to inform you that . . ._
Making a request	• _We would be grateful if you could . . ._
Responding to a request	• _We would be happy to . . ._ • _I am afraid we are unable to . . ._
Complaining	• _I am writing to complain about . . ._
Responding to an invitation	• _We would be very happy to come to . . ._ • _I am afraid I will be unable to attend._

Unit 6 | Page 76, Exercise 9a

Autobiographical statements

1. Read the autobiographical statement. Which summary is the most accurate?

   a. The writer is applying for a job at a design company.

   b. The writer is explaining how she became a graphic designer.

   c. The writer is trying to enroll in an academic program.

I was born in Miami, but I grew up in Reed City, which is a small town with not much to do, so my two sisters and I had to improvise and invent a lot of games. This is probably one reason I was good at making things. As a child, I always enjoyed designing objects to put in rooms, and my teachers encouraged me to develop my artistic abilities. I also found that I had a particular aptitude for math.

At the age of 18 I began an apprenticeship with a design company. I worked for Bilosh Design Solutions for two years, mainly doing clerical work in the office, but also observing some of the projects. During this time I learned a lot, especially from Judith Baker, who was my manager. She taught me how to solve problems by looking at things in a different way. From her I learned how to "think outside the box."

In 2011 I felt that I needed a new challenge, so I decided to enroll in a cartoon animation course. I spent a very enjoyable month working on film animation. It was at this time that I realized that my true vocation was designing graphics for advertisements and commercial films. For this reason, I have applied to the School for Design graphic design program. I hope to develop my skills so that I will be able to work in this field for the foreseeable future.

Cheryl Nemeth

Writing skill | redrafting

2. Here are some sentences and phrases that Cheryl wrote originally and then changed. Which sentences and phrases did she replace them with? Why are the rewritten sentences and phrases better (think about formal vs. informal, style, economy of words, repetition)?

Example: *"the town is incredibly boring"* she rewrote *"which is a small town with not much to do."* She changed this because the first version sounds too negative.

   1. I always enjoyed designing things

   2. I was also really good at math

   3. doing tasks like photocopying, sending faxes, mailing letters and ordering materials

   4. I'd had enough of Bilosh

   5. I will be able to work in graphic design

Useful Phrases	
Organizing time and sequence	• *as a child,* • *at the age of . . .* • *during this time,* • *I spent a month/year . . .* • *it was at this time that . . .* • *. . . for the foreseeable future*
Explaining stages in your career path	• *had an aptitude for . . .* • *began an apprenticeship* • *enroll in a program* • *apply to a program* • *my true vocation*

Cause and effect essays

1   Read the essay. Which title best fits the essay?

   a. Insomnia—Causes and Effects

   b. How Stress Affects Your Sleep

   c. Five Ideas for a Better Sleep

1 It has been estimated that around 90 percent of adults in the developed world have, at some time in their life, suffered from a period of insomnia of at least one week. Other recent research has shown
5 that women are nearly twice as likely as men to have it. There are a number of causes, which can be roughly put into three categories: lifestyle, environment, and health.

Lifestyle greatly affects the way we sleep. People
10 who smoke or drink alcohol and coffee (or other drinks with caffeine) close to bedtime are more vulnerable to insomnia. Another aspect of lifestyle that affects our sleep is physical activity. People who exercise are more likely to sleep soundly than those
15 who do no physical exercise. Also, those who work in highly stressful jobs, under a lot of pressure, often have trouble "turning off" and relaxing, and this affects the quality and quantity of their sleep.

The second cause is environment. Bedrooms
20 should be quiet, dark, and cool. Furthermore, they should not be used as an office or a place of work. Instead, the bedroom should be a retreat from our daily activities. While many people report that they get used to living in noisy neighborhoods, for others
25 silence is essential for a good night's sleep.

The third cause of insomnia is health. Both physical and mental health affect the way we sleep. Pain, illness, and an unhealthy diet leading to excess body fat can all cause insomnia. Regarding
30 mental health, any stressful situation causing emotions such as fear, panic, and nervousness may keep us from sleeping.

So what are the effects of insomnia? Many insomniacs report feeling drowsy during the
35 day. This prevents them from learning, recalling information, and concentrating to their full capacity. One potentially dangerous side effect of this may occur when they are handling machinery. A large number of car accidents take place because
40 of the effects of insomnia.

A further effect is irritability. Insomniacs may experience mood swings during which they feel angry for no reason, while long-term lack of sleep may lead to depression. For this reason, people who
45 are living with the insomniac need to be aware of the effects.

Writing skill | reference words

2   What do these words refer to?

   1. *it* (line 6)

   a. sleep   **b.** a partner who suffers from insomnia

   c. insomnia

   2. *those* (line 14)

   a. people   **b.** exercises   **c.** types of drink

   3. *they* (line 20)

   a. environments   **b.** people   **c.** bedrooms

   4. *this* (line 35)

   a. insomnia   **b.** feeling drowsy   **c.** the day

   5. *they* (line 42)

   a. feelings of depression   **b.** insomniacs

   c. mood swings

Useful Phrases

Text organization	• *The second . . .* • *The third . . .*
Adding information	• *Another* (aspect) • *Also* • *Furthermore* • *A further* (effect)
Referring	• *Regarding* • *For this reason*

Phrasal Verbs

A phrasal verb consists of two or more words: a verb + a particle (an adverb or a preposition) [+ a preposition]. The meaning of a phrasal verb is usually very different from the meaning of the verb alone. For example, the phrasal verbs *look up* (search for in a book or other source) and *look after* (care for) have very different meanings from *look*. Some phrasal verbs are intransitive, (they cannot take an object). The majority are transitive (they take an object). Sometimes the object can come after the particle or after the verb. For example, *hand in* your papers / *hand* your papers *in* / *hand* them *in*. These phrasal verbs are known as *separable*. With other phrasal verbs the words in the phrase cannot be separated; they are known as *inseparable*.

Some common phrasal verbs

Separable

Ask out	ask someone on a date
Bring up	1) raise children 2) mention a subject
Call back	return a phone call
Call off	cancel
Call up	make a phone call
Figure out	find the solution
Fill in	give detailed information
Fill out	writing information on a form
Fill up	fill completely
Give back	return
Hand out	give to each person in a group; distribute
Hold up	keep waiting
Look over	examine carefully
Look up	search for information in a book or other source
Make up	Invent (a story)
Pick up	1) lift 2) collect in a car
Put away	put something where it belongs
Put back	return to the place it was found
Put off	Delay doing something you don't want to do; procrastinate
Shut off	turn off; stop
Show up	make someone feel stupid or bad
Split up	to end a relationship
Take back	return
Tear down	destroy
Try on	put something on to check the fit
Turn around	change direction
Turn down	refuse
Turn in	1) produce a great result 2) tell the police about a criminal 3) go to bed
Turn up	increase the volume
Work out	resolve a problem

Inseparable

Catch on	1) understand 2) become popular
Come across	find by chance
Come by	visit
Come from	born in a place; originate
Come up with	invent or create something
Cut back/down on	use less; reduce
Fit in	be accepted by others
Get along with	have a friendly relationship
Get away from	escape
Get away with	go unnoticed or unpunished
Get in	enter
Get over	recover
Get up	get out of bed
Give up	stop trying
Go on	1) continue 2) happen
Go for	choose
Go through	1) experience 2) spend 3) check 4) be approved
Grow up	become an adult
Hang up	end a phone conversation
Keep out of	stay away from; not be involved
Make off with	steal
Make up	apologize after a quarrel
Look into	investigate
Look forward to	anticipate
Look up to	admire
Put up with	tolerate
See to	deal with someone or something
Take after	look or behave like a relative
Turn up	appear suddenly
Work out	exercise

Audioscript

UNIT 1 Achieving goals

▶ **1.02** (Page 9)

A: Mark, you speak seven languages.

B: That's right.

A: Can you tell us a little about your level of fluency and proficiency in the languages?

B: Well, Russian is probably my best language. I speak it pretty well because I spent a lot of time there, but it's a little rusty. I have a good ear, which is a good thing and a bad thing, because my accent makes people think that I know more than I really do. The other languages are mainly Latin-based: Spanish, Portuguese, Italian, but also French and Polish.

A: You learned the languages through a combination of techniques.

B: That's right: classes, travel, private study . . .

A: Did you use any special techniques? Any magic secrets?

B: Magic secrets, no. But I did do some interesting things, like memory training. I watched movies in their original languages, and at some point I tried sticking lists of words around the house. But I think for me it was more a case of being motivated. My biggest motivator was a love of languages and pleasure in communicating with people from other countries.

A: Would you say it's easier to learn new languages if you already know languages in that family? For example, you speak Spanish and French, so was it easy to pick up Portuguese?

B: I wouldn't say it was easy, but yeah, I would definitely say it helps. Occasionally it gets confusing, though. You might be speaking in one language and suddenly a word from another language slips out, causing complete confusion.

A: Is there any little word of encouragement you could offer those poor souls who are trying to master a language?

B: Hmm . . . that's a tricky one. What I would say is that knowing how to read and write a language doesn't mean you can speak it. You really have to get out there and try to speak at every opportunity. Take risks. Don't be afraid to look stupid, because that's the only way you're going to learn. And everyone has to start somewhere. When I was young, I went to France, after years of studying French, and, to my complete embarrassment, I couldn't speak the language or understand anything. All I could do was order breakfast in my hotel!

▶ **1.03** (Page 12)

To continue our series on famous firsts . . .

If you ask a Brazilian who first flew an airplane, she'll tell you it was Alberto Santos Dumont. Ask an American, and he'll answer the Wright brothers. In 1906, Santos Dumont was widely believed to have flown the first plane that was heavier than air. Others say that the Americans Wilbur and Orville Wright first flew in 1903. The truth is, we don't really know who flew first, though Santos

Dumont was certainly a colorful character. He's said to be the first person to have owned a flying machine for personal use. He kept his balloon tied up outside his Paris apartment and regularly flew to restaurants!

Question 2 . . . It's commonly assumed that Alexander Graham Bell invented the telephone, but now we're not so sure. Many people believe that Antonio Meucci, an Italian immigrant, got there first. And in 2003, files were discovered which suggest that a twenty-six-year-old German science teacher, Philipp Reis, invented the phone fifteen years before Bell.

Now, who was the first to the North Pole? In 1908, Dr. Frederick Cook said he'd done it, but it's commonly believed that he lied, and that a man named Robert Peary made it first. There are others who claim that neither of them reached the North Pole.

The light bulb. It's widely assumed that Thomas Edison invented it, but we don't really know for sure. Edison based a lot of his inventions on other people's ideas. Also, he worked with a team, and he never shared the credit.

Moving on to our soccer question, it's widely assumed that South America's soccer glory belongs to Brazil and Argentina. But it was Uruguay that hosted and won the first World Cup in 1930. They beat Argentina 4–2 in the final, in front of 93,000 people in Montevideo. The cheering of the crowd is said to have been the loudest noise ever heard in Uruguay.

Speaking of sports, it is often thought that rugby and sheep are the main claims to fame for New Zealand. Not many people know that in 1893 New Zealand became the first country to allow women to vote.

OK, question 7: Ellen MacArthur is sometimes wrongly assumed to be the first woman to sail around the world. She wasn't. She was the fastest but not the first. That honor goes to Naomi James, who did it in 1979. Apparently, she got so seasick that soon afterward she gave up sailing altogether.

And our final question. The ancient Olympic Games were of course first held in Greece. They were very different from the Games today. Instead of medals, the winners received a crown of laurel leaves. They were also said to be allowed to put their statue up on Olympus.

▶ **1.04** (Page 13)

In the news today . . .

A conservation institute has produced kittens by cross-breeding cloned adult wild cats. It is believed to be the first time that clones of wild animals have been bred. Researchers at the Audubon Center for Research of Endangered Species say that the development holds enormous potential for the preservation of endangered species.

Australian teenager Jessica Watson has succeeded in her attempt to become the youngest person to sail solo around the world. The 16-year old battled raging storms and monster 40-foot waves during her 7-month journey. In an interview following her triumphant arrival in Sydney Harbor, Ms. Watson stressed that teenagers, girls in particular, can do so much more than people generally expect of them.

And finally, the story of a man who has entered the record books as the world's most renowned eater of burgers. It is estimated that Don Gorske has eaten over 15,000 Big Macs, and he even proposed to his girlfriend Mary in the parking lot of a McDonald's. In fifteen years, he says, he has missed a Big Mac on only seven occasions, including the death of his mother, a snowstorm and a 600-mile drive without a McDonald's in sight.

▶ **1.05** (Page 16)

1. When I was in college, a friend of mine was injured in an accident while playing football. He was paralyzed and needed to spend the rest of his life in a wheelchair. Together with some friends I decided to organize a sponsored bike ride to raise money for his family and other people in similar situations. So we set up a charity called "One Step Ahead" and arranged to bike from Scotland to Gibraltar. I'd never done anything like that before, so it was a fantastic learning experience. I'd always thought it would be great to bike across a whole country, but this exceeded my expectations. There were about twenty or thirty of us on bikes, and the rest of the crew in vans with all the equipment and camping gear. It was very tough, especially in Spain where we had to battle against the heat. But we had a fantastic time, and at the end, when we arrived, there was a huge party. We were even on the news! We felt we'd accomplished something really important, and most importantly, we raised lots of money for people with spinal injuries.

2. I've been doing volunteer work here in the rain forest, in Brazil, for a while now. Next week I'll have been here for three months, helping to teach English to the young children in the village. It's been an amazing experience. I'd never even left the U.S. before, so you can imagine how different things are for me here. When I arrived I really didn't know what to expect. It was a real culture shock, and I was here on my own for the first couple of months. Now my girlfriend has joined me, and things are a little bit easier. I've been living with a small tribe of people in the forest. I'd never done any teaching before, so the whole thing has been quite a challenge, and I've learned a lot. But some of the children are speaking pretty good English with me now, and a few of them are actually starting to write little stories, so I feel a real sense of achievement.

3. I ran the Cracovia Marathon last year. It was my first marathon, and it was great. It felt like a major achievement. I had to train really hard, getting up early in the morning to run before going to work. And as the distances got longer I had to get up earlier and earlier. It was incredibly hard, because I'd never done any training like that before. I've always run, just for myself, to relax and keep fit, but this was a chance to be more competitive and really push myself to the limit. It was a fantastic run, because Cracovia is a beautiful city, and there's such a special atmosphere as you go

along the route, with people cheering you on. My parents even came over from Australia to see me cross the finish line. I couldn't move for about a week afterwards, but I was glad I'd done it, and I'm looking forward to the next one.

▶ 1.06 (Page 16)

1. Jake, this is my friend Amy, whom I've known forever.
2. I asked what had happened, but nobody could tell me.
3. I chose this school because I'd heard it was the best.
4. Before I came to the U.S., I'd never been abroad.
5. I'm so exhausted. I've been working really hard.
6. By the time she retires, she'll have been working there for more than fifty years.

▶ 1.07 (Page 18)

If you chose mostly (a), then you are very comfortable as you are, and you're not too interested in new challenges. I think you need to make an effort to get off the couch. Go on! Take a risk—it might have a positive effect!

Now, if your answers were mainly (b), it means you love a challenge and you take advantage of your opportunities. You're willing to try anything and everything. So, good luck, but be careful!

Those of you who chose mainly (c), well, you tend to check everything out before committing yourself. You are very cautious. You may live a long, safe life, but a bit of a challenge from time to time won't do you any harm!

UNIT 2 Places and communities

▶ 1.08 (Page 20)

1. I'm from South Africa. I spent two and a half years, actually more like two years, living in Vancouver, Canada. My wife and I were trying to set up our own business there as packagers in the publishing industry. Unfortunately, things weren't going very well economically. Canada wasn't in a depression, but it wasn't a very good time to try and start your own business in publishing. What did I like about Vancouver? Well, Vancouver is one of the most beautiful cities in the world. In fact, Vancouver is regularly named as one of the best places in the world to live. It's stunningly beautiful, with mountains, sea, forests and natural beauty. Vancouver is a city where you can walk to the beach on your lunch break if you want to. You can take a bus and go skiing in the mountains forty minutes later. Canadian food is not at the top of the world's list of good food, but Vancouver has very large Chinese and Indian populations, as well as people from all over the world, so you can eat some very good food in Vancouver. The only food that people might consider uniquely Vancouverite is what they would call "fusion" cuisine, which mixes Asian, European, and local cuisines. My best memories about

Canada? Well, the open spaces, the vastness, and the friendly people.

2. I'm from Mexico originally, but over the past ten years I've lived in Spain, Austria, France, and other parts of the UK. I lived in Austria for a year when I was about twenty-two. I was studying German, so I wanted to spend a year in a German-speaking country. I was a teaching assistant. I worked in a school four days a week, which meant I had long weekends. I usually traveled with my friends on the weekends. We went to Slovenia, The Czech Republic, Italy, and Germany. Some other great things about living there were skiing and ice skating on lakes. The scenery was spectacular, and the people were really welcoming. The thing I didn't really like was the food, because I'm vegetarian, and in Austria they eat a lot of meat. Apart from that, everything else was great. I think my favorite memories of Austria are the scenery, being able to go off into the mountains after school every afternoon, and going skiing or swimming in the lakes in the summer. I'd definitely like to go back one day.

3. I lived in Japan, actually in Tokyo, for about two years. It was, as you can imagine, a completely crazy experience for me, coming from my small, quiet home town. I was living in Tokyo because I was working as an English language teacher for a language school in a suburb of Tokyo. I really loved Tokyo. It was such an interesting experience. It was like being dropped into a lifestyle that was completely different from my own. Even going to the supermarket was an adventure, because I couldn't read anything. I got a few surprises, a few foods that I'd never seen before, but they were usually good. I think my favorite memories of the country would have to be the people. Because I was teaching English, I knew a lot of Japanese people as students and as colleagues in the school. They were friendly, funny, and really interested in what a foreigner like me was doing in Tokyo. They were very helpful when it came to explaining things like social customs in Japan. It was a really rewarding experience, some of the best times of my life.

▶ 1.09 (Page 23)

A: The Internet has made a big difference in my life. I mean, communication is so much easier than it was before.
B: Sure, I'd agree with that. But I still say that face-to-face communication is better. Sending an email is not nearly as personal and meaningful as a conversation.
A: Well, it depends . . .
B: On what?
A: Well, an email isn't as good as seeing someone you love, or your friends, but I'd much rather email my clients then go to meetings or talk on the phone. It saves time.
B: True, but I just think the more we use email, the more we need it. It's like an addiction, with people checking their emails every five minutes, even in meetings.

A: Yeah, but I'd still rather have it than not.
B: And, there's so much false information. Do you use it to do research?
A: All the time. I think it's OK. Maybe it's not quite as good as looking in books. It's not as reliable, but it's considerably faster.
B: I'd say that looking something up on the Internet is only slightly less reliable than shouting out the window, "Does anybody know the answer to this?" It's not regulated. Anyone can publish anything on the Internet, and it may or may not be true.
A: Well the best thing about the Internet is that it lets you do things more cheaply than before, like buying plane tickets, and buying stuff on e-bay.
B: I've never used e-bay.
A: Or Amazon. You love buying books . . .
B: Yeah, but I'd rather go to a second hand bookstore. I'm not into the idea of giving my credit card information over the Internet. No way.
A: There're lots of security measures these days . . .

▶ 1.10 (Page 30)

1. I'm a member of an alumni club, which is basically a way to keep in touch with your old friends from school. Every five or ten years we have a reunion and remember the old days, some good, some bad . . . We also get involved in some charity events. Recently, we actually sponsored some events to save our old school, which was going to be closed. I felt really great about that. We meet only once every two years as a group. We have a big party and reunite with all the people that we remember, and some of the teachers as well. What's really interesting about the group is that we've all known each other now for about 20 years. It's so interesting to meet people every two years and see how they've changed. I'm sure that if I hadn't seen those people for 20 years, I wouldn't recognize them on the street now. Hmm . . . if there's something that I don't like, it's that it's very difficult to keep in touch when you only meet every two years. And sometimes people aren't as involved as they should be, sometimes you don't hear anything for a year or two. But I will definitely stick with it, because it keeps me better connected than I probably would be if I weren't a member.

2. I'm a member of a ballroom dancing club. There are lessons, but it's also social. There's about . . . oh I suppose . . . it must be about thirty people in the club, and I think I'm the youngest there. I go with a friend of mine, who's my dance partner. It's really fun. I joined about six months ago on a whim because I just had an urge to try ballroom dancing. I've never been very coordinated as a dancer, and I'm not very good at choreography, but it's been really great. There are a lot of beginners in the class, so I never feel out of place. We meet once a week, in a local school gym. We meet in the evenings after work, and it can be hard to get out of

the house in the evening, but it's so much fun, it's well worth the effort. So far we've been learning . . . the Waltz, the Foxtrot, and some Latin dances like the Jive and the Tango. I love it.

UNIT 3 Stories

▶ 1.11 **(Page 33)**

1. In 1957 a news program called *Panorama* broadcast a story about spaghetti trees in Switzerland. While the reporter told the story, Swiss farmers in the background were picking spaghetti from trees. Following this, thousands of people called the show, asking how to grow spaghetti trees.

2. In 1998 large numbers of Americans went to Burger King asking for a new type of burger. The food company had published an ad in USA Today announcing the new "left-handed Whopper," a burger designed for left-handed people. The following day, Burger King admitted that they had been joking all along.

▶ 1.12 **(Page 35)**

1. My favorite fictional character is Linda Hammerick, in the book *Bitter in the Mouth*, by Monique Truong. Linda, or Lin Dao, as we later learn is her real name, is a really strong-minded girl growing up in North Carolina, in the U.S. The story is partly about her difficult relationship with her mother and grandmother, and partly about the problems that Linda has to overcome. She has a condition known as synesthesia, which in her case means that almost every word triggers an actual taste in her mouth. For example, every time she hears her own name, Linda, she tastes mint. Every time she hears the word *you*, she tastes canned green beans, and so on. The thing is, it's not until the end of the book that she learns that this is a condition that other people have, that she's not alone. So she spends the first 30 years of her life trying to hide what's going on from everyone except Kelly, her best friend. (The name Kelly tastes like canned peaches, by the way.) One of the other really interesting things about the character is we don't learn until halfway through the book that she's Vietnamese American. So, even though the book describes her as having long, dark hair, the picture I had in my mind changed slightly halfway through the book. I thought that was kind of cool. Anyway, I admire Linda for her strength, and also for her ability to empathize with others, to see things from their perspective.

2. I think my favorite fictional character has to be the lead character, the heroine of Jane Austen's *Pride and Prejudice*. I think she's one of the best-drawn characters in literature. She is of course Elizabeth Bennett. She's lively, she's feisty, and when you think that this is a book that's set in the 1800s, it's really remarkable that such a modern woman is the heroine. I mean, she talks back to all these men who are older than her and in more authority than her. It's great. She's a good role model for today's women too. I imagine her as being pretty tall, with a lively face and dark hair. Hmm . . . memorable things that she does: well, the thing that I really like about her is the way that she takes control of her own life in a period of history when women really had very little power and very little control over who they married. She sort of comes to a self-realization through the events of the novel and decides to go for the guy that she really likes. She has problems along the way: people who think she's socially unacceptable, or people who have very typical views about class and society. But, of course, she succeeds and wins Mr. Darcy, her true love, in the end.

3. I think my favorite fictional character is the old man from *The Old Man and the Sea*, by Ernest Hemingway. I still have a strong visual image of this man. The whole story takes place in a boat off the coast of Cuba, with just this one character, mostly. I imagine him to be pretty old. He was a lifelong fisherman. He had a tough life, so I imagine he had really big strong hands that were . . . cut and bruised from hauling in nets every night out in the ocean. I imagine him with a little bit of grey hair, old and wise, somebody who took a lot of pride in his work. He is down on his luck in the story. He hasn't caught anything for a long time, but he still drags himself out every night and casts his nets and hopes that he'll catch something.

In a way, he sort of reminds me of my father, somebody who had limited opportunities in life, but found a job that he could do and did it to the best of his ability.

▶ 1.13 **(Page 39)**

Groucho Marx didn't want to be a comedian at first. He loved reading and singing, and he wanted to become a doctor. But his mother had other ideas. She persuaded Groucho and his brothers to start a group called The Six Mascots. During a radio show they started making jokes, and that's when they decided to become a comedy act. Their popularity grew quickly. But in 1926 the boys' mother died, and the Great Depression began. In the 1930's a man called Irving Thalberg helped the Marx Brothers to get on television. They made their most famous movies, the last of which was called *A Day At the Races*. After this, Groucho became a radio host and he also made more movies, but without his brothers. In the 1970's he toured with a live one-man show, but by now in his nineties he was getting weaker, and he died in 1977.

▶ 1.14 **(Page 40)**

Three colleagues, a photographer, a journalist and an editor are covering a political convention. One day, during their lunch break, they walk along a beach, and one of them sees a lamp. He picks it up and rubs it, and a magic genie suddenly appears. The genie says "You can each have one wish." So the photographer says, "I want to spend the rest of my life in a big house in the mountains with a beautiful view, where I can take photographs." Poof!

Suddenly the photographer is gone to his home in the mountains. Then it's the journalist's turn. "I want to live in a big house in the countryside with an enormous garden where I can sit and write for the rest of my life." Poof! The journalist is gone. Finally, the genie says to the editor, "And what about you? What's your wish?" So the editor says, "I want those two back before lunch. We've got a deadline at 6:00 tonight."

UNIT 4 Moving forward

▶ 1.15 **(Page 43)**

Resistance to antibiotics is on the increase. Research out today shows an increase in the number and strength of superbugs, resistant to normal antibiotics. Analysis of particularly resistant strains, kept in laboratory test tubes, shows that in the last twelve months . . .

A new virus, developed by hackers in South East Asia has been crashing computer networks around the globe. The virus penetrates standard firewalls to affect computer software and eventually data stored in the microchip. Experts have warned that . . .

A breakthrough in genetic engineering technology means that human cloning can now enable scientists to re-build damaged organs in children. Cells taken from skin tissue are used to provide the necessary genes, which are then implanted . . .

The ongoing budget crisis has been cited as the reason for the latest delay to the space mission. The new shuttle, Discover XVIII, which was originally due to launch last Thursday, is set to orbit Mars, scanning the surface for evidence of early life-forms.

▶ 1.16 **(Page 44)**

A: It says name four superheroes. Can you think of any?

B: Well, there's . . . let's see . . . Superman . . .

C: Spiderman, Batman . . .

B: The Incredible Hulk . . .

C: The Fantastic Four . . .

B: The Incredibles . . .

A: Well, that's definitely more than four . . . Should we move on? The next one is about the color of the Incredible Hulk . . .

C: He was green, wasn't he?

B: I heard the original comic book version was actually grey, but a printing error made him appear green, and the comic's writers decided that it suited him, so they let it stay.

A: Oh . . . what do you know? OK — can you name four of Spiderman's special powers?

B: Well, he can walk up walls using his spider-grip, he has super-strength . . .

C: . . . and can lift up to 10 tons . . .

B: He has web shooters which he can fire to catch villains and . . . he has spider-sense . . .

C: Yes . . . a kind of ESP that allows Parker to sense when danger is afoot, and spider-speed, so he can run fast to escape danger.

A: OK . . . the name of the planet where Superman was born was . . .

C: . . . Planet Krypton, wasn't it?

A: Of course! OK, what was the name of the movie released in 2002 that broke all box office records in the first weekend?

B: Oh, that must be Spiderman, without a doubt!

A: Great! And last, the name of the female character who has super-strength, bullet-proof bracelets and . . .

C: . . . a lasso that makes people tell the truth . . . Wonder Woman!

▶ **1.17** (Page 46)

A: Legendary veteran comic writer Stan Lee co-created Spiderman and the Fantastic Four, among others.
We asked him how he thought of Spiderman, and this was his response.

B: In trying to create a superhero, the first thing you have to think of, or at least the first thing I have to think of, is a super-power. What super-power would be different, that people hadn't seen before? I had already done the Hulk, who was the strongest character on Earth; I had done a group called the Fantastic Four: one of them could fly, one was invisible, and one's body could stretch, and I was trying to think: what else can I do? And I've told this story so often that for all I know it might even be true! But I was sitting and watching a fly crawling on the wall, and I thought "Gee—that would be great—what if a character could crawl on walls like an insect?" So I had my super-power, but then I needed a name. So I thought, "Insectman" . . . that didn't sound good. Crawlingman? I went on and on . . . Mosquitoman? . . . and then somehow I said "Spiderman" and it just sounded dramatic and mysterious to me, so that was my name.

A: When asked why he made Spiderman a scientist, he replied . . .

B: I had always resented the fact that in most superhero stories and actually, in most comic books the hero is some sort of a rugged, muscular outdoorsman, a sportsman . . . an adventurer. And anybody who was literate or scholarly, they were . . . he was always considered to be somewhat of a nerd. And I thought, my gosh, people don't have enough respect for intelligence. So again, in trying to be different, and in trying to be realistic, I thought I would make my teenage hero a scholarship student, extra-bright—he was studying science. And just to show that there's no reason why a hero couldn't also be a kid who likes science and is good in school and is smart . . . and that was the thinking behind it.

A: When asked if he was at all scientific, he replied . . .

B: I'm not much of a scientist. I love reading science-fiction but when it comes to actual science, I'm . . . I'm a dummy. But I like to make things seem scientific!

A: Our final question asked if Stan Lee thought there would ever be real superheroes.

B: I believe that they will be able, through cloning . . . through genetics they will be able to find a way to abolish most diseases. They will be able . . . they will have to . . . see, once these wars are finished with, if they ever are, we're going to want to go to the planets, they're going to want to go to Mars. Now, it's such a long trip, and it'll be so hard to get back again, they're going to have to make human beings able to adapt to Mars, adapt themselves . . . or is it adopt? I never . . . I always get those two mixed up. But at any rate, I believe that they will find a way to make people able to live in the atmosphere of Mars, through altering them genetically . . . Because of genetics, I think we can do virtually anything.

▶ **1.18** (Page 48)

1. Do you think you'll still be studying English?
2. Do you think you'll have the same lifestyle?
3. Do you think you'll be living in the same place?
4. Do you think your country will have a different government?
5. Do you think you'll have changed much?
6. Do you think you'll have the same interests?
7. Do you think you'll have the same close friends?
8. Do you think you'll have seen more of the world?

▶ **1.19** (Page 49)

Conversation 1

A: Hello?

B: Hi, Kevin. It's Tina.

A: Oh hi, Tina. How are you?

B: Great. You?

A: Pretty good.

B: Are you busy this Saturday?

A: Um . . . sort of. I'm playing soccer.

B: Oh, I didn't know you played soccer.

A: I don't really. Well, once in a while.

B: Are you playing all day Saturday?

A: Yeah, pretty much all day.

B: What are you up to in the evening?

A: I might be free. Let me think. Mm, maybe about eight-ish. What are you thinking?

B: We're thinking of going to Riverside Café. . .

A: Oh yeah? I used to go there every so often when I was a student. Do you want me to pick you up?

B: Um, or should I drive?

A: I don't mind driving.

B: Actually, it'll be easier if I take my car. I think I'll drive . . .

Conversation 2

C: Lauren James.

D: Hi, sweetheart.

C: Oh, hi.

D: Still working?

C: Yep.

D: Hard day?

C: Kind of. Nothing major, just the usual.

D: Such as?

C: Filling out forms, replying to emails, that kind of thing.

D: Uh-huh.

C: Going over the schedules again, checking budgets, etcetera. Actually, there were tons of mistakes.

D: Really?

C: Yeah. But I'm almost finished.

D: Would you like me to get dinner started?

C: That would be great.

D: Pasta maybe? Or there's chicken in the fridge.

C: Chicken sounds good. I'll be home in an hour or so.

D: OK, I'll put the chicken in the oven . . . [fade out]

▶ **1.20** (Page 52)

A: Can you tell us a little bit about the case and what made it so special?

B: The case concerned a pair of twins called John and Michael. They were in their late teens, but they were very small for their age, and they wore thick glasses. They used to get laughed at in school, because, in a conventional sense, they weren't very bright or social.

A: They were outsiders.

B: Well, that's right. Outsiders. But they had an amazing gift. You could name any date in the past or future forty thousand years and they would be able to tell you what day of the week it was.

A: So I could say, for example, June 5th 1376, and they could tell me it was Sunday or Monday, etcetera?

B: That's right. But that wasn't all. During one interview, the psychologist dropped a box of matches on the floor and the twins immediately called out "one hundred and eleven." The psychologist counted the matches and there were exactly one hundred and eleven.

A: And the twins hadn't counted them?

B: No. There was no time. As soon as the matches hit the floor, they knew there were one hundred and eleven. Now another thing the twins could do was remember extremely long sequences of numbers. You could say a number of up to three hundred digits, and they were able to repeat it back to you perfectly.

A: So they basically have an extraordinary ability with numbers.

B: Not only with numbers. They have another talent, which is that you can name any day of their lives since they were about four years old, and they are able to tell you what the weather was like, what they did, and other events in the wider world. They can remember absolutely everything about that day.

A: Just any ordinary day.

B: Any and every ordinary day.

A: Obviously the twins, John and Michael, were studied at length by various psychologists, educators . . .

B: Yes, they were.

A: What progress did these people make in coming up with explanations of their ability?

B: I think the main thing is that we realize that John and Michael's ability is actually visual as well as mathematical. If you ask them how they do it, they say they can "see" the answers. When the box of matches fell, they "saw" one hundred and eleven. It wasn't a calculation. Similarly, they can "see" themselves as five year-olds. Somehow they have an ability to record incredible numbers of things in the mind. Of course, we have no idea how it works, but it would be very interesting to learn.

▶ 1.21 (Page 54)

1. Great discoveries of our time . . . well, in the last one hundred years or so, I guess it would be medical advances, like the use of x-rays, or the discovery of penicillin by Fleming. I mean, he made that discovery almost by mistake, and it changed modern medicine completely. Or perhaps the discovery of the structure of DNA by Watson and Crick in the fifties. That paved the way for genetics and genetic engineering . . .

2. I would say that sending man to the moon was one of the greatest scientific achievements. The man who invented the liquid-fuelled rocket, Robert Goddard, was fascinated by the idea of sending a rocket into space, and he spent years researching his ideas, until he developed the first rocket, called Nell. It was 10 feet tall, and he fired it from his aunt's farm in the U.S. At first nothing happened, but when the fuel finally ignited, the rocket was launched. It only reached a disappointing 14 yards into the air though, and scientists were skeptical of its success. When the newspapers got hold of the story they wrote the headlines "Moon rocket misses target by 238,799 miles." But later, engineers in Germany and America used his ideas, and the film footage of Nell to develop military and space exploring rockets. The *New York Times* had to write Goddard a public apology.

3. Computers, definitely, especially information technology and the Internet. The whole way that information is distributed and kept has been revolutionized by information technology. And things have happened so quickly. I mean, the first computer was built in 1948, I think. And was so big it took up a whole room! If you think about the designs now, and the capacity, it's just amazing. And it has made the world a smaller place, because it is so easy now to get information about almost anything.

4. I don't think we should underestimate the importance of domestic appliances, like the washing machine, dishwasher, etcetera. These timesaving inventions made it easier for women to enter the workforce, and that has had a huge impact on society. Or maybe it should be the advances in travel, with the bicycle, then the car and the airplane. The world must have been a very different place when the fastest way to get anywhere was on a horse! . . .

UNIT 5 Making money

▶ 1.22 (Page 57)

1. He can't complain. It's his own fault he didn't get a raise.
2. We are by no means certain that it is the same man committing the crimes.

3. What I really miss is having enough time to spend with friends.
4. They didn't understand what we wanted at all.
5. The employees actually love coming to work.
6. It was always Sammy who got into trouble.
7. Keith wasn't the least bit annoyed when we cancelled the meeting.

▶ 1.23 (Page 58)

While we're on the subject of choosing business partners, I cringe whenever I hear that two old friends or family members are planning to start a business together as fifty–fifty partners. It isn't that doing business with friends and family is a bad idea—many very successful businesses are family-owned. It's just that being someone's friend or relative is one of the worst reasons I can think of for making that someone your business partner. One of the problems is that once someone becomes your business partner, there is generally only one way to get rid of them (legally, of course) if things don't work out.

You must buy them out for the fair value of their interest in the business. And that can be an expensive proposition.

There are a few ways to determine if someone has what it takes to be your business partner, however.

Firstly, you need to decide, are you a visionary, or an operations person? Successful partnerships combine those two kinds of people. A visionary is a strategic, "big picture" thinker who understands the business model, the market, and the overall business plan. An operations person is someone who rolls up their sleeves, wades up to their hip boots in the details and executes the strategy that the visionary comes up with. You are either one or the other—it is almost impossible to be both. Once you have determined if you are a "visionary" or an "operations person," look for your opposite number. That way your business is more likely to strike the right balance between strategy and tactics.

Do you have all the skills you need on board to make the business work? Perhaps you are an inventor who is excellent at product design but clueless about selling. Perhaps you have a strong marketing background but need someone to help you crunch the numbers and make sure your products or services can be delivered within budget. Your partners should complement your set of business skills, not duplicate them. Keep in mind that you can acquire someone's skills without making them a partner. If a particular skill, such as contract negotiation or bookkeeping, is not critical to the success of your business, you may be better off hiring a lawyer, accountant, or consultant to do it for you and keeping ownership of your business.

Can you communicate directly and honestly with this person, without pulling any punches? Communication between partners can often get rough; disagreements and arguments break out all the time. It is difficult to criticize someone harshly, yet sometimes you must be cruel with your business partners in order to do the right thing for your business. Your business may

well suffer if you consistently hold back important information for fear of offending your partner or jeopardizing the underlying friendship or emotional bond between you.

Sometimes the most successful business partnerships are those where the partners do not socialize outside the office.

And lastly, is your business partner willing to hang around for the long haul? This is the critical test of a business partner. Many people are happy to help out with a business during its start-up phase, only to lose interest later on when something more attractive (like a job offer from a big corporation) comes along, a life-changing event (like the birth of a new child) occurs, or the going is getting tougher and the business isn't as much "fun" as it used to be. If you are not sure if someone is committed to the long-term success of your business, make them an employee or independent contractor, with perhaps an 'option' to acquire an interest in your business at a date two or three years down the road . . . provided, of course, they are still working for you at that time and you continue to be satisfied with their performance.

▶ 1.24 (Page 58)

Section 1

While we're on the subject of choosing business partners, I cringe whenever I hear that two old friends or family members are planning to start a business together as fifty–fifty partners. It isn't that doing business with friends and family is a bad idea—many very successful businesses are family-owned. It's just that being someone's friend or relative is one of the worst reasons I can think of for making that someone your business partner. One of the problems is that once someone becomes your business partner, there is generally only one way to get rid of them (legally, of course) if things don't work out.

You must buy them out for the fair value of their interest in the business. And that can be an expensive proposition.

Section 2

There are a few ways to determine if someone has what it takes to be your business partner, however.

Firstly, you need to decide, are you a visionary, or an operations person? Successful partnerships combine those two kinds of people. A visionary is a strategic, "big picture" thinker who understands the business model, the market, and the overall business plan. An operations person is someone who rolls up their sleeves, wades up to their hip boots in the details and executes the strategy that the visionary comes up with. You are either one or the other—it is almost impossible to be both. Once you have determined if you are a "visionary" or an "operations person," look for your opposite number. That way your business is more likely to strike the right balance between strategy and tactics.

Section 3

Do you have all the skills you need on board to make the business work? Perhaps you are an inventor who is excellent at product design but clueless about selling. Perhaps you have a strong marketing

background but need someone to help you crunch the numbers and make sure your products or services can be delivered within budget. Your partners should complement your set of business skills, not duplicate them. Keep in mind that you can acquire someone's skills without making them a partner. If a particular skill, such as contract negotiation or bookkeeping, is not critical to the success of your business, you may be better off hiring a lawyer, accountant, or consultant to do it for you and keeping ownership of your business.

Section 4

Can you communicate directly and honestly with this person, without pulling any punches? Communication between partners can often get rough; disagreements and arguments break out all the time. It is difficult to criticize someone harshly, yet sometimes you must be cruel with your business partners in order to do the right thing for your business. Your business may well suffer if you consistently hold back important information for fear of offending your partner or jeopardizing the underlying friendship or emotional bond between you.

Section 5

Sometimes the most successful business partnerships are those where the partners do not socialize outside the office.

And lastly, is your business partner willing to hang around for the long haul? This is the critical test of a business partner. Many people are happy to help out with a business during its start-up phase, only to lose interest later on when something more attractive (like a job offer from a big corporation) comes along, a life-changing event (like the birth of a new child) occurs, or the going is getting tougher and the business isn't as much 'fun' as it used to be. If you are not sure if someone is committed to the long-term success of your business, make them an employee or independent contractor, with perhaps an 'option' to acquire an interest in your business at a date two or three years down the road . . . provided, of course, they are still working for you at that time and you continue to be satisfied with their performance.

▶ **1.25** (Page 64)

A: 98 percent of staff working at Blue Skies Recruitment say they laugh a lot with their team. As many as 95 percent say that they are excited about where the company is going. So what do they have to smile about? Last month this small San Francisco-based company won a prestigious award for being one of the best small companies to work for in the U.S. With us today is Will Counts, CEO of Blue Skies. Will, first of all, tell us a little bit more about the company and what you do.

B: Good morning. Well, Blue Skies is more than just a normal recruitment agency. The difference is that we actually train and then place college graduates in sales jobs. That means we have a lot of young people working for us, so it's a bit like a continuation of college, but with a salary. We're only a small company, with as few as sixty employees, but there's a great deal of energy in our office.

A: Yes, your employees have said that it's a fun atmosphere, with smart outgoing people. You have regular parties, an annual ski weekend, a present for the most-appreciated employee of the month, and plenty of other benefits. I'm not much of an expert on these things. Why such an emphasis on staff incentives?

B: Well, our employees are young and highly qualified. They are good at what they do, and they believe in it. We have trained sales people going into companies to try and place graduates. Quite a few of them get offered the job themselves. If we didn't treat our employees well, they would quickly get poached by other companies. So the incentives need to be good to keep people.

A: So how are your salaries?

B: Salaries are high and there are monthly, performance-related cash bonuses. Employees also set their own targets for the coming year, and for the most part they have a say in their incentives as well.

A: And how about the atmosphere in the office. How do you influence that?

B: We have a company café, where we offer free breakfasts, and cappuccino all day long. People spend a lot of time in there discussing ideas over coffee, but it's very productive.

A: The vast majority of your employees say that they admire their managers, and feel that they can actively contribute to the future success of the company. How did you achieve this?

B: Well, one of the things is that we help them with finding somewhere nice to live. Rent is very expensive in San Francisco, and as a lot of our employees are just fresh out of college, with a lot of debt, they don't have a large budget for rent. So, we bought some homes, and quite a few employees rent them from us at reasonable rates. It makes a real difference. It means that working for the company becomes a lifestyle choice. They are involved personally. Also, we like to give people a say in the company. We have monthly meetings to discuss big issues, when we all sit around and talk about things. Initially, only a handful of people would come to the meetings. So we decided to offer free food, sandwiches and pizza, and now everyone comes, and everyone has something to say.

▶ **1.26** (Page 64)

1. As many as 95 percent say that they are excited about where the company is going.

2. Will, first of all, tell us a little bit more about the company and what you do.

3. We're only a small company, with as few as sixty employees, but there's a great deal of energy in our office.

4. You have regular parties, an annual ski weekend, a present for the most-appreciated employee of the month, and plenty of other benefits.

5. I'm not much of an expert on these things.

6. Employees also set their own targets for

the coming year, and for the most part they have a say in their incentives as well.

7. The vast majority of your employees say that they admire their managers.

8. So, we bought some homes, and quite a few employees rent them from us at reasonable rates.

9. Initially, only a handful of people would come to the meetings.

▶ **1.27** (Page 66)

A: Well, if we had a million dollars, I'd replace these chairs for a start. No wonder I've got a backache.

B: Oh come on, we can do better than that. How about an all-expense-paid trip to the Bahamas or something?

A: Would you really want to go on a vacation with our co-workers?

B: Well, no, but . . .

A: I think it should be spent on day-to-day things that'll make a difference here, like renovating the office.

B: That is so boring!

A: Or maybe . . . what d'you mean boring?!

B: Well, it's lots of money—let's have some fun! The company could get a house on the beach that the employees could use whenever they wanted.

A: Yes, but that would only be useful once every few years for each person. It wouldn't make the least bit of difference for most of us. My first priority would be to do something practical with the money . . .

UNIT **6** Understanding power

▶ **1.28** (Page 69)

A: "La Tour Eiffel" in Paris was built in 1889 to commemorate the 100th anniversary of the French Revolution. The Industrial Revolution in Europe had brought about a new trend—the use of metal in construction. The tower, built from a lattice made from very pure iron, is light and able to withstand high wind pressures. For 40 years from the time that it was built, it stood as the tallest tower in the world, and today it is still the tallest building in Paris.

B: The Pentagon, covering 34 acres, is thought to be the largest office building in the world. It takes a person fifteen to twenty minutes to walk around the building once. It was built in five concentric rings, in record time during the Second World War, in order to relocate employees of the War Department from the seventeen buildings they occupied within Washington D.C.

A: Built between 1406 and 1420 during the Ming dynasty, The Forbidden City, also called the Purple Forbidden City, or Gugong Museum in Chinese, is located in the center of Beijing. Occupying a rectangular area of more than 720,000 square meters, the Forbidden City was the imperial home of twenty-four emperors of the Ming (1368–1644) and Qing (1644–1911) dynasties. It is one of the largest and best-preserved palace complexes in the world, with over a million rare and valuable objects in the museum.

B: The CN Tower, a communications and observation tower in Toronto, Canada, was named for Canadian National, the railway company that built it. Completed in 1976, the 553-meter CN Tower was the world's tallest tower for 34 years. It remains the tallest free-standing structure in the Western Hemisphere and attracts more than two million visitors each year. From its Sky Pod, which is the second-highest public observation deck in the world, it is possible to see up to 120 kilometers away, to the mist rising from Niagara Falls.

A: The Great Pyramid is arguably the most accomplished engineering feat of the Ancient World. Built to house the body of the dead pharaoh, the base of the Great Pyramid in Egypt is 230 meters square, large enough to cover ten football fields. According to the Greek historian Herodotus, it took 400,000 men twenty years to construct this great monument. They used 2.3 million blocks of stone, some of which weighed as much as 50 tons!

B: Chan Chan, the largest adobe city in the Americas, was built about 1200 years ago in what is now northern Peru. It was the capital of the Chimu civilization, which lasted from A.D. 850 to around 1470. Chan Chan consisted of 10,000 structures, some with walls as high as 9 meters—including the huge, elaborately decorated palaces of the Chimu kings. The city covered 20 square kilometers and, though it was built on a coastal desert, boasted a sophisticated network of irrigation canals and wells. Efforts are currently underway to preserve Chan Chan, which is threatened with erosion by increased rainfall in recent years.

A: The Sydney Harbor Bridge is one of Australia's best known, and most photographed landmarks. It is the world's largest (but not the longest) steel arch bridge with the top of the bridge standing 134 meters above the harbor. Fondly known by the Australians as the "coathanger," Sydney Harbor Bridge celebrated its 70th birthday in 2002. Nowadays, a group of twelve people leave every ten minutes to climb to the top of the bridge and admire spectacular views of the city, and out to the Tasman Sea.

▶ 1.29 (Page 71)

A: I think, with technology, it was Microsoft that started it.
B: "It" being the use of teenagers . . .
A: Using teenagers to find out what's in and what isn't, what the market wants next. Around the year 2000, they started observing kids to find out what they were doing with technology. They went all over the place observing kids: from street markets in Seattle to skating rinks in London, bars in Tokyo, anywhere they thought trends might start.
B: So the idea was to watch teenagers, and learn what they wanted to do with their cell phones, with software . . .
A: That's right. Because it's teenagers that really drive technology. Kids have no

fear of technology. They experiment, and they automatically home in on the new. One thing that became clear is that teenagers want technology they can carry around. Anything bigger than a few inches is out.
B: And now we have tiny phones and tablets that are practically computers—they do almost everything.
A: Yup. Text messaging caught on because kids wanted to pass notes to each other during class. And now texting is almost more popular than actual face-to-face talking. What else . . . the lights that you find on keyboards are there because tech companies noticed that kids take notes in the dark during lectures.
B: So all of these things came about because of the needs of kids.
A: That's right. And don't forget about Facebook—it was developed first as a way for college students to share information. And now it, along with Twitter, has revolutionized the way almost the entire world communicates.
B: So is it just technology with these kids?
A: You mean where teenagers are leading the market?
B: Yes.
A: Not at all. I mean, fashion has been youth-led for years and years, but in particular, sneakers. Now, if you want to keep up with the latest style, who do you ask? You don't ask anyone over twenty, that's for sure. And I think it was Converse who used to do lots of their market research on the streets, on the basketball courts of New York, anywhere you find teenagers. They may still do it, I don't know.
B: And, what, they just talk to these kids?
A: Talk to them, watch what they are wearing, the colors, the styles, and maybe bring in a prototype, ask the kids if they'd wear them. If not, why not?

▶ 1.30 (Page 72)

Conversation 1
A: Well, it depends on the age.
B: I agree.
A: When they're young teenagers, no I don't think so.
B: What kind of limits would you put on, say, a fifteen year old?
A: It depends. There are some places that are not OK for teenagers.
B: Such as?
A: I wouldn't let my fifteen-year-old go to a bar, for instance.

Conversation 2
C: Teenagers? I don't think so.
D: Really? Why not?
C: Because . . .well, I think there are still things that they shouldn't see, that are inappropriate. Plus, they could be doing other things.
D: It's not that good for their eyes either, is it?

Conversation 3
E: Oh, definitely, yeah. They're our friends.
F: Me too. If parents can choose who they hang out with, then we should too.
E: What's the difference?
F: Exactly. It's not like we're stupid and can't judge someone's character.

Conversation 4
G: I think if it's a school day the next day, then it makes sense to have some kind of limit.
H: Yeah, but who sets the limit? If you know you're going to be OK on six hours' sleep or something . . .
G: Yeah, you should discuss it, but if you're going to be exhausted in the morning then that's not really . . .
H: I'm saying it's not up to the parents to decide. We're old enough—we know how to turn off the lights, don't we?

▶ 1.31 (Page 73)
Example
A: Whatever you do, don't forget to turn off the power.
1
B: Whenever you feel down, give me a call.
2
A: Wherever we go, they're always close behind.
3
B: Whenever I can, I'll see her.
4
A: Whoever we hire, he'll have to work miracles.
5
B: Whatever those children do, they make a success of it.

▶ 1.32 (Page 76)
1. She's very charismatic.
2. I find him inspirational.
3. He's very dignified.
4. She's pretty aloof.
5. He's so idealistic.
6. They are tireless.
7. He's not very trustworthy.
8. She's extremely resolute.
A. She doesn't have much drive or energy.
B. He wavers in the face of problems.
C. He's very approachable.
D. He's corrupt.
E. She's fairly nondescript.
F. She's very down-to-earth and practical.
G. She's not very inspiring.
H. She lacks gravitas.

UNIT 7 The natural world

▶ 2.02 (Page 82)
1. Taking care of pet rabbits is really easy. You just need to do a little planning. The first thing you need to do, before you even get the rabbits, is to buy a hutch, which is like a little house for the rabbit. Put the hutch in a place where it won't be exposed to cold winds or hot summer sun. Once you have your rabbits, basically you feed them twice a day. You have to make sure to get food that they like. It can be a little tricky, because they're sort of picky about what they eat. You have to clean out the hutch once a week or more, so you need fresh straw and hay.

And you need to have them vaccinated against myxomatosis, a disease that affects rabbits. So, that's about it- they're a pretty easy pet to take care of.

2. It seems pretty straightforward, but actually there are a lot of things that can go wrong when you choose a dog. A lot of people, for example, just go for the cutest dog they can find, which is understandable, but really not the right way to choose a dog. The first thing you need to do is to ask yourself a few questions. Will you have enough time to walk the dog and give her attention? Can you afford a dog? People often forget that there are expenses involved in owning a dog—you have to pay a vet for vaccines and if the dog gets sick. Do you have enough space in the house? Once you've answered these questions, the next thing to think about is what type of dog would be best for you. If you buy a puppy, you need to consider how big and active it will be once it's grown up. Different breeds have different characteristics. If you have an active lifestyle it's OK to get a Chihuahua or a Doberman, but if you spend most of your time at home watching TV, get a less active dog, like a Saint Bernard. The most important thing is to do your research before you buy. Talk to other dog owners and vets, and read as much as you can.

▶ **2.03 (Page 82)**

1
A: The first thing you need to do . . .

2
B: You just need to do a little planning.

3
A: You have to make sure to get food that they like.

4
B: You have to clean out the hutch once a week or more . . .

▶ **2.04 (Page 82)**

1. A lot of people, for example, just go for the cutest dog they can find.
2. The first thing you need to do is to ask yourself a few questions.
3. The next thing to think about is what type of dog would be best for you.
4. If you spend most of your time at home watching TV, get a less active dog.

▶ **2.05 (Page 83)**

A: The first thing I noticed when I entered the bureaucrat's office was that it was bright white, like a doctor's surgery or the cell of a madman. There were a few filing cabinets next to the desk and a huge photo of the king staring at us from the wall. The air was thick, and a fan droned weakly, whirring overhead as a gang of flies zig-zagged across the air.

The bureaucrat behind his desk looked up to greet me.

"How can I help you?" he said. I told him I needed a visa for my trip to the Danakil Depression, and he asked me if I'd ever been in a desert. "I've been in many," I replied. He shifted in his chair and said, "The Danakil Depression is the world's hottest place. It's not a tourist site. There's nothing there but hot air and salt." I told him I knew that, and that's why I wanted to go there.

"Typical American," he said. "Obsessed by the weather."

He asked me what I'd do if I got lost, and I told him I wouldn't. "And what about the three s's?" he said. "What three s's?" "Snakes, spiders, and scorpions. What if you get bitten?" "I won't." He stared at me again, glanced at my passport, and with a resounding thump, stamped it. "One visa," he said. "This will get you into Danakil, but it won't get you out."

▶ **2.06 (Page 83)**

A: Going to the Danakil Depression means walking into hell on Earth. The land is sunk more than 300 feet below sea level and the place is a furnace. The air shakes, warped by the sun. Even the wind brings no relief from the heat. Almost everything around you is dead: stumps of trees, cracked earth, the occasional white glow of animal bones.

Along the way we saw a group of bandits on camels, brandishing their weapons. They waved and went on riding. Salt statues loomed out of the spectacular landscape, nine feet high, vibrant colors and shapes from another world. An active volcano was hunched on the horizon, biding its time. We stopped to visit a ghost town, with its abandoned shacks stripped bare by the wind and the nomads and the scavenging animals. This was Danakil, where an American company had tried to set up a business in the sixties and had been defeated by the heat. The ruined buildings made of salt blocks were now crumbling away, and there were metal tracks in the ground where they had tried to build a railway but which now led nowhere.

For three days my shirt was drenched and my mouth parched. Even covered up against the sun, my skin baked and burned, and there seemed no escape from the cauldron of heat. They tell you to drink twelve liters of water a day, to remember to drink even when you're not thirsty, but it's never enough.

When we finally arrived at our destination I felt empty, as if everything had been a mistake. I didn't regret going to Danakil, but the land was so inhospitable that permanent settlement seemed impossible, and it felt wrong being there, as if we were trespassing on a place nature had intended only for itself.

▶ **2.07 (Page 86)**

A: Sharon Edwards once spent a day in an airplane, looking for a cat. The plane flew around the world for three weeks before she found it. They sent the cat home first-class. Another time, she found two suitcases full of birds from Turkey. But her strangest experience was when she pulled a snake out of a man's clothing.

B: I'm an animal health inspector at Heathrow Airport. I look after the animals that pass through Heathrow. I check that they are healthy and legal, and sometimes I look after them when they are waiting for a connecting flight.

Here are the areas for dogs, cats, reptiles, birds and fish. Over there is the area for very big animals. The biggest we ever had here was a black rhino, absolutely enormous.

At the Animal Center here, we receive all types of animals—we've had chimpanzees, wild cats, poisonous spiders, and it's impossible for one person to know about all of these. It keeps you on your toes because you're always picking up new information about different breeds of animal. But there are twenty people working here and between us we share our expertise. There is also a library and the Internet if we have any problems. I recently had to feed a group of toucans, but luckily, Tesco's is open twenty-four hours, so I had to go out at 2 A.M. to buy bananas.

The most common animals are cats and dogs. They come in all the time. And also lots of little children arrive at Heathrow carrying their pet hamster in their pocket, so I have to look after it for a while. The children always look very contrite when they're caught, but we usually don't take any action. It's not what you'd really call smuggling!

I often work at night. It's very quiet between 1 and 4 A.M. because we don't have any night flights. We try and give the animals a night-time. We dim the lights, and it's peaceful. And you never know what the new day will bring.

▶ **2.08 (Page 87)**

1. A monkey costs as little as that?
2. It's as big as an elephant.
3. We're as happy as can be.

▶ **2.09 (Page 90)**

A: Well, it's a piece of land that's about 31 square miles, so there's really a lot you could do with it, but I don't really know much about managing land. Do you have any ideas about what we could do with it?

B: Well, when I see 31 square miles of land, I think money. I think . . .

A: Ha, that's typical!

B: Well, yeah. I think a hotel would be great there. There's enough room for it, and we could really sell the whole unspoiled-island aspect.

A: Yeah, but the problem with the hotel is that the land is so beautiful as is. It would be a shame to mess with that. Maybe it would be nicer to do something that's kind of more geared toward the environment. We could leave it wild and just let the animals roam free, or start an animal sanctuary.

B: What would we get out of that?

A: It's good for the environment, Greg. I mean, it's doing something good, and giving something back to the earth, and making sure that there's a little wildness left in this world.

B: Mm. OK. Maybe not a hotel then, but I think we could think of a commercial use that would fit in more with the environment. What about some kind of health resort, maybe?

A: Well that's a nice idea because there's so much land, and people could go walking in the hills, and we could do nature trails through the forest. We could even have a little organic garden or, provide food that's really fresh and healthy because the land's really good for growing vegetables and things like that. We could have an organic health spa. What do you think?

B: Hm . . . yeah, that's a nice idea.

UNIT 8 Problems and issues

▶ **2.10** (Page 94)

1. That's a good question. Hmmm. I think I'd like some kind of robot to clean the house and do the laundry. Either that or get a maid.

2. A time machine. Not so I could go back and see earlier civilizations and dinosaurs—I mean, who cares about dinosaurs?—but so I could go back this morning and get to work before that guy who took my parking space.

3. That's a difficult question. I'd have to think about it. Well, I wouldn't mind a weather machine, with me in control, of course. So when my friends go on vacation, I could make it rain every day and they'd stop telling me how beautiful the weather was.

4. That's tricky. How about a pill that you can substitute for food, so no one would need to starve? And so I wouldn't have to cook.

5. Let me see. You could have a pill that makes you extremely intelligent. You'd take it just before every test or whenever the computer breaks down.

6. Well, I'd like to invent a special device that could take you to other places but only in your mind. Like a hat or glasses that give you all the sensations of being there. Then I'd use the glasses to go straight to a beach in Hawaii and spend the week there.

7. I'd invent a clock that extends hours of the day when you need it. Like every morning when I'm lying in bed and don't want to get up.

▶ **2.11** (Page 95)

A: I was on a business trip in Rome a few years ago. I'd been having dinner with a client all evening, and afterwards I found myself desperately looking for a late-night Internet café to check my emails from the office. So there I was at midnight, wandering around one of the most beautiful cities in the world, and I was tearing my hair out trying to get access to a computer. Anyway, I went back to the hotel and thought, do I really have to live like this? Are those emails really so important? So I started to reassess my life.

The world is one stressed-out place. When I go to cities now, I see everybody rushing around with their smart phones and laptops, and everyone's scared they're going to miss something. Y'know, no one ever looks back on their life and says, "I wish I'd spent more time working in the office."

After leaving my job, I moved to the beach. I sell surfing gear now. It doesn't make much money, but then money isn't the be-all and end-all. I'm happier than ever before, I think because living by the ocean gives you a certain perspective on life. The waves will be rolling in every morning long after we're gone. And it makes you realize all that hurrying isn't going to make any difference.

B: I've been working at an investment company for about four years. It's a very competitive business, of course, and you have to know about every fluctuation in the market right as it's happening. So I live a very fast-paced, high-pressure lifestyle. Actually, my friends tell me I suffer from a disease called "running out of time syndrome."

A lot of my work is done on the move, so I carry my office around with me: laptop, smart phone, electronic notepad. I suppose you could call these my weapons of war! They're a security blanket really.

I don't live a particularly healthy lifestyle: I grab a sandwich when I can, and drink far too much coffee. But it's not going to be like this forever. Most people in my profession burn out after three and a half years. In fact, the statistics are getting worse—I think it's under three years now. So by the time I'm forty, forty-five, I'll be slowing down a bit. But I don't think I'll ever live on a farm in the middle of nowhere growing vegetables. I'd hate that. I enjoy the buzz too much.

▶ **2.12** (Page 99)

Conversation 1
A: This stupid thing keeps getting jammed.
B: What, again?
A: I can't get it to make any copies.
B: It happened to me yesterday. Give it a good kick. Is that better?
A: Well, I feel better, yeah, but it's still not working.

Conversation 2
C: See? I always get the same message.
D: You have performed an illegal operation. That sounds bad.
C: See? I don't know how to make it shut down normally.
D: Have you tried dropping it on the floor?
C: What?
D: Or shouting at it? That works sometimes.
C: You're not funny.

Conversation 3
E: I'm having a problem turning it on.
F: Oh really?
E: This thing seems to be stuck. It won't turn.
F: Oh.
E: Which means I can't get any air in here. And it's so hot.
F: The middle of summer is a bad time for it to break. You can always open the windows.
E: Oh! Yeah, thanks.

UNIT 9 People with vision

▶ **2.13** (Page 106)

A: What can you tell us about what happens when geniuses relax?
B: Without a doubt, we can be sure that great scientists don't always make their discoveries in the lab. Archimedes's famous Eureka moment came while he was having a bath. Physicist Richard Feynman saw a plate flying through the air in a college cafeteria, and was inspired to calculate electron orbits. He later won the Nobel Prize. And Alexander Fleming was making mold for his hobby, microbe painting, when he accidentally came across *Penicillium notatum*, later known as penicillin.
A: So what does this tell us?
B: Well, a recent study by Robert Root-Bernstein compared the hobbies of 134 Nobel prize winning chemists to those of other scientists. He found that the Nobel prize winners were accomplished outside the lab as well. Over half were artistic, and almost all had a long-lasting hobby. Twenty-five percent of the Nobel prize winners played a musical instrument, and eighteen percent drew or painted regularly. Of the non-Nobel winners, under one percent had a hobby.
A: Fascinating. So should we conclude that only a creative person can be a genius?
B: Well, I think that's debatable. Perhaps it's true up to a point, but I don't think it's as clear-cut as that. What we do know is that to a certain extent, creative thinking can help people to solve problems, even scientific ones. That if you are thinking about a problem all the time, often the answer eludes you. But it may come in an inspiration when you are least expecting it—perhaps when you're asleep, or thinking about other things, doing a hobby, for example. It's not 100 percent certain, but it seems that the mind has the ability to make connections from one part of your life to another, so that actually stepping back from a problem can often provide the answer. And people who are good at making these connections, people who pursue creative hobbies and interests, often excel in their particular fields.

▶ **2.14** (Page 107)

Every year, at the National Portrait Gallery in London, there is a competition for the best portrait. The winner is decided democratically: everyone who visits the exhibition can vote for their favorite portrait. Listen to some visitors to the exhibit.

Conversation 1
A: What do you think of this one?
B: Um . . . it's OK. To be honest, it's not really my taste. It sort of looks like a photo to me.
C: Yeah, you have to get up really close to it to see that it's a painting.
A: What do you think of it?
C: I really like it, actually.
A: Me too.

C: I like the colors, and the expression on her face is kind of intense.

A: It's a little bit enigmatic, isn't it? You don't really know what she's thinking. And the details are great, too—You can almost see the pores of her skin.

B: Well, as I was saying, it really does look like a photo—the detail is amazing. But to tell you the truth, I still wouldn't want it hanging on my bedroom wall.

Conversation 2

A: I love this one.

C: He has such an interesting face, doesn't he? He looks like a hippie poet from the Seventies.

A: That's some beard.

B: I like the blanket over his shoulders.

C: And the medallion.

A: Oh yeah, I didn't notice that.

C: As a matter of fact, I like this one better than the other one. At any rate, I think it's more interesting.

A: How about this one for your bedroom wall?

B: Nope. 'Fraid not.

Conversation 3

B: I think this one's great.

C: It's kind of menacing isn't it?

B: For me, what's interesting is that they are in a group, almost like a gang. And they're all dressed pretty much the same.

C: The jeans and white T-shirt.

B: Exactly, except for the guy sitting in the middle. He's the only one sitting and looking directly at us, sort of challenging us, so maybe he's the boss.

A: Well, what I noticed is that, as you said, they're in a group, but somehow they look isolated. They're all facing in different directions, and they don't seem to relate to each other at all.

C: And I wonder why it's called La Familia. They obviously aren't a family in any traditional sense. At any rate, they don't look like a family, so it's kind of intriguing. I think this one should win, actually.

A: Me too.

▶ **2.15** (Page 107)

C: So which one won in the end?

A: Which do you think?

C: Well, as I said before, my favorite is La Familia, but . . .

A: That one didn't win.

C: Oh really?

A: The winner was Giulietta Coates, the one that looks like a photo.

C: Well, I think it's really good too, but it isn't my favorite.

▶ **2.16** (Page 114)

A: Clarence Birdseye was a taxidermist from New York. On a visit to the Arctic he saw how the native people preserved their food by putting it in barrels of sea water, which froze quickly. This way, the food maintained its freshness for later. So in 1923 he bought a seven-dollar electric fan, some ice, and some buckets of salt water and experimented by putting food in them. Birdseye's

experiments worked, and he went on to become the pioneer of frozen foods in the western world. In 1929 he sold the patent for 22 million dollars and in 1930 frozen food went on sale for the first time in the United States.

B: As a young man, Chester Carlson's job involved making multiple copies of patent documents by hand. Writing everything down was difficult for Carlson because he was short-sighted and had arthritis, so in 1938 he invented a machine to make copies. He tried to get funding for his idea from all sorts of well-known companies, including IBM and General Electric, but they turned him down. Eventually the company that became Xerox bought his idea, and the first photocopier was manufactured in 1959. Now there's hardly an office in the world that doesn't contain his invention.

UNIT **10** Expressing feelings

▶ **2.17** (Page 116)

A: Today we have psychologist Walter Bright with us to talk about optimism and pessimism. Welcome, Dr. Bright.

B: Thank you, Kathryn. It's a pleasure to be here.

A: So, Dr. Bright—Optimism vs. pessimism. My mom is the queen optimist. She waltzes her way through life blissfully happy. She sees a positive side to everything. My dad is the polar opposite—he can't see the positive in anything. When I had a car accident as a teen and crashed the family car, Mom focused on the fact that I was OK. Dad, on the other hand, almost had a nervous breakdown because the car was totaled. He reprimanded me for being a careless driver and didn't let me behind the wheel for six months. (He still won't let me forget that incident, either.) (chuckle)

B: Well, what a perfect example of seeing the glass half full or half empty! We are all born with a predisposition to a more positive or negative way of thinking. Optimists believe that they influence positive events in their lives, but that negative events just happen.

A: So in my mom's eyes, the accident wasn't my fault.

B: Exactly. There must have been some other reason for the accident. Whereas pessimists believe that they are responsible for the negative events that happen to them. So your dad clearly saw you as being responsible for the car accident. And being a pessimist, he most likely saw more such failures for you ahead.

A: That about sums up my dad . . .

B: Now, in turn, if something good happens, an optimist believes that she is directly responsible. So, let's use your mom as an example. What was her reaction when you got your first job?

A: She was beyond thrilled, of course.

B: And in her optimistic thinking, it was proof that more good things will happen to you. Now, what was your dad's reaction when you got that job?

A: Well, he was shocked. I mean, he was happy, I guess. But clearly he thought it was a total fluke that someone would hire me.

B: Classic! When something good happens, pessimists see it as chance and as something that probably won't happen again.

A: Wow, seems like pessimists would be more prone to depression.

B: Well, depression is complex, with a variety of different causes—mental, physical, social. But, yes, a person with a negative outlook is more likely to be depressed than an optimistic person.

A: So what is the verdict? Clearly the optimists out there will be OK. Are all of us pessimists doomed?

B: Ha ha. No, you're not doomed. We're not doomed. I'm a pessimist by nature, too! While we tend to be predisposed to think negatively, we can learn positive patterns of thinking.

A: I don't know. As much as my mom tried to instill her optimism in me when I was growing up, her Mary Sunshine disposition was lost on me. I'm sure I'm even further gone now in adulthood.

B: Not necessarily. With cognitive restructuring, you can train yourself to become more optimistic. You just need to be aware of your negative thoughts and replace them with positive thinking. I can't exactly call myself a converted optimist, but I have significantly improved my pessimistic ways, thanks to cognitive restructuring.

A: So, what would I do to think more positively?

B: You need to define positive things that happen in your life as being caused by you and as proof that more good things are bound to happen to you.

A: So, getting a talented psychologist to do this interview was my doing, and I should look forward to landing more interesting people to interview.

B: That's right, exactly! And negative events that occur, you might think about whether they are due to something you did, or whether they are just isolated occurrences that will not have an effect on the future. You must guard against assuming that you are automatically responsible for everything bad that happens.

A: So, my poor tennis game this past week—I shouldn't be too bummed about that?

B: Definitely not! Think of extenuating circumstances that might have contributed to the game. Were you worried about something? Maybe sleep deprived? Or maybe you just had an off day. Whatever it was, the temporary failure wasn't a reflection of personal weakness! Also, part of cognitive restructuring is the idea that you have endless opportunities to improve in the future.

A: Well, if you put it that way, then I'm inspired. Looking forward to my next potential success! (cynical)

B: That's the idea. And no need to be cynical! Remember, if you can embrace optimism at least on some level, you will reap all sorts of benefits: physical health, greater achievement, emotional health, increased longevity, less stress, and on and on . . .

A: True! Well, thank you for being our guest, Dr. Bright. This was truly informational! And can I ask you—your name, by the way—did you change it as part of your cognitive restructuring?

B: Ha, ha. No. But let's say it's been an inspiration trying to live up to my name!

▶ 2.18 **(Page 119)**

1. I've often wondered what it was like to have been in the first airplane to take off and really fly, not just like the Wright Brothers' first plane going for a ten or thirty second hop, but really climbing into the air. It couldn't have been easy, because those aircraft were not very sophisticated. They must have been difficult to fly—physically and even mentally—and they would've had to do lots of calculations that no one else had done before. But of course it would have been so exhilarating as they got higher and higher. And then coming in for the landing. How would that have been? It must have been something close to a controlled crash. Even so, what a thrill.

2. It must have been amazing to be the first modern person to see Machu Picchu, after it had been covered by jungle for so long. I think it must have been pretty hard to get there, because nowadays they've built a train, and it's easier to get to. But, the first modern people that went there had to climb right up the side of the huge mountain without knowing that there was anything there at the top, so they must have been really driven. But, although they might have felt the same atmosphere when they arrived, it couldn't have been quite as spectacular as it is today because the ruins now are there for you to see as soon as you arrive. It must have had more of a mysterious air when they discovered it covered in vegetation and all hidden, without really knowing what it was.

3. I think Yuri Gagarin must have had mixed emotions about being the first person in space. On the one hand, there's that sort of thrill and excitement of space travel, and the absolute awe of what he was experiencing, being the first person to see Earth from space, having never even had any concept of what it might look like. The vastness of space must have been amazing, too. But on the other hand, he was up there on his own, basically in a tin can—anything could have happened up there. He probably didn't know if he would get back home or not. He must have felt alone and I would think pretty scared as well.

▶ 2.19 **(Page 122)**

1. During my childhood my parents moved a lot, so I was always changing schools. In fact, in about six years I think we moved three times. It was hard, because just when I'd made new friends and gotten used to the teachers and the school, I had to do it all again. I got pretty lonely, and I found it difficult to relate to other children, especially because they all knew the area, they already had their small groups of friends, and I was slightly out of it. But it also made me very outgoing, because if I wasn't going to be outgoing and energetic, and entertaining, I was never going to make friends. So, I suppose that's one good thing that came from all those moves—I have lots of friends in many places.

2. I think one of my worst memories from childhood is probably a sports-related memory. I'm not very athletic, you see. I grew up in a pretty big city, and our gym teacher used to make us go cross-country running every week, so we'd be out there, in the rain, and the wind, in the middle of the city, with the traffic roaring by, running around in our gym clothes—I hated it. I used to dread Mondays, because that's when we had gym class. I'm still the same. I still hate sports, and running is one of the sports I hate the most. I know some people love it, but I just can't seem to enjoy it no matter what. So I would say running in gym class is one of the worst memories from my childhood.

3. When I was a child we used to go to Majorca nearly every year. It was a family vacation—my grandparents came, too. I think the last time I was there I was about seven. Maybe eight. The thing I remember most vividly is arriving in Majorca, and this wall of heat that would hit us when we got off the plane. The air smelled so different from home. It was a wonderful smell. And I remember the things that children remember about vacations—I remember the pool, and how blue it was—we used to swim every day. And the breakfasts that went on forever—the routine was completely different from what we did at home. We met people there from all over the world. We made friends with a Norwegian family one year and kept in touch with them for many years. I haven't been back since then, because I don't really want to spoil my memories of it. I think the magic might be lost if I were to see it now as an adult.

4. During the summer, I lived in the woods. Well, actually, our property was next to a beautiful forest. I used to climb over the fence, and my friends and I used to play in the woods all day. We used to climb trees, run in and out of bushes, and basically run around free all summer. It was such a great feeling of freedom—something every kid should have.

▶ 2.20 **(Page 126)**

1. Wow. I went to the most amazing restaurant last night. You would not believe it. I'd never been anywhere like that before. The name of the restaurant was Aria. It was on one of those cute little streets down by the river—the owners had renovated one of those adorable old buildings. It's such a wonderful blend of old and modern— the old architecture, with very modern décor in the dining rooms. The service was incredible—the servers were all really polite and charming, but not too obtrusive. The food was what I would call modern French, and it was out of this world. We had what they call a "tasting menu," which consisted of lots of small courses. It was pretty expensive but sooo delicious that it was worth it.

2. I cannot stand public transportation in this country. I mean, despite the fact that it's expensive and unreliable, it's just so unnecessarily complicated. Just look at trains, for example. There must be about twenty different ticket types. And it all depends on when you're traveling, what time of day, how far in advance you buy your ticket, etc. It's just ridiculous. For example, you could be sitting on a train, and the person sitting next to you could've paid twice as much for their ticket just because they happened to buy it on a different day. I don't understand why we don't have a system like in other countries, where you just pay one price for each distance, and maybe a little more for an express train. As it stands now, it's just too complicated.

3. I really hate smoking, and I think it should be banned altogether. It's really unfair for those of us who don't smoke—you go to a restaurant or café, and you have to breathe in other people's smoke. Then you smell like smoke for the rest of the day. I mean, smoking is obviously not good for the smoker of course, but it's not good for the non-smokers, either. If you don't smoke, it's really disgusting to have to breathe in second-hand smoke. And I don't buy it when smokers say, "Well, we'll just sit in a part of the restaurant where it doesn't affect you, or we'll go outside." You know what, it does affect us, because even if you're outside, and you're walking behind somebody who is smoking, you're breathing in their smoke. And don't get me started on people who smoke around children. I think it should just be banned, because it's one of the few bad habits that really does affect everybody else.